by the editors **CONSUMER GU**

THE ULTIMATE
FOOD PROCESSOR
COOKBOOK
International Recipes & Menus

A Fireside Book
Published by Simon and Schuster
New York, New York

Contents

Copyright © 1979 by Publications International, Ltd.
All rights reserved.
This book may not be reproduced or quoted in whole or in part by mimeograph or any other printed means or for presentation on radio or television without written permission from:

Louis Weber, President
Publications International, Ltd.
3841 West Oakton Street
Skokie, Illinois 60076

Permission is never granted for commercial purposes.

Manufactured in the United States of America
1 2 3 4 5 6 7 8 9 10

Library of Congress Cataloging in Publication Data
Main entry under title:

The Ultimate Food Processor Cookbook
(A Fireside Book)
Includes index.
1. Food Processor Cooking.   2. Cookery, International.   I. Consumer guide.
TX840.F6F67   641.5'89   79-10240
ISBN 0-671-24591-0
ISBN 0-671-24592-9 pbk.

A Fireside Book
Published by Simon and Schuster
A Division of Gulf + Western Corporation
New York, New York 10020

Cover and Book Design: Barbara Griffler
Color Photography: Dave Jordano Photography Inc.
Recipe Development: Linda Carter, Barbara Grunes and Judy Vance

Introduction

The *Ultimate Food Processor Cookbook* opens many, many worlds to everyone who cooks and entertains. There is the world of food processor cooking, with all of its special tricks and techniques. And the world of menus planned for successful family meals, parties and feasts. Most importantly, there is the globe-spanning variety of all kinds of international cuisines. And the excitement of discovering the exciting world of flavors that each holds.

To experience the world of cuisines at jet-age speed, you first need to master the time-saving miracles offered by the food processor. It is important that you get used to using every shortcut the machine has to offer—from instant slicing, shredding, chopping and mincing to bread, pastry, sauce and salad making. These techniques will be your passport to the great menus and recipes in this book.

So before you begin to cook, read through the Food Processor Techniques sections. Note that the general guidelines are presented in four parts: General Guidelines for Using Your Food Processor; Guidelines for Using the Slicing Disc; Guidelines for Using the Shredding Disc; and Guidelines for Using the Steel Blade. These guidelines apply to all food processors. They discuss in detail uses for each of the three basic cutting attachments, describe the most commonly encountered problems, and answer such questions as which blade to use, how to position foods in the machine, how to get the most attractive results and how to combine ingredients most effectively. You may be surprised to discover that you can get far better performance from your food processor than you realize. Our guidelines are more comprehensive than most of the operating manuals that come with the machines, but it is extremely important that you read your operating manual as well for manufacturer's use and safety recommendations that apply specifically to your model.

For spectacular evidence of the food processor's versatility, turn to the section of photographed techniques. Here you will find, arranged in alphabetical order by name of food, dozens of specific kinds of food preparation—everything from slicing an apple to creating julienne strips of zucchini. Turn to sequence 50. PASTRY DOUGH for step-by-step illustration of how to combine flour and shortening, how to add the liquid through the feed tube and how to process the dough. And learn the do's and don'ts of chopping raw beef in the sequence labeled 39. MEAT (Raw)—Chopped. You can prepare any cookie recipe in seconds by following the sequence of photographs under 24. COOKIE DOUGH—General Method. Or if you want a quick sandwich spread, turn to 29. EGG SALAD or 33. HAM SALAD for directions that apply to any combination of chopped ingredients.

You'll find yourself referring to the photographed techniques for all kinds of food processor uses—whether you simply want to grate Parmesan cheese for your favorite spaghetti dish or prepare one of the luscious homemade pasta recipes in this book.

In very little time, the food processor will come to play a routine role in all the cooking you do. You'll find it so easy and convenient to use that you will want to take advantage of its speed to prepare many foods that you otherwise would buy ready-made or enjoy only in restaurants. Not only can the machine spare you the expense of the packaged products, and enable you to experience such unique pleasures as fresh, home-baked breads, but it also makes it possible for you to dine on the best French, Italian, Chinese, Indian, Japanese or German food at home.

The Ultimate Food Processor Cookbook brings the magnificent flavors and fragrances of twenty great cuisines into your kitchen. And each recipe is placed in the context of an authentic menu. There are thirty-six travelogue menus in all, each with specific serving suggestions for appropriate wines and other beverages. If you long for the unparalleled flavor of homemade pasta, you'll find four complete menus, ranging from a Homestyle Italian Supper to a Do-Ahead Italian Buffet and an Italian Holiday Dinner, that feature this scrumptious fare. If you have always wanted to entertain friends with a luxurious, seafood-laden Spanish Paella or French Bouillabaise, you'll find menus that include not only the formulas for these festive dishes but also recipes for salads and desserts to accompany them.

The food processor whizzes around the globe to China, Japan, Indonesia, Korea and India to make quick work of the chopping chores intrinsic to colorful, economical Asian cooking. You will be amazed at how easy it is to present guests with a traditional Chinese Dim Sum Brunch or an Indian Curry Dinner when all the ingredients are machine-ready in seconds. Displaying equal talents with mouth-watering sauces, the food processor translates fabulous French, German, Russian, Greek and Turkish dishes into a language of fast efficiency that we all can understand. And you needn't speak Swedish, Norwegian or Danish to present a magnificent Scandinavian Smörgåsbord, complete with a Danish Fish Mousse, Marinated Herring, Lucia Buns, Beef à la Lindstrom and half a dozen other treats. If your sweet tooth longs for the satisfaction of Austrian tortes or your family craves the unique spiciness of Mexican enchiladas, you will find satisfying recipes in this book.

While you are traveling around the world in your kitchen, you should become acquainted with metric measurements, since these are used in almost all foreign countries and will soon be adopted universally. All of our recipes provide easy lessons: Every measurement is given in the units we are accustomed to—pounds, ounces, cups and teaspoonfuls—as well as in metric equivalents. The metric equivalents are rounded off to the nearest convenient metric measurements. Thus, although not exact conversions, the *proportion* of ingredients remains the same. (For your convenience, we have included some basic metric conversion charts you may wish to use for your own recipes.) So if you want to become "bi-lingual," all you have to do is obtain a metric measuring cup and a set of metric measuring spoons and start using them. In no time at all, you'll be thinking in terms of liters and milliliters instead of fluid ounces and spoonfuls.

We present *The Ultimate Food Processor Cookbook* as a special Bon Voyage! and a warm welcome home. For with these menus and recipes, you can experience a wonderful taste of the world—right at your own table.

METRIC EQUIVALENTS FOR VOLUME AND WEIGHT MEASURES

Volume measure	Metric equivalent
¼ teaspoon	1 mL
½ teaspoon	2 mL
1 teaspoon	5 mL
1 tablespoon (3 teaspoons)	15 mL
2 tablespoons (1 fluid ounce)	30 mL
¼ cup (4 tablespoons) (2 fluid ounces)	60 mL
⅓ cup	80 mL
½ cup (8 tablespoons) (4 fluid ounces)	125 mL
⅔ cup	160 mL
¾ cup (6 fluid ounces)	180 mL
1 cup (8 fluid ounces)	250 mL
1 pint (2 cups)	500 mL
1 quart (4 cups)	1 L

Weight measure	Metric equivalent
1 ounce	30 g
2 ounces	60 g
3 ounces	85 g
¼ pound (4 ounces)	115 g
½ pound (8 ounces)	225 g
¾ pound (12 ounces)	340 g
1 pound (16 ounces)	450 g

METRIC EQUIVALENTS FOR OVEN TEMPERATURES

°Fahrenheit	°Celsius
250 °F	120 °C
275 °F	140 °C
300 °F	150 °C
325 °F	160 °C
350 °F	180 °C
375 °F	190 °C
400 °F	200 °C
425 °F	220 °C
450 °F	230 °C
475 °F	250 °C
500 °F	260 °C
550 °F	290 °C

METRIC EQUIVALENTS FOR DIMENSIONS

½ inch	1.5 cm
1 inch	2.5 cm
1½ inches	4 cm
2 inches	5 cm
3 inches	8 cm
4 inches	10 cm
5 inches	13 cm
9 inches	23 cm
11 inches	28 cm
13 inches	33 cm

Metric abbreviations are as follows:

mL = milliliter   L = liter (1000 milliliters)   g = gram   kg = kilogram   cm = centimeter

Food Processor Techniques

The following guidelines and photographed techniques will provide you with general directions for the correct and most efficient use of your food processor. Some techniques may differ for various food-processor brands and models. Read your operating manual carefully for specific instructions.

General Guidelines for Using Your Food Processor

1. When you are unsure of which blade or disc to use, consider how you want the food to be processed. Unless the food is to be sliced or shredded, the steel blade is the one to use. The steel blade is used for about 80 percent of all food processing.

2. If your food processor has a plastic blade, it can be used for mixing liquids and soft mixtures, such as puddings. The steel blade can also be used for these functions. On some food-processor models, the plastic blade is meant to be used for mixing doughs; check your operating manual.

3. Special discs for fine shred, thin slice, julienne cut, crinkle cut and French-fry cut are available for some food processors. Check your operating manual for availability and use.

4. If your food processor features speed selection, check the operating manual for proper speeds to use in processing various foods.

5. Your food processor may have a circuit breaker that will stop the machine if it is overloaded with food or overheated. Check your operating manual for information and procedures.

6. CHECK YOUR OPERATING MANUAL FOR SAFETY DIRECTIONS BEFORE USING YOUR FOOD PROCESSOR. Never attempt to operate the machine without the cover in place. Never attempt to open the machine while it is running.

7. You'll find that using a long-handled brush will make cleaning the food processor much easier, since most bowls and covers have "hard-to-get-at" nooks and crannies. Use the brush to clean discs and blades, too, so that you don't have to handle the sharp cutting surfaces with your hands. Check your operating manual to find out which food-processor parts may be dishwasher safe.

Guidelines for Using the Slicing Disc

1. Select ripe but firm fruits and vegetables. Soft foods will not slice well and the quality of the slices will be inconsistent.

2. Check your operating manual to see if you can slice citrus fruit, tomatoes, raw and cooked meats and hard sausage with your food processor. Some manufac-

turers recommend that you do not slice these foods; slicing them could damage the machine.

3. Do NOT slice frozen or extremely hard foods such as ice; these can cause damage to the disc or the machine.

4. A thin slicing disc or adjustable slicing feature is available for many food processors. Use the regular or thin slicing disc as desired; however, best results can be attained for soft foods, such as strawberries or bananas, with the regular slicing disc.

5. All foods except raw meat should be refrigerator temperature for best slicing results. Hard sausage contains a large amount of fat and will be too soft to slice at room temperature. Cheese is also too soft at room temperature and will stick to the blade.

6. Semi-hard cheeses, such as Cheddar, can be sliced. Soft, processed and hard cheeses cannot be sliced.

7. Raw meat and poultry must be PARTIALLY, but not completely, frozen for slicing. Cut meat into pieces that will fit into the feed tube. Wrap in plastic wrap or waxed paper. Place in freezer; remove when very firm to the touch. (If you cannot insert the tip of a knife into meat, it is too hard.) Remove paper before slicing. Do not use thin slicing disc with raw meat.

8. Trim large foods, such as potatoes, to fit diameter of feed tube. Cut foods into lengths slightly shorter than that of the feed tube, so that the pusher can be positioned above them (see 59. ZUCCHINI—Sliced).* You can insert some foods, such as a small whole lemon or onion, through the bottom of feed tube if they will not fit through top (see 46. ONIONS—Sliced). Do not pack feed tube too tightly or food will not be able to move through tube smoothly.

9. Cut a thin slice from bottom of foods to create a flat surface that will rest on slicing disc when food is inserted into feed tube. This will help to keep food upright in tube and ensure even slices.

10. Use firm, steady pressure on pusher. Hard foods require more pressure, soft foods require less.

11. Generally, you can fill the bowl with sliced food to the level of the slicing disc; but food must not touch disc. If food begins to touch the disc, it can force the disc to move upward on the shaft, causing damage to the disc or the machine. Some food-processor bowls are marked with a "fill level"; sliced food should not exceed this level.

12. If your food processor features speed selection, check your operating manual for the correct speed to use for slicing various foods.

13. A "holding tool" for guiding a single item, such as a carrot, through the feed tube is available for some food processors. You can also slice a single food item by

*References are to the photographed techniques that begin on page 9.

placing it correctly in the feed tube (see 14. CARROTS—Sliced). If the disc turns clockwise, position the food on the left side of the feed tube; if it turns counter-clockwise, place food on the right side. The disc will then move against the food, helping it to remain upright.

14. NEVER USE YOUR FINGERS TO GUIDE FOOD THROUGH THE FEED TUBE. Always use the food pusher.

Guidelines for Using the Shredding Disc

1. Select ripe but firm fruits and vegetables. Soft foods, such as melons and tomatoes, will not shred well.

2. Fruits, vegetables and semi-hard cheese should be refrigerator temperature for best shredding results.

3. Do not shred raw or cooked meat or hard sausage. These foods can be chopped or sliced if these procedures are recommended in your operating manual.

4. Semi-hard cheeses can be shredded. Soft and processed cheeses cannot be shredded. Do not shred any cheese softer than mozzarella. Check your operating manual to see if hard cheeses can be shredded; some manufacturers recommend that you do not shred hard cheese because it could cause damage to some machines. Hard cheese should be at room temperature for shredding.

5. Do not shred frozen or extremely hard foods such as ice; these could damage the disc or the machine.

6. A thin shredding disc is available for many food processors. Use the regular or thin shredding disc, depending upon texture desired.

7. Trim large foods, such as potatoes, to fit diameter of feed tube. Cut foods into lengths slightly shorter than that of the feed tube, so that the pusher can be positioned above them (see 13. CARROTS—Shredded). Do not pack feed tube too tightly or food will not be able to move through tube smoothly.

8. It can be helpful to cut a thin slice from bottom of foods to create a flat surface that will rest on shredding disc when food is inserted into feed tube. This will help to keep the food upright in the tube and produce even shredding.

9. Position foods vertically in the feed tube for short shreds, horizontally in the feed tube for long shreds.

10. Use firm, steady pressure on pusher. Hard foods will require more pressure, soft foods less.

11. Generally, you can fill the bowl with shredded food to the level of the shredding disc, but food must not touch disc. If food begins to touch the disc, it can force the disc to move upward on the shaft, causing damage to the disc or the machine. Some food-processor bowls are marked with a "fill level"; shredded food should not exceed this level.

12. If your food processor features speed selection, check your operating manual for the correct speed to use for shredding various foods.

13. A "holding tool" for guiding single items, such as a carrot, through the feed tube is available for some food processors. You can also shred a single food item

by placing it correctly in the feed tube. If the disc turns clockwise, position the food on the left side of the feed tube; if it turns counter-clockwise, place food on the right side. The disc will then move against the food, helping it to remain upright (see 14. CARROTS—Sliced).

14. NEVER USE YOUR FINGERS TO GUIDE FOOD THROUGH THE FEED TUBE. Always use the food pusher.

Guidelines for Using the Steel Blade

1. Generally, food to be processed with the steel blade should be cut into 1-inch (2.5 cm) pieces. The size of the pieces must be consistent; if large and small pieces are processed together, the finished food will be uneven in texture (see 11. CARROTS—Chopped).

2. To chop or grate some foods, such as Parmesan cheese, ice and garlic, you drop them through the feed tube with the machine running [see 19. CHEESE (Hard)—Grated]. Your operating manual will recommend which foods to process in this manner.

3. Soft foods and those that have a high moisture content, such as green peppers, onions, tomatoes and raw and cooked meats, should be processed with an on/off or "pulse" technique to control texture. These foods process quickly and can be processed more finely than desired unless the on/off technique is used. Some food processors have a "pulse switch" that performs this technique automatically. If your food processor does not have a pulse switch, turn the machine on and off manually, leaving the machine on about one second each time, until desired texture is achieved.

4. Process no more than one cup (250 mL) of raw meat or two cups (500 mL) of other foods at one time for best results. Check your operating manual for recommended amounts of food, as the capacities of different food processors do vary.

5. Use no more than 2 to 2½ cups (500 to 625 mL) of flour in bread or dough recipes unless your operating manual recommends otherwise. Most blades and bowls are not designed to handle larger amounts.

6. Some food processors can be used for beating egg whites and whipping cream, but neither the steel nor the plastic blade is designed to incorporate as much air as a wire whisk, hand beater or electric mixer. Therefore, the volume of the processed food will be less than if beaten conventionally.

7. Most food processors will not grind coffee beans; check your operating manual. Purchased ground coffee can be ground to a finer texture.

8. Do not attempt to process grains or hard foods, such as whole nutmeg. These can damage the machine.

9. Cheese should be refrigerator temperature for chopping or grating.

10. You can chop raw meat for hamburgers, meatballs or meatloaf in the food processor. You'll find that the hamburgers will have a more "solid" texture than those made with purchased ground beef. You will soon become accustomed to the difference and will enjoy the

chewier texture. Do not trim all the fat from meat for hamburgers or meat loaf; some fat (about 10 percent) is necessary for moistness and juiciness. All fat can be trimmed for recipes in which the meat is not cooked, such as Steak Tartare. The food processor will not chop tendons or gristle in meat; after removing the meat from the machine, remove the tendons with a fork.

11. Fruits, vegetables and herbs, such as parsley, should be dry before you chop or mince them. Remove stems from herbs; most food processors will not chop stems. Herbs will become moist when chopped; spread chopped herbs on paper toweling and let dry at room temperature, about 15 minutes. Chopped fresh herbs can be frozen for year-round use.

12. Several foods can be combined in the food processor for salads and spreads (see 33. HAM SALAD). If the mixture will contain both hard and soft foods, process the hard foods, such as celery, first. Then add the soft foods, such as hard cooked eggs or tuna, and use the on/off technique to combine ingredients (see 29. EGG SALAD and 20. CHEESE SPREAD).

13. If a piece of food becomes stuck on the blade, stop the machine and remove the blade. Carefully remove the food from the blade with a spatula. Empty the bowl, reassemble the machine and continue processing.

14. You can make fresh bread crumbs from any kind of bread, such as whole wheat, rye, white or French. Use dry or toasted bread for dry bread crumbs. Or make fresh crumbs and dry them in a warm oven. Process fresh or dried herbs with bread crumbs to make herb-seasoned crumbs (see 5. BREAD CRUMBS).

15. Peanut butter and other nut butters can be made in your food processor (see 51. PEANUT BUTTER). You can use any kind of nut that has not been dry-roasted. The butter will become thinner and smoother the longer it is processed. Usually, it is not necessary to add oil; if it is necessary, add vegetable oil one teaspoon (5 mL) at a time through the feed tube with the machine running, until desired texture is achieved. You can keep nut butters refrigerated up to three weeks.

16. You can puree any soft food, such as strawberries and bananas, or any food that has been cooked until it is soft. Cut food into 1-inch (2.5 cm) pieces and place up to two cups (500 mL) in the bowl. Add liquid, if necessary, through feed tube with machine running, until desired texture is achieved. The longer a puree is processed, the smoother it will become. The plastic blade will produce a coarser-textured puree than the steel blade. Seasonings can be mixed into purees.

17. You'll enjoy the freshly-squeezed flavor of frozen fruit juices reconstituted in the food processor. Soft fruits, such as bananas, strawberries or peaches, can be processed with the reconstituted juice for blended fruit beverages (see 35. LIQUID MIXTURES).

18. After processing purees or liquids, remove the bowl from the machine with the blade in place. Insert your finger in the hole in the bottom of the blade to hold blade in place while you pour liquid from bowl. This procedure eliminates the possibilities of the blade falling out and of the food running out through the hole in the bottom of the bowl (see 35. LIQUID MIXTURES).

19. You can use the food processor to make baby food. Control the texture of the food by length of processing time. As the baby grows, food can be processed less time for coarser texture.

20. Usually, the butter used in food processor bread and pastry recipes should be frozen. Check your operating manual for pastry and dough recommendations for your machine.

21. Pastry and most (but not all) bread doughs will form a ball when processing is completed. If dough is too dry to form a ball, add a few drops of water and continue processing; if dough is too wet to form a ball, add a little more flour and continue processing.

22. You can make any favorite cookie dough in your food processor as long as the recipe contains no more than two cups (500 mL) of flour. (Divide recipe in half and process in two batches for larger amounts.) Process butter and sugar until fluffy; add egg; then add remaining ingredients (see 24. COOKIE DOUGH).

23. When you are mixing only one or two eggs, processing may be more successful if the machine is propped up to tilt it at an angle (see 36. MAYONNAISE).

24. When you are making mayonnaise, add the oil slowly at first. You can add the oil more rapidly when the mayonnaise begins to thicken in the bowl. The longer the mayonnaise is processed, the thicker it will become. Mayonnaise can be kept refrigerated up to two weeks. Mayonnaise made with egg yolks will be thicker than that made with whole eggs.

25. If your food processor features speed selection, check the operating manual for correct speed to use when processing various foods with the steel blade.

You will notice that the recipes in this book have been organized to minimize food processor clean-up. Whenever possible, we process dry foods before wet ones, so that the bowl does not have to be washed between steps. When you are preparing your own recipes, you might want to follow similar procedures. If you are making a meatloaf, for example, process the bread crumbs, parsley or other fresh herbs and the meat in that order; then you needn't wash the bowl until after the meat has been processed.

Use the following photographed techniques as a guide for processing foods from "Apples" to "Bread Dough" to "Meat" to "Pastry Dough" to "Zucchini." The alphabetical order makes it easy to refer to these techniques whether you are preparing recipes in this book or your own favorites.

Each technique has been numbered for cross-referencing throughout this book. When you come to a tricky food processor step in one of the recipes, you will see this symbol beside it. Turn to the technique number indicated in the symbol for a clear illustration of the method you should use.

1. APPLES—*Chopped*

Insert steel blade. Cut apples into wedges; place up to 2 cups (500 mL) of apples in bowl.

Process until desired texture is achieved. Use chopped apples in salads or to make applesauce.

2. APPLES—*Sliced*

Insert slicing disc. Cut apples into halves or quarters and core. Pare if desired. Cut a small slice from side of apple to create a flat edge, if using halves. Position in feed tube horizontally with flat edge on disc.

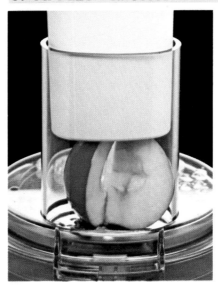

Apple halves positioned horizontally will yield attractive slices, as shown above, for tarts and salads. (For slices with a semi-circular shape, position half an apple upright in feed tube.)

3. APPLES—*Shredded*

Insert shredding disc. Position halved or quartered apples vertically in feed tube.

The regular or fine shredding disc can be used, depending upon the fineness of texture desired. The apple above was shredded with regular disc.

4. BANANAS—*Sliced*

The curved shape of a banana will yield some oblong slices. For perfectly even slices, gently mold banana with hands to straighten ends. Insert slicing disc. Cut banana in half; position in feed tube with flat edges on disc.

Use firm bananas for best quality slices. Sprinkle slices with lemon juice to prevent them from turning brown.

5. BREAD CRUMBS

Insert steel blade. Cut or tear bread into pieces; it is not necessary to remove crusts. Use fresh or dry bread, depending upon recipe.

Process until crumbs of desired texture are formed. Fresh or dried crumbs can be used as a topping for casseroles or coating for fried or baked meats.

Fresh or dried herbs, such as parsley, can be added to bread crumbs.

Process until herbs are finely chopped. Herb-crumbs are a delicious coating for fish or chicken. (For buttered crumbs, melted butter can be added through feed tube with machine running.)

6. BREAD DOUGH—General Method

Insert steel or plastic blade. Cut butter into pieces; place flour and butter in bowl.

Process until butter is mixed into flour.

Add yeast mixture or liquid ingredients through feed tube with machine running.

The dough will form a ball in most bread recipes. Follow specific recipe directions.

7. CABBAGE—Shredded

Insert shredding disc. Cut cabbage into wedges to fit feed tube; core if desired. Position upright in feed tube.

Use regular or thin shredding disc, depending upon the fineness of texture desired. The cabbage above was shredded with regular disc.

8. CABBAGE—*Sliced*

Insert slicing disc. Cut cabbage into wedges to fit feed tube; core if desired. Position upright in feed tube.

Use regular or thin slicing disc, depending upon the fineness of texture desired. The cabbage above was sliced with regular disc.

9. CAKE BATTER

Insert steel or plastic blade. Place all ingredients in bowl. Process several seconds; then stop machine. Scrape down sides of bowl with spatula.

Continue processing, using on/off technique, until completely blended.

10. CANDIED FRUIT—*Chopped*

Insert steel blade. Place fruit in bowl, cutting larger fruit into pieces, if necessary. Place about ½ cup (125 mL) of the amount of flour or sugar called for in recipe in bowl; subtract amount of flour or sugar used from remainder of recipe procedure.

Process until desired texture is achieved. Chopped fruit is ready to stir into cake or cookie recipe. If making recipe in food processor, add chopped fruit last; mix into batter or dough using on/off technique.

11. CARROTS—*Chopped*

Insert steel blade. Cut raw carrots into 1-inch (2.5 cm) pieces; place up to 2 cups (500 mL) of carrot pieces in bowl.

Process until desired texture is achieved. Use chopped carrots in vegetable and molded salads, casseroles and soups.

When chopping food, be sure to cut evenly-sized pieces. If you start with food cut into uneven pieces, the resulting mixture will contain large and small pieces, as shown above.

12. CARROTS—*Puree*

13. CARROTS—*Shredded*

To make carrot puree, place up to 2 cups (500 mL) cooked carrots, cut into 1-inch (2.5 cm) pieces, in bowl with plastic or steel blade. Process to desired texture, adding cooking liquid, milk, broth or other liquid through feed tube. Texture will vary according to blade used, amount of liquid added and processing time.

Insert shredding disc. Cut carrots into lengths to fit feed tube. Position carrots in feed tube with flat edges on disc. Foods should be cut the same length so that pusher can rest evenly on top.

Position carrots vertically in feed tube for short shreds, as above. Position carrots horizontally in feed tube for longer shreds.

14. CARROTS—*Sliced*

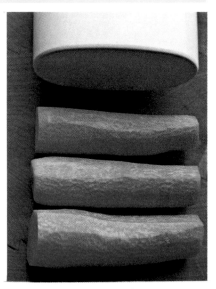

Insert slicing disc. Cut and position carrots in feed tube, as shown for shredding carrots. To slice single carrot or other food, place on left side of feed tube if disc turns clockwise or on right side of feed tube if disc turns counterclockwise. The disc will move against the food, helping it to stay in an upright position.

Position carrots vertically in feed tube for round slices, as shown above. Position horizontally in feed tube for lengthwise slices (see 60. ZUCCHINI—Julienned).

Use food pusher as a guide for measuring width and height of feed tube to cut foods to correct size. Trim one end of food to create a flat edge that can be positioned to rest on disc.

15. CELERY—*Sliced*

Insert slicing disc. Cut celery into lengths to fit feed tube. Remove strings, if desired, for smoother slices. Position celery vertically in feed tube with flat edges on disc.

Use regular or thin slicing disc, depending upon the thickness of slices desired. The celery shown above was sliced with regular disc. Do not position celery horizontally in feed tube; due to the curved shape of the celery, slices would be uneven.

Sometimes pieces of food will catch on the disc, as shown above. This is normal. Excessive food caught on the blade may indicate that the feed tube has not been properly loaded.

16. CHEESE—*Shredded*

Insert shredding disc. Cut chilled semi-hard cheese, such as Cheddar, into pieces to fit feed tube. Position in feed tube with flat edge on disc. Do not shred any cheese softer than mozzarella.

Use regular or thin shredding disc, depending upon texture desired. The cheese above was shredded with regular disc. Shredded cheese can be used for pizza and casseroles and in salads. Extra shredded cheese freezes well.

Cheese may stick to the disc, as shown above. This is normal. Excess cheese on the disc indicates that cheese was not properly chilled or that too soft a cheese was used.

17. CHEESE—*Sliced*

18. CHEESE (Soft)—*Grated*

Insert slicing disc. Cut chilled semi-hard cheese, such as Cheddar, into pieces to fit feed tube. Position in feed tube with flat edge on disc, as shown for shredding cheese. Use slices for appetizers, cold-cut platters or as a topping for casseroles.

Insert steel blade. Cut chilled soft or semi-hard cheese into 1-inch (2.5 cm) pieces. Place up to 2 cups (500 mL) of cheese in bowl.

Process until desired texture is achieved. Processor does not actually "grate" cheese, but "chops" it to a very fine texture.

19. CHEESE (Hard)—*Grated*

Insert steel blade. With machine running, drop 1-inch (2.5 cm) cubes of chilled cheese through feed tube.

Process until desired texture is achieved.

If piece of cheese should get stuck on blade, stop machine immediately. Remove blade; carefully remove cheese from blade with spatula. Reassemble machine and continue processing.

20. CHEESE SPREAD

To make a tangy cheese spread, process 4 ounces (115 g) of Parmesan cheese until grated; leave cheese in bowl.

Cut one 8-ounce (225 g) package cream cheese, at room temperature, into pieces; add to Parmesan cheese in bowl.

Process until mixture is well mixed and soft. Spread on toast squares or crackers. This is an example of how a hard food can be combined with a soft food by processing the hard food first and then processing the two together.

21. CHICKEN—*Sliced*

Roll chicken pieces to fit feed tube; wrap in plastic wrap and place in freezer until very firm, but not completely frozen. (If you cannot insert tip of knife into chicken, it is too hard.) Unwrap chicken; position in feed tube.

Use chicken slices in Oriental cooking or casseroles.

22. CHOCOLATE—*Grated*

Insert steel blade. Break chocolate into pieces no larger than 1-inch (2.5 cm). Place up to 2 cups (500 mL) of chocolate pieces in bowl.

23. COCONUT—*Shredded*

Process until desired texture is achieved. Chocolate can also be shredded if flakier texture is desired; place chocolate in feed tube and process with shredding disc.

Insert shredding disc. Cut peeled coconut into pieces to fit feed tube. Position in feed tube. (See recipe for Spicy Eggs in the Indian Curry Dinner for preparation of fresh coconut.)

For shreds smaller than those shown above, use smaller pieces of coconut. If a grated texture is desired, process like grated chocolate.

24. COOKIE DOUGH—*General Method*

Insert steel or plastic blade. Cut butter or shortening into pieces; place in bowl with sugar.

Process until mixture is soft and fluffy. Add egg to bowl; process until mixed.

Add flour to bowl, about ½ cup (125 mL) at a time; process until blended after each addition.

25. CRACKER AND COOKIE CRUMBS

After final addition of flour, mix until all flour is incorporated and mixture is smooth. If using nuts, raisins or chocolate chips, mix in last, using on/off technique.

Insert steel blade. Break graham crackers, vanilla wafers or other cookies or crackers into pieces; place up to 2 cups (500 mL) in bowl.

Process until crumbs of desired texture are formed. Use to make crumb crusts for pies and cheesecakes.

26. CUCUMBERS—*Shredded*

Insert shredding disc. Cut cucumbers to fit feed tube. Pare and seed if desired. Position vertically in feed tube with flat edge on disc.

If shredded cucumber is too moist, drain on paper toweling. Use shredded cucumber in relishes and salads.

27. CUCUMBERS—*Sliced*

Insert slicing disc. Cut cucumbers to fit feed tube. Pare if desired; seed if desired. Position vertically in feed tube with flat edge on disc.

Seeded cucumbers yield arc-shaped slices that are attractive in salads. Small cucumbers can be sliced whole, pared or unpared, for round slices (see 59. ZUCCHINI—Sliced). To obtain lengthwise slices, position cucumbers in feed tube horizontally (see 60. ZUCCHINI—Julienned).

28. EGGS—*Chopped*

Insert steel blade. Cut eggs into halves or quarters; place in bowl. (Egg yolks and whites can be chopped separately, if desired.)

Process, using on/off technique, until desired texture is achieved. Use in salads or as garnish.

29. EGG SALAD

Insert steel blade. Cut firmer foods for egg salad, such as celery, carrots, pickles and green onions, into 1-inch (2.5 cm) pieces; place in bowl.

Process firmer foods until mixture is desired texture. Add hard-cooked eggs, cut in half, and generous spoonful of mayonnaise to bowl.

Process, using on/off technique, to chop egg and combine ingredients.

30. EGGPLANT—*Sliced*

Insert slicing disc. Pare eggplant; cut into thirds or quarters to fit feed tube. Position in feed tube with flat edge on disc.

Before using eggplant slices in recipe, sprinkle with salt; let stand 30 minutes to remove excess moisture. Rinse; dry with paper toweling.

31. GARLIC—*Minced*

To chop small foods, like garlic or gingerroot slices, insert steel blade. Drop food through feed tube with the machine running. You can then add other foods, such as celery, onion or carrot, to the bowl and continue processing until these are chopped.

32. GREEN BEANS—*French-Cut*

Insert slicing disc. Trim ends from beans; position horizontally in feed tube. Small spatula may be used to help arrange beans in feed tube.

Use only fresh green beans for French-cut beans. Canned and frozen beans are too soft to slice well.

33. HAM SALAD

All ingredients for ham salad—ham, cheese, green pepper, onion and parsley—are similar in texture; so they can be placed in bowl with mayonnaise and seasonings and processed together with steel blade.

34. ICE—*Chopped*

Process, using on/off technique, until ingredients are chopped to desired texture. This technique applies to all meat salads and other combinations of similarly-textured food.

Insert steel blade. Drop ice cubes through feed tube with machine running. It is not unusual for machine to move on counter during this process; so do not position near edge.

Process ice to desired texture. One or two large pieces of ice may remain; discard them.

35. LIQUID MIXTURES

You can mix-blend liquids or a liquid and a soft fruit with the plastic or steel blade. Reconstitute frozen orange juice in food processor for freshly-squeezed flavor; add pieces of banana or other fruit.

Process until banana is pureed. Pour this refreshing fruit beverage over ice cubes or crushed ice.

Check operating manual for capacity of bowl when processing liquid mixtures. If bowl is overfilled, mixture will leak through lid during processing.

36. MAYONNAISE

Finger can be placed in bottom of bowl to hold blade in place when pouring liquids from bowl.

Insert steel or plastic blade. When making mayonnaise with 1 or 2 eggs, place egg and lemon juice in bowl; tilt the machine with a book, so that the egg can be more easily mixed. It is not necessary to tilt the bowl when using more eggs.

With machine running, slowly pour in oil through feed tube. When mayonnaise begins to thicken, you can add remainder of oil more quickly.

37. MEAT (Lunchmeat)—*Sliced*

The longer the mayonnaise is processed, the thicker it will become.

Insert slicing disc. Fold lunchmeat in half; use enough slices to pack feed tube tightly. Insert meat through bottom of feed tube.

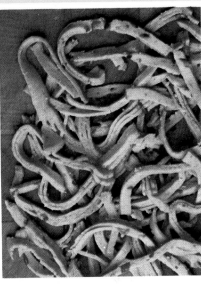

Use lunchmeat strips in vegetable or meat salads or in casseroles.

38. MEAT (Raw)—*Sliced*

Insert slicing disc. Cut raw beef or other meat into pieces to fit feed tube; wrap in plastic wrap and place in freezer until very firm, but not completely frozen (if you cannot insert tip of knife into meat, it is too hard). Unwrap meat; position in feed tube.

Slice raw meat only with regular slicing disc; do not use thin slicing disc. Use meat slices in Oriental cooking or other recipes that specify slices.

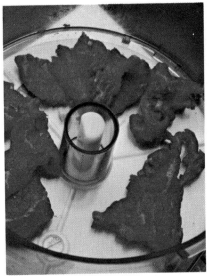

Uneven or ragged slices, as above, indicate that meat was too soft when sliced.

39. MEAT (Raw)—*Chopped*

Insert steel blade. Cut raw beef or other meat into 1-inch (2.5 cm) cubes; place up to 1 cup (250 mL) in bowl. Trim fat from meat according to use: leave some fat for juicy hamburgers; trim all fat for steak tartare.

Process, using on/off technique, until desired texture is achieved. Remove meat from bowl; remove any tendons or gristle, which will not be chopped during processing.

You must use on/off technique to chop meat. On/off technique was not used to process meat shown above; so it is nearly pureed.

40. MEAT (Cooked)—*Chopped*

Insert steel blade. Cut ham or other cooked meat into 1-inch (2.5 cm) pieces; place up to 2 cups (500 mL) in bowl. Process ham until desired texture is achieved. Use in salads, sandwich spreads or casseroles. Cooked meat may be processed with other foods (see 33. HAM SALAD).

Use on/off technique to control texture carefully. Meat can be chopped to coarse, medium or fine texture.

41. MEAT (Cooked)—*Sliced*

Insert slicing disc. Cut chilled ham or other meat into pieces to fit feed tube. Position in feed tube with flat edge on disc.

42. MEAT (Sausage)—*Sliced*

Use slices on sandwiches or canapés or on meat platters. If meat is soft in texture or not chilled, slices will have ragged edges.

Insert slicing disc. Remove casing from chilled sausage; cut into lengths to fit feed tube. Position in feed tube with flat edges on disc.

Use sliced sausage for salads, appetizers and pizza.

43. MUSHROOMS—*Sliced*

Small pieces of meat may stick to the slicing disc; this is normal. If meat is not chilled well enough, an excess amount may stick to the disc.

Insert slicing disc. Trim stems and stack mushrooms randomly in feed tube.

Sliced mushrooms can be used in soups, salads and casseroles.

44. NUTS—*Chopped*

Insert steel blade. Place up to 2 cups (500 mL) shelled nuts in bowl. Process until desired texture is achieved. You can control texture more easily by using on/off technique.

Nuts can be chopped to coarse, medium, fine or ground texture for use in any recipe.

45. ONIONS—*Chopped*

Insert steel blade. Peel onion; cut into pieces. Place in bowl.

Process, using on/off technique, until desired texture is achieved.

Be careful to use on/off technique with onions and other foods that have a high moisture content. Otherwise, onions may be chopped more finely than intended, as shown above.

46. ONIONS—*Sliced*

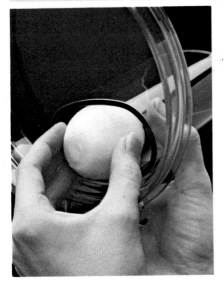

Insert slicing disc. Cut small slice from end of onion. If onion is too large to fit through top of feed tube, insert from bottom (bottom of feed tube is slightly larger than top). Small lemons, limes, potatoes and similarly-shaped foods can be inserted the same way. Cut large onions into halves or quarters to fit feed tube.

47. ONIONS (Green)—*Sliced*

Insert slicing disc. Trim onions into even lengths to fit feed tube. Position vertically and pack tightly into feed tube.

Use slices in salads, Chinese dishes and as a garnish for soups.

48. ORANGES—*Sliced*

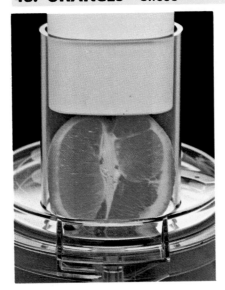

Insert slicing disc. Cut small slice from end of orange; cut in half lengthwise. Insert through top or bottom of feed tube; position in feed tube with flat edge on disc.

Use orange slices to garnish cakes, pies, salads and fruit punches. Oranges may be peeled before slicing for use in salads.

49. PARSLEY—*Chopped*

Insert steel blade. Remove stems from parsley and other leafy herbs. Make sure sprigs are dry before placing in bowl.

Process until desired texture is achieved. Herbs will become moist when processed; dry them on paper toweling. Chopped, dried herbs may be frozen.

50. PASTRY DOUGH

Insert steel blade. Cut frozen butter into pieces; place flour and butter in bowl.

Process until butter is mixed into flour.

Add cold water through feed tube with machine running.

Stop adding liquid when dough has formed a ball. Refrigerate dough 30 minutes to make it easier to roll out. Follow specific recipe directions.

51. PEANUT BUTTER

Insert steel blade. Place up to 2 cups (500 mL) shelled peanuts (or other nuts) in bowl (do not use dry-roasted nuts). Process until nut butter is formed. It will be very thick at first, as shown above.

Continue processing until nut butter reaches desired consistency. For chunky peanut butter, add a handful of nuts after butter has been processed; process with several on/off motions. Honey or jelly can be added to peanut butter and processed until combined.

Cut top off pepper; remove seeds. If pepper is too large to fit feed tube, slit it from top to bottom on one side.

Carefully fold pepper, overlapping edges, to fit feed tube.

Insert slicing disc. Position folded pepper in feed tube with flat edge on disc.

Use slices to garnish salads, sandwiches and casseroles.

53. PEPPERS (Halved)—*Sliced*

Large peppers can also be cut in half and sliced. Insert slicing disc. Arrange one or both halves in feed tube with flat edge on disc. (Do not position peppers horizontally to slice; due to the curved shape of the pepper, slices would be uneven.)

Use slices as ingredients in Oriental cooking and salads or for garnish.

54. POTATOES—*Shredded*

Potatoes may be shredded pared or unpared. Insert shredding disc. Leave potato whole, if small, or cut to fit feed tube. Insert into feed tube from top or bottom.

Rinse shredded potatoes with water and drain on paper toweling to remove excess starch. Chop shreds with steel blade, using on/off technique, if shorter shreds are desired for foods such as potato pancakes.

55. POTATOES—*Sliced*

Potatoes may be sliced pared or unpared. Insert slicing disc. Cut small slice off end of potato to create a flat edge. Leave whole, if small, or cut to fit feed tube. Insert into feed tube from top or bottom; position with flat edge on disc.

Rinse sliced potatoes with water and drain on paper toweling to remove excess starch. Use for fried or scalloped potatoes. (A French-fry slicing disc is available with many food processors; it may be used to cut carrots or zucchini strips as well as French-fried potatoes.)

56. RADISHES—*Sliced*

Insert slicing disc. Unevenly shaped or round small fruits and vegetables such as radishes, mushrooms and strawberries are difficult to place evenly in the feed tube. Trim ends and place in feed tube randomly.

Slices are attractive for use as a garnish or in salads.

57. SPINACH—*Sliced*

Insert slicing disc. Rinse spinach; dry on paper toweling. Remove stems. Stack leaves and fold; position tightly in feed tube.

Sliced spinach can be used raw in salads or cooked in recipes.

58. STRAWBERRIES—*Puree*

Process up to 2 cups (500 mL) of hulled strawberries with plastic or steel blade to desired texture. Strawberries and other foods with high moisture content may not require additional liquid to process into a puree.

Use strawberry puree as a sauce or mix with fruit juice or milk for beverages.

59. ZUCCHINI—*Sliced*

60. ZUCCHINI—*Julienned*

Insert slicing disc. Cut zucchini into lengths to fit feed tube. Position in feed tube with flat edges on disc.

Zucchini slices can be used raw in salads or pickles, steamed or used in Oriental recipes. Zucchini can be sliced with regular slicing disc (left) or with thin slicing disc (right).

To make julienne strips without a special disc, trim zucchini or other foods to fit horizontally into feed tube. Insert slicing disc. Position zucchini in feed tube.

Lengthwise slices can be used with dips or reinserted into feed tube and resliced for julienne strips.

To reslice lengthwise slices, place them together and insert tightly in bottom of feed tube; slice.

Sauté julienne strips as a vegetable side dish or use in salads.

France

Ratatouille and Country Pâté

French Dinner as Fresh as Spring

Liver Pâté

Cream of Carrot Soup

Herbed Leg of Lamb

Spinach Mousse

Potato Puffs

Apple Charlotte

There are few signs of spring as tempting as the appearance in the market of young, tender lamb. So take advantage of the season to serve a bountiful dinner that also features bouquets of fresh vegetables prepared in interesting ways.

The food processor has turned the famous pâtés of France into accessible cosmopolitan treats. So we offer a classic, fluffy chicken-liver blend scented with cognac and spices. This recipe is superb because the strong flavor of the chicken livers is perfectly balanced by butter and whipped cream. You can serve it without the Aspic, but there are few touches as elegantly enticing as the appearance of the decorative vegetable garnish beneath their shimmering topping. For the sake of convenience, make this course a day in advance and refrigerate covered with plastic wrap.

The same miracles of chopping and pureeing that the processor performs with pâtés are repeated in smooth, satiny soups like the Cream of Carrot Soup. Although it fits beautifully into the harmony of this spring menu, this recipe will prove to be a year-round meal-saver because carrots are almost always available.

The most important thing to remember about lamb is not to overcook it; truly, it is best served rare. Slivers of garlic randomly implanted in the surface of the lamb contribute a very subtle yet important flavor dimension. The sauce for this Herbed Leg of Lamb is a nouvelle cuisine specialty of the food processor; it is simply a puree of vegetables that have been roasted with the lamb and processed with the pan juices. You can't improve on its honest flavor!

Accompanied by a delicate, yet foolproof, Spinach Mousse and fried Potato Puffs and followed by a heavenly Apple Charlotte, this spring lamb will prove memorable. So match it with an excellent Médoc Claret or a full-bodied Saint-Emilion.

LIVER PÂTÉ
Makes 8 to 10 servings

1 onion
¾ pound (340 g) chicken livers, cleaned, trimmed
2 parsley sprigs
1 cup (250 mL) chicken stock
½ small onion, cut in half
½ pound (225 g) butter or margarine, room temperature
1 teaspoon (5 mL) cognac
½ teaspoon (2 mL) ground nutmeg
¼ teaspoon (1 mL) ground cloves
½ teaspoon (2 mL) salt
⅛ teaspoon (0.5 mL) pepper
½ cup (125 mL) whipping cream
Aspic (recipe follows)
Pimiento, carrots, radishes, ripe olives, green onions for decoration
French Bread (see Index for page number)

1. Using slicing disc, slice 1 onion.

2. Combine sliced onion, the chicken livers, parsley and chicken stock in small saucepan. Heat to boiling; reduce heat. Simmer covered 10 minutes. Drain. Reserve livers; reserve liquid for Aspic.

3. Using steel blade, process ½ onion, using on/off technique, until finely chopped. Add reserved chicken livers, the butter, cognac, nutmeg, cloves, salt and pepper to bowl. Process until mixture is smooth, stopping to scrape sides of bowl occasionally.

4. Refrigerate mixture 15 minutes. Mix well with spoon. Refrigerate 15 minutes longer.

5. Whip cream with electric mixer until stiff. Gently fold into liver mixture. Pour mixture into small terrine or serving dish. Refrigerate until firm, about 3 hours.

6. Make Aspic.

7. Cut vegetables into decorative shapes. When pâté is firm, arrange vegetable cutouts on top of pâté. Spoon Aspic over top. Refrigerate at least 5 hours before serving.

8. Serve from terrine with French Bread.

Aspic

1 envelope unflavored gelatin
1 egg white, slightly beaten
Reserved cooking stock

1. Stir gelatin and egg white into reserved cooking stock. Heat to boiling, stirring constantly. A crusty film will form on the top. Remove pan from heat.

2. Pour mixture through strainer lined with paper toweling. Let stand until cool. Refrigerate until Aspic is consistency of heavy syrup, about ½ hour.

CREAM OF CARROT SOUP
Makes 6 servings

½ cup (125 mL) parsley
   sprigs
1 pound (450 g) carrots,
   cut into 1-inch (2.5
   cm) pieces
2 onions, cut into
   quarters
2 ribs celery, cut into
   1-inch (2.5 cm)
   pieces

3 tablespoons (45 mL)
   butter or margarine
1 tablespoon (15 mL)
   all-purpose flour
4 cups (1 L) chicken
   stock
3 egg yolks
½ cup (125 mL)
   whipping cream
Pinch black pepper

1. Using steel blade, process parsley until chopped; reserve.

2. Using steel blade, process carrots, onions and celery until finely chopped.

3. Sauté chopped vegetables in butter in large saucepan until tender, 10 to 15 minutes. Stir in flour; cook 2 to 3 minutes.

4. Stir in chicken stock. Cook covered over medium heat until carrots are soft, 15 to 20 minutes.

5. Strain soup; return stock to saucepan.

6. Using steel blade, process cooked vegetable mixture, 2 cups (500 mL) at a time, until smooth. Add to stock, stirring until smooth.

7. Using steel blade, process egg yolks and cream until blended. With machine running, gradually add 1 cup (250 mL) hot soup through feed tube. Stir egg yolk mixture gradually into remaining hot soup.

8. Stir in pepper. Simmer until slightly thickened and hot. Do not boil.

9. Just before serving, sprinkle with chopped parsley.

HERBED LEG OF LAMB
Makes 8 servings

4 cloves garlic
½ cup (125 mL) parsley
   sprigs
1 carrot, cut into 1-inch
   (2.5 cm) pieces
1 onion, cut into
   quarters
1 rib celery, cut into
   1-inch (2.5 cm)
   pieces
2 tablespoons (30 mL)
   butter or margarine
2 tablespoons (30 mL)
   olive oil
1 leg of lamb (5 to 6
   pounds or 2250 to
   2700 g)
Salt

Pepper
1 cup (250 mL) red
   wine
1 to 1½ cups (250 to
   375 mL) beef stock
¼ teaspoon (1 mL)
   dried basil leaves
⅛ teaspoon (0.5 mL)
   dried thyme leaves
⅛ teaspoon (0.5 mL)
   dried oregano leaves
½ to 1 teaspoon (2 to 5
   mL) salt
⅛ teaspoon (0.5 mL)
   pepper
Parsley or watercress
   sprigs

1. Using steel blade, process 2 cloves of the garlic, ½ cup (125 mL) parsley, the carrot, onion and celery until finely chopped.

2. Sauté chopped vegetables in butter and oil until soft, 10 to 15 minutes; place in bottom of roasting pan.

3. Heat oven to 450 °F (230 °C). Cut remaining 2 cloves of garlic into tiny slivers. Pierce lamb in several places with knife and insert garlic slivers. Sprinkle lamb with salt and pepper. Place lamb on rack in roasting pan. Roast lamb 15 minutes.

4. Reduce oven temperature to 350 °F (180 °C). Mix wine, 1 cup of the stock, basil, thyme and oregano; add to roasting pan. Roast 15 to 20 minutes for every pound of lamb. [For rare, 145 to 150 °F (63 to 66 °C) on meat thermometer; for well done, 160 to 165 °F (71 to 74 °C).]

5. Remove lamb to serving platter. Let stand 20 to 30 minutes before carving.

6. Skim fat from pan juices.

7. Using steel blade, process pan juices until pureed. Strain through fine sieve, if desired. If mixture is too thick, add beef stock to desired consistency. Season with ½ to 1 teaspoon (2 to 5 mL) salt and ⅛ teaspoon (0.5 mL) pepper.

8. To serve, slice lamb and arrange on heated serving platter. Spoon a little sauce over top. Garnish with parsley sprigs. Serve remaining sauce on the side.

SPINACH MOUSSE
Makes 6 servings

1 slice dry white bread,
   broken into pieces
1 onion, cut into
   quarters
3 tablespoons (45 mL)
   butter or margarine
1 pound (450 g) fresh
   spinach, stems
   trimmed

2 teaspoons (10 mL)
   flour
1½ cups (375 mL)
   half-and-half
1 teaspoon (5 mL) salt
¼ teaspoon (1 mL)
   pepper
⅛ teaspoon (0.5 mL)
   ground nutmeg
4 eggs

1. Using steel blade, process bread to fine crumbs; reserve.

2. Using steel blade, process onion, using on/off technique, until chopped. Sauté in butter until tender, 5 minutes.

3. Rinse spinach; place in large saucepan with water clinging to leaves. Cook covered over medium heat until tender, about 5 minutes. Drain. Using steel blade, process spinach, using on/off technique, until coarsely chopped.

4. Add flour to cooked onions; cook over medium heat, stirring constantly, 2 to 3 minutes. Gradually stir in half-and-half. Heat to boiling; reduce heat. Cook,

stirring constantly, until thickened. Stir in chopped spinach, salt, pepper and nutmeg.

5. Using plastic or steel blade, process eggs until foamy. Stir into spinach mixture.

6. Heat oven to 350°F (180°C). Coat buttered 6-cup (1.5 L) casserole or mold with bread crumbs. Pour spinach mixture into prepared mold. Place mold in pan of hot water.

7. Bake until knife inserted into center comes out clean, 35 to 40 minutes. Remove mold from water bath. Let stand 5 minutes.

8. To serve, run knife around inside of mold and invert onto serving platter.

POTATO PUFFS
Makes 6 to 8 servings

3 potatoes (1 pound or 450 g), pared, cut into quarters
2 cups (500 mL) water
½ teaspoon (2 mL) salt
*1 ounce (30 g) Gruyère cheese
1 cup (250 mL) warm Pâte à Choux (recipe follows)
¾ teaspoon (4 mL) salt
Vegetable oil

1. Boil potatoes in water and ½ teaspoon (2 mL) salt until tender. Drain; let dry a few minutes.

2. Using shredding disc, shred potatoes and cheese. Transfer to mixing bowl.

3. Make Pâte à Choux.

4. Mix Pâte à Choux and potato mixture thoroughly. Stir in ¾ teaspoon (4mL) salt. Heat 3 inches (8 cm) vegetable oil to 350°C (180°C). Drop batter, 2 teaspoonfuls (10 mL) at a time, into hot oil; cook, turning occasionally, until light brown. Drain on paper toweling. Serve immediately.
   *Note: *Grated Parmesan cheese can be substituted for the Gruyère cheese.*

Pâte à Choux

½ cup (125 mL) milk
3 tablespoons (45 mL) butter or margarine, cut into pieces
¾ teaspoon (4 mL) salt
Pinch pepper
Pinch ground nutmeg
½ cup (125 mL) flour
2 eggs

1. Heat milk, butter, salt, pepper and nutmeg to boiling; cook until butter melts. Remove from heat.

2. Add flour all at once. Stir vigorously with wooden spoon until mixture forms into ball and cleans side of pan. Let cool 5 minutes.

3. Insert steel blade. Transfer mixture to bowl; add eggs. Process until mixture is blended, smooth and shiny, 30 to 45 seconds.

APPLE CHARLOTTE
Makes 6 to 8 servings

10 large red or golden delicious apples (3½ to 4 pounds or 1600 to 1800 g), pared, cored, cut into halves
½ cup (125 mL) sugar
Grated rind of 1 lemon
2 tablespoons (30 mL) dark rum
6 tablespoons (90 mL) butter or margarine
½ teaspoon (2 mL) ground cinnamon
¼ teaspoon (1 mL) ground ginger
1 teaspoon (5 mL) vanilla
10 to 12 slices firm white bread, crusts removed
Apricot-Rum Sauce (recipe follows)

1. Using slicing disc, slice apples.

2. Cook apples, sugar, lemon rind and rum in 4 tablespoons (60 mL) of the butter in large skillet over medium heat until juices have evaporated and apple mixture is quite thick, 20 to 30 minutes. Stir in cinnamon, ginger and vanilla.

3. Melt remaining butter. Coat bottom and sides of 1½-quart (1.5 L) charlotte mold or soufflé dish with melted butter.

4. Heat oven to 425°F (220°C). Cut 3 slices bread into small triangles. Arrange triangles, points facing toward center, in bottom of charlotte mold. Trim to fit where necessary. (If desired, cut off tips of triangles in center of mold with a small round cutter; cut a circle of bread with the same cutter and fit into center.)

5. Reserve 1 slice of bread; cut remaining slices in half. Arrange slices around sides of charlotte mold, overlapping them slightly (see photo 1).

Photo 1. Arrange bread triangles in bottom of charlotte mold. Arrange half-slices of bread around sides of mold, overlapping slices slightly.

6. Fill mold with apple mixture, mounding mixture in center. Cover with reserved slice of bread trimmed to fit top. Apple mixture should be completely enclosed by bread.

7. Bake until top is golden, 30 to 35 minutes. Let stand at least 1 hour before unmolding.

8. While mold is baking, make Apricot-Rum Sauce.

9. Just before serving, invert mold onto serving platter and coat with a thin layer of Apricot-Rum Sauce. Cut into wedges. Pour a little sauce over each serving.

Note: This dessert may be served warm or cold. Always serve Apricot-Rum Sauce hot.

Apricot-Rum Sauce
Makes about 1½ cups (375 mL)

1 jar (12 ounces or 340 g) apricot preserves
2 tablespoons (30 mL) water

3 to 4 tablespoons (45 to 60 mL) rum
2 tablespoons (30 mL) lemon juice
Pinch ground ginger
Pinch ground nutmeg

1. Heat apricot preserves and water in small saucepan to boiling, stirring until smooth. Strain through fine sieve. Return to saucepan. Stir in rum, lemon juice and spices. Keep warm.

Dinner from the South of France

Green Salad Vinaigrette

Bouillabaise

French Bread

Orange-Cheese Tart

Even if you choose to serve this hearty fish-stew dinner on a cold, blustery winter night, you can't help feeling the sunniness of the south of France in this menu.

We cannot stroll along the quai in Marseilles to select the pick of the catch from seaside vendors. But we can prepare a Bouillabaise to rival the local classic from the best fresh fish available here. Garlic, tomatoes and saffron give the broth an irresistible Mediterranean fragrance. You can prepare the Fish Stock and the Rouille up to a week in advance and keep them tightly covered in the refrigerator. The Rouille is a heady garlic sauce that adds an absolutely essential dimension to the fish stew.

Equally essential to any French meal are long, crusty loaves of bread. If kneading has discouraged you from bread-making previously, then this food-processor recipe provides a perfect invitation to fill your kitchen with the uniquely marvelous aroma of fresh-baked loaves. You can't fail so long as you keep in mind a couple of baking facts: The water in which the yeast is dissolved must be at the temperature specified; yeast needs just the right amount of warmth to "grow" and "raise" the bread. You cannot judge how much flour to use except by watching the texture of the dough; the amount required will depend on the kind of flour and the humidity in the air. Where you leave the dough to rise will determine how long the process takes; it will rise fastest in a warm place, like an unheated oven with a pilot light; but many cooks prefer to let the dough rise slowly, at room temperature, for optimum texture.

Like the French Bread, the Green Salad Vinaigrette is sure to become a staple at your dinner table. You can, as the French would, serve the refreshing salad following the entree in any French menu.

Chablis (Premier Cru) has been labeled the "fish wine" of France, making it the perfect dry accompaniment to the Bouillabaise.

GREEN SALAD VINAIGRETTE
Makes 6 to 8 servings

1 hard-cooked egg, cut in half
1 clove garlic
2 large parsley sprigs
⅛ teaspoon (0.5 mL) dried chervil leaves
⅛ teaspoon (0.5 mL) dried tarragon leaves
1 teaspoon (5 mL) Dijon-style mustard

1 tablespoon (15 mL) wine vinegar
1 tablespoon (15 mL) lemon juice
3 tablespoons (45 mL) olive oil
3 tablespoons (45 mL) vegetable oil
¼ teaspoon (1 mL) salt
⅛ teaspoon (0.5 mL) pepper
1 large head romaine, broken into pieces

1. Using steel blade, process egg until finely chopped; reserve.

2. Insert steel blade. With machine running, drop garlic through feed tube; process until minced. Add parsley to bowl; process until chopped.

3. Add remaining ingredients except egg and romaine to bowl. Process until thoroughly blended.

4. Arrange romaine in salad bowl; toss with dressing. Sprinkle chopped egg over top.

BOUILLABAISE
Makes 6 to 8 servings

Fish Stock (recipe
   follows)
Rouille (recipe
   follows)
½ cup (125 mL) parsley
   sprigs
2 large cloves garlic
3 onions, cut into
   quarters
1 leek, trimmed, cut
   into 1-inch (2.5
   cm) pieces
1 rib celery, cut into
   1-inch (2.5 cm)
   pieces
¼ cup (60 mL) olive oil
4 large tomatoes,
   peeled, seeded
½ cup (125 mL) tomato
   sauce
2 bay leaves
1 piece orange rind, 2-
   inches (5 cm)
   square
½ teaspoon (2 mL)
   saffron threads
½ teaspoon (2 mL)
   dried thyme leaves

Pinch dried rosemary
   leaves
4 pounds (1800 g)
   assorted fresh fish
   (whitefish, red
   snapper, striped
   bass, scrod,
   seabass or porgy),
   cut into serving
   pieces
½ pound (225 g)
   uncooked shrimp,
   shelled, deveined
½ pound (225 g)
   scallops, rinsed
12 cherrystone clams,
   rinsed
2 tablespoons (30 mL)
   anise-flavored
   liqueur
1 to 2 teaspoons (5 to
   10 mL) salt
¼ teaspoon (1 mL)
   pepper
6 to 8 slices dry French
   Bread, 1-inch (2.5
   cm) thick (see
   Index for page
   number)

1. Make Fish Stock.

2. Make Rouille.

3. Using steel blade, process parsley until chopped;
   reserve.

4. Insert steel blade. With machine running, drop garlic
   through feed tube; process until minced. Add onions
   to bowl. Process, using on/off technique, until
   chopped.

5. Using steel blade, process leek and celery until finely
   chopped.

6. Sauté garlic and onions, leek and celery in olive oil in
   large saucepan until soft, about 15 minutes.

7. Using steel blade, process tomatoes until chopped.
   Add tomatoes, tomato sauce, bay leaves, orange
   rind, saffron, thyme and rosemary to saucepan. Heat
   to boiling; reduce heat. Simmer uncovered 30
   minutes.

8. Add Fish Stock; heat to boiling. Add fish, shrimp,
   scallops and clams to stock. Simmer covered until
   fish is tender and opaque, 10 to 15 minutes. Do not
   overcook.

9. Transfer seafood to heated platter; keep warm. Stir
   liqueur, salt and pepper into saucepan. Sprinkle with
   chopped parsley.

10. To serve, place bread slice in each individual bowl,
    ladle soup into bowl and top each bowl with spoonful
    of Rouille. Set platter of fish on table; let each person
    serve himself.

*Note: Bouillabaise may also be served
without bread slices. Ladle soup and
seafood into serving bowls; pass dish
of Rouille.*

Fish Stock
Makes 10 cups (2.5 L)

½ cup (125 mL)
   parsley sprigs
2 onions, cut into
   quarters
3 carrots, cut into
   1-inch (2.5 cm)
   pieces
1 leek, trimmed, cut
   into 1-inch (2.5
   cm) pieces
3 ribs celery, cut into
   1-inch (2.5 cm)
   pieces

2 pounds (900 g) fish
   bones, heads and
   skins
1 bay leaf
½ teaspoon (2 mL)
   dried thyme leaves
10 peppercorns
2½ quarts (2.5 L) water
2 cups (500 mL) dry
   white wine

1. Using steel blade, process parsley, onions, carrots,
   leek and celery, using on/off technique, until
   chopped.

2. Combine chopped ingredients with fish bones, bay
   leaf, thyme, peppercorns, water and wine in large
   stockpot. Heat to boiling; reduce heat. Simmer uncovered 30 minutes. Strain. Discard solids.

Rouille

4 cloves garlic
1 medium potato, boiled,
   pared, cut into pieces
1 teaspoon (5 mL)
   cayenne pepper

4 to 6 tablespoons (60 to
   90 mL) olive oil
Salt
Pepper

1. Insert steel blade. With machine running, drop garlic through feed tube; process until minced. Add
   potato and cayenne pepper to bowl. Process until
   blended.

2. With machine running, add olive oil in slow steady
   stream through feed tube. Process until mixture is
   smooth and the consistency of mayonnaise. Add salt
   and pepper to taste.

FRENCH BREAD
Makes 2 loaves

2 packages active dry yeast	1 tablespoon (15 mL) melted butter or margarine
2¼ cups (560 mL) warm water (105 to 115°F or 40 to 45°C)	5 to 6 cups (1250 mL to 1.5 L) all-purpose flour
Pinch sugar	Cornmeal
2 teaspoons (10 mL) salt	1 egg white
	1 tablespoon (15 mL) cold water

1. Combine yeast and warm water in 1-quart (1 L) measuring cup. Stir to dissolve yeast. Sprinkle with pinch of sugar. Let stand 3 to 5 minutes. Add salt and butter; stir until salt is dissolved.

2. Insert steel blade. Place 2 cups (500 mL) flour in bowl. With machine running, add half the yeast mixture through feed tube. Process a few seconds until blended. Add ½ to 1 cup (125 mL to 250 mL) more flour, about ¼ cup (60 mL) at a time, until dough forms smooth and slightly sticky ball. Let dough spin around bowl 20 to 30 seconds. Turn dough onto lightly floured board. Knead for a minute; shape into smooth ball.

3. Repeat step 2 with remaining flour and yeast mixture.

4. Place each ball of dough in greased bowl; turn the dough to grease the top of the ball. Let stand covered in warm place until doubled, about 1 hour.

5. Punch down dough. Turn onto lightly floured board. Knead for 1 to 2 minutes. Shape dough into long tapered loaves. Place on greased baking sheet lightly sprinkled with cornmeal.

6. Let stand covered in warm place until doubled, about 1 hour.

7. Heat oven to 400°F (200°C). Score surface of dough in 3 diagonal cuts with sharp razor blade or knife. Mix egg white and cold water. Brush loaves with mixture.

8. Bake until golden and bread sounds hollow when tapped, 50 to 55 minutes. Remove from pan; cool on wire rack.

Note: French Bread freezes very well. Let loaves cool. Wrap cool loaves tightly and freeze. To thaw, unwrap and place on baking sheet in cold oven. Heat at 400°F (200°C) until hot, about 20 minutes.

ORANGE-CHEESE TART
Makes 8 servings

Sweet Tart Pastry (see Index for page number)	2 egg yolks
¼ cup (60 mL) butter or margarine	1 tablespoon (15 mL) flour
½ cup (125 mL) sugar	4 tablespoons (60 mL) Grand Marnier or orange-flavored liqueur
1 cup (250 mL) cottage cheese	4 large navel oranges
3 ounces (85 g) cream cheese	¾ cup (180 mL) apricot preserves
2 eggs	

1. Make Sweet Tart Pastry. Heat oven to 400°F (200°C).

2. Roll dough on lightly floured surface into 11-inch (28 cm) circle. Ease pastry into 9-inch (23 cm) tart pan. Line shell with aluminum foil. Fill with pie weights, dried beans or rice.

3. Bake 10 minutes. Remove foil and weights. Bake until shell is light brown, 6 to 8 minutes; cool on wire rack.

4. Heat oven to 375°F (190°C). Insert steel blade. Place butter and sugar in bowl. Process until mixture is creamy. Add cottage cheese and cream cheese; process until smooth. Add eggs, egg yolks, flour and 2 tablespoons (30 mL) of the liqueur. Process until mixture is thoroughly blended. Pour cheese mixture into partially-baked shell.

5. Bake until filling is firm, about 30 minutes. Let stand until cool.

6. While tart is baking, peel and section oranges.* Marinate oranges in remaining liqueur.

7. When baked tart is cool, drain oranges. Heat drained liqueur and apricot preserves in small saucepan until preserves have melted. Stir frequently until mixture is smooth. Strain through fine sieve. Arrange orange sections on top of tart. Brush orange sections with apricot glaze.

*Note: *To section oranges, peel oranges with a sharp knife so that no white membrane is left. Cut out whole sections from between membranes.*

Bouillabaise and French Bread

Country French Picnic—for Indoors or Out

Country Pâté

Cream of Watercress Soup

Broiled Herbed Chicken

Ratatouille

Fresh Peach Tart

Although you may not wish to transport this complete menu to distant woods, you'll find that many of the herb-fragrant dishes suggest a lush setting on a warm summer evening.

The coarse-textured Country Pâté is quite different in mood and taste from the pâté of the spring menu. But here, too, the food processor proves invaluable for chopping chores. A casing of bacon strips moistens the mixture of veal, chicken, pork and chicken livers as it bakes; similarly, surrounding the terrine with boiling water in a roasting pan moderates the effect of the oven's dry heat. Weighted after it's baked, the terrine invariably turns out dense, rich, moist and aromatic. Make it a week in advance and your only problem will be to keep from devouring every crumb of it before serving time!

In contrast to the pâté, the Cream of Watercress Soup is as beautifully delicate as its primary ingredient. You can make it a day in advance and serve it cold or reheat it.

Two food-processor assets contribute to the tantalizing flavor of Broiled Herbed Chicken. First, fresh bread crumbs for the crust take only seconds to process. Secondly, you can blend the mayonnaise-like, mustard-tanged sauce with equal speed. You will want to pack up this chicken in many a picnic basket and keep it on hand for quick lunches and suppers, too.

Remember this Ratatouille recipe when the garden and market abound with delicious fresh peppers, tomatoes and zucchini. You could even omit the eggplant and savor the splendid mélange with twice the quantity of zucchini specified. The same harvest season will yield enough ripe peaches to make the Fresh Peach Tart a menu must.

Regardless of where you spread this picnic, enjoy it with a dry, full-bodied white wine, like a Chassagne-Montrachet.

COUNTRY PÂTÉ
Makes 18 to 20 slices

¾ pound (340 g) sliced bacon
Water
2 ounces (60 g) pistachio nuts, shelled
Boiling water
1 slice boiled ham, ½-inch (1.5 cm) thick
⅓ cup (80 mL) cognac or brandy
2 cloves garlic
1 onion, cut into quarters
2 tablespoons (30 mL) butter or margarine
½ pound (225 g) lean veal, cut into 1-inch (2.5 cm) cubes
½ pound (225 g) chicken, cut into 1-inch (2.5 cm) cubes
½ pound (225 g) lean pork, cut into 1-inch (2.5 cm) cubes
¼ pound (115 g) chicken livers, cleaned, trimmed
½ pound (225 g) pork fat, cut into pieces
2 eggs
½ teaspoon (2 mL) dried thyme leaves
½ teaspoon (2 mL) dried savory leaves
½ teaspoon (2 mL) ground allspice
½ teaspoon (2 mL) ground cinnamon
¼ teaspoon (1 mL) ground cloves
¼ teaspoon (1 mL) ground nutmeg
½ teaspoon (2 mL) salt
¼ teaspoon (1 mL) pepper
2 bay leaves
Boiling water
French Bread (see Index for page number)
Cornichons or other pickles

1. Place bacon in skillet. Cover with water; simmer 10 minutes. Drain; pat dry on paper toweling.

2. Drop pistachio nuts into small pan of boiling water; simmer 1 minute. Remove with slotted spoon. Rub pistachio nuts with paper toweling to remove skins.

3. Cut ham into ½-inch (1.5 cm) wide strips. Pour cognac over ham in shallow bowl.

4. Insert steel blade. With machine running, drop garlic through feed tube; process until minced. Add onion to bowl; process, using on/off technique, until chopped.

5. Sauté garlic and onion in butter in small skillet until tender, about 5 minutes.

6. Using steel blade, process veal, chicken, pork, chicken livers and pork fat separately until finely chopped; place in large mixing bowl.

7. Stir in onion mixture, eggs, thyme, savory, allspice, cinnamon, cloves, nutmeg, salt, pepper and pistachio nuts. Drain ham; pour cognac into meat mixture.

8. Heat oven to 350°F (180°C). Arrange blanched bacon slices over bottom and up sides of 4-cup (1 L) terrine or baking dish. Spread ⅓ meat mixture in bottom. Place half the ham strips over meat. Repeat layers. Cover with remaining meat mixture. Fold bacon slices over top. Pâté should be completely enclosed by bacon. Place bay leaves on top. Cover terrine with lid or aluminum foil.

9. Place terrine in baking pan; add boiling water halfway up side of terrine.

10. Bake until juices are clear when knife is inserted in center and meat shrinks away from sides of terrine, 1¼ to 1½ hours.

11. Remove terrine cover; pour off juices. Cover with aluminum foil. Place heavy weights on top (a brick wrapped in foil or heavy cans). Cool to room temperature; refrigerate 24 hours before serving.

12. To serve, remove pâté from terrine. (If it sticks, place terrine over low heat until bacon fat melts.) Cut into ½-inch (1.5 cm) slices. Serve with French Bread and pickles.

Note: Pâté improves in flavor after 2 to 3 days. Securely wrapped, pâté will keep 8 to 10 days in refrigerator.

CREAM OF WATERCRESS SOUP
Makes 6 servings

3 green onions and tops, cut into 1-inch (2.5 cm) pieces
3 tablespoons (45 mL) butter or margarine
2 large bunches watercress, stems trimmed
3 tablespoons (45 mL) all-purpose flour
5½ cups (1375 mL) chicken stock
½ cup (125 mL) heavy cream
Pinch white pepper
Pinch ground nutmeg
2 apples, pared, cored, cut into quarters

1. Using steel blade, process green onions until chopped. Sauté green onions in butter in large saucepan until tender, 5 to 10 minutes.

2. Reserve 6 sprigs of watercress for garnish. Stir remaining watercress into green onions; cook covered over low heat 5 minutes.

3. Add flour; cook, stirring constantly, 3 minutes. Remove from heat; stir in chicken stock. Heat to boiling; reduce heat. Simmer until watercress is tender, about 10 minutes.

4. Strain soup; return stock to saucepan. Using steel blade, process watercress mixture until smooth. Return to saucepan.

5. Stir in cream, pepper and nutmeg; heat to simmering. Refrigerate until cold.

6. Using shredding disc, shred apples.

7. To serve, ladle chilled soup into individual cups. Sprinkle each serving with shredded apple. Top with watercress sprig.

Note: This soup is also delicious hot; omit shredded apple.

BROILED HERBED CHICKEN
Makes 6 servings

2 broiling chickens (2½ pounds or 1125 g each), cut into serving pieces
¼ cup (60 mL) butter or margarine
¼ cup (60 mL) olive oil
6 slices fresh white or whole wheat bread, broken into pieces
2 green onions and tops, cut into 1-inch (2.5 cm) pieces

2 fresh parsley sprigs
6 tablespoons (90 mL) Dijon-style mustard
1 tablespoon (15 mL) lemon juice
¼ teaspoon (1 mL) dried basil leaves
¼ teaspoon (1 mL) dried tarragon leaves
⅛ teaspoon (0.5 mL) dried thyme leaves
⅛ teaspoon (0.5 mL) pepper

1. Heat oven to 550°F (290°C) or broil. Wash and dry chicken thoroughly. Heat butter and olive oil in small saucepan until butter is melted. Arrange chicken in broiling pan. Baste with 2 tablespoons (30 mL) of the butter mixture.

2. Broil chicken 6 inches (15 cm) from heat source until light brown, 5 to 8 minutes per side. Baste chicken with 2 tablespoons (30 mL) of the butter mixture after turning.

3. While chicken is broiling, insert steel blade; process bread to fine crumbs; reserve.

4. Using steel blade, process green onions and parsley until finely chopped. Add mustard, lemon juice, basil, tarragon, thyme and pepper to bowl. With machine running, gradually add half the remaining butter mixture through feed tube. Mustard mixture should have mayonnaise-like consistency.

5. Brush chicken with mustard mixture. Roll chicken in bread crumbs.

6. Return chicken to broiler pan. Baste with remaining butter mixture. Broil until chicken is tender, 8 to 10 minutes per side. Serve hot or cold.

RATATOUILLE
Makes 6 servings

2 cloves garlic
½ cup (125 mL) parsley sprigs
1 small eggplant (¾ pound or 340 g), pared, cut lengthwise into quarters
½ cup (125 mL) olive oil
2 small zucchini (¾ pound or 350 g)

3 onions
2 green peppers
6 tomatoes, peeled
1 teaspoon (5 mL) dried basil leaves
2 teaspoons (10 mL) salt
¼ teaspoon (1 mL) pepper

1. Insert steel blade. With machine running, drop garlic through feed tube; process until minced. Add parsley to bowl; process until chopped. Reserve.

2. Using slicing disc, slice eggplant. Sauté eggplant slices in 3 tablespoons (45 mL) of the olive oil in large skillet until light brown, about 5 minutes.

3. Using slicing disc, slice zucchini. Sauté in 2 tablespoons (30 mL) of the olive oil in skillet until light brown, 3 to 5 minutes.

4. Using slicing disc, slice onions and green peppers. Sauté in remaining olive oil in skillet until tender, about 10 minutes.

5. Cut tomatoes crosswise in half; gently squeeze out seeds. Slice tomatoes by hand into ½-inch (1.5 cm) slices.

6. Arrange ⅓ of the tomato slices in bottom of Dutch oven. Layer half the eggplant, zucchini, onion and green pepper on top. Sprinkle with ⅓ of the garlic and parsley, basil, salt and pepper. Repeat layers. Top with remaining tomato slices. Sprinkle with remaining garlic and parsley, basil, salt and pepper.

7. Cook covered over low heat 15 minutes. Uncover and baste with juices. Cook uncovered until juices have evaporated, 10 to 15 minutes.

   Note: Ratatouille may be served warm or cold. It is best when made a day in advance. Heat covered over low heat. Be careful vegetables do not burn.

FRESH PEACH TART
Makes 8 servings

Sweet Tart Pastry (recipe follows)
4 egg yolks
½ cup (125 mL) sugar
⅓ cup (80 mL) all-purpose flour
1½ cups (375 mL) scalded milk, cooled to 115°F (45°C)
1 tablespoon (15 mL) butter or margarine

1 teaspoon (5 mL) vanilla
3 tablespoons (45 mL) kirsch
12 ounces (340 g) apricot preserves
*6 to 8 firm ripe peaches, peeled, cut in half
2 tablespoons (30 mL) lemon juice

1. Make Sweet Tart Pastry.

2. Heat oven to 400°F (200°C). Roll dough on lightly floured surface into 13-inch (33 cm) circle. Ease pastry into 11-inch (28 cm) quiche or tart pan. Line shell with aluminum foil or parchment paper. Fill with pie weights, dried beans or rice.

3. Bake 12 minutes. Remove foil and weights. Bake until shell is light brown, 10 to 12 minutes. Cool on wire rack.

4. Insert steel blade. Place egg yolks in bowl. With machine running, gradually add sugar through feed tube. Process until thick and lemon-colored, about 1 minute. Add flour; process until blended.

5. With machine running, gradually add milk through feed tube; process until blended.

6. Place mixture in saucepan. Cook over low heat, stirring constantly, until very thick, about 10 minutes.

7. Remove from heat; stir in butter, vanilla and 1 tablespoon (15 mL) of the kirsch. Cover custard with plastic wrap. Refrigerate until cold.

8. Heat apricot preserves and remaining kirsch in small saucepan until preserves are melted and smooth. Strain.

9. Brush baked pastry shell with thin coating of apricot glaze. Let stand 5 minutes.

10. Spread custard in pastry shell.

11. Using slicing disc, slice peaches. Toss with lemon juice.

12. Arrange sliced peaches over custard. Brush peaches with apricot glaze.

*Notes: *Any fresh fruit can be substituted for the peaches. If using red fruits, substitute red currant jelly for the apricot preserves. This tart should not be assembled more than 1 hour before serving.*

Sweet Tart Pastry

1½ cups (375 mL) all-purpose flour
2 tablespoons (30 mL) sugar
½ cup (125 mL) butter or margarine, frozen, cut into 8 pieces

Pinch salt
4 to 5 tablespoons (60 to 75 mL) ice water

1. Insert steel blade. Place flour, sugar, butter and salt in bowl. Process until butter is mixed into dry ingredients. With machine running, add ice water through feed tube. Process until mixture forms ball.

French Family-Style Dinner

Spinach-Mushroom Eggs Mornay

Onion Soup with Cheese

Stuffed Breast of Veal

Brussels Sprouts Polonaise

Cherry and Pineapple Clafouti

Hearty provincial fare highlights a menu that might grace the table of a Sunday family dinner in France.

Begin the meal with either the Spinach-Mushroom Eggs Mornay or the Onion Soup. The eggs are more traditional, but soup-lovers will relish the richness of the cheese-laden onion soup, which could also serve as a luncheon or light-supper entree on another occasion.

The food processor comes to the fore in the preparation of stuffings and gravies. All the chopping of the myriad ingredients that make stuffings so savory is accomplished in seconds in the machine. You'll find the blend of pork, pistachio nuts and herbs featured in the Stuffed Breast of Veal to be especially delightful. Best of all, processing the onion-seasoned pan juices from the meat yields a naturally flavorful sauce that requires no thickener.

You may wonder how the term "polonaise," as in Brussels Sprouts Polonaise, entered the realm of French cuisine. The answer is that French chefs who traveled to Poland to cook for the royal court brought back the trick of sprinkling vegetables with buttered bread crumbs. Unquestionably native French is the famous fruit dumpling from Limousin called clafouti. Cherries are the favorite regional filling, but you can use virtually any fruit and prepare this rustic dessert in advance.

A fresh, young Beaujolais-Villages will complement the veal entree with appropriate spirit.

SPINACH-MUSHROOM EGGS MORNAY
Makes 6 servings

1 ounce (30 g)
  Parmesan cheese,
  cut into 1-inch (2.5
  cm) cubes
3 shallots, peeled
2 tablespoons (30 mL)
  butter or margarine
¼ pound (115 g)
  mushrooms
½ pound (225 g) fresh
  spinach, stems
  trimmed

6 hard-cooked eggs
½ teaspoon (2 mL) dried
  tarragon leaves
½ teaspoon (2 mL) salt
⅛ teaspoon (0.5 mL)
  pepper
Pinch ground nutmeg
Mornay Sauce (recipe
  follows)

1. Insert steel blade. With machine running, drop Parmesan cheese through feed tube; process until finely grated.

2. Using steel blade, process shallots until finely chopped. Sauté in butter until soft, about 3 minutes.

3. Using steel blade, process mushrooms until finely chopped. Add to shallots.

4. Rinse spinach; place in medium saucepan with water clinging to leaves. Cook covered over medium heat until tender, about 5 minutes. Drain. Using steel blade, process spinach until chopped. Add to shallots. Cook spinach mixture uncovered over medium heat until moisture has evaporated.

5. While spinach is cooking, cut hard-cooked eggs lengthwise in half. Remove yolks.

6. Using plastic or steel blade, process egg yolks, spinach mixture, Parmesan cheese, tarragon, salt, pepper and nutmeg to a pastelike consistency.

7. Fill egg whites with mixture, mounding the tops.

8. Make Mornay Sauce.

9. Heat oven to 350°F (180°C). Spread thin layer of Mornay Sauce in shallow baking dish. Place filled eggs on top. Pour sauce over all.

10. Bake until hot and beginning to brown, about 10 minutes.

Mornay Sauce
Makes about 2½ cups (625 mL)

1 ounce (30 g)
  Gruyère or Swiss
  cheese
2 tablespoons (30 mL)
  butter or
  margarine
3 tablespoons (45 mL)
  all-purpose flour

2½ cups (625 mL) milk
½ teaspoon (2 mL) salt
⅛ teaspoon (0.5 mL)
  pepper
Pinch ground
  nutmeg

1. Using shredding disc, shred cheese.

2. Melt butter in saucepan. Stir in flour to make smooth paste; cook, stirring constantly, 2 to 3 minutes. Remove pan from heat; stir in milk gradually. Stir in salt, pepper and nutmeg. Heat to boiling; reduce heat. Cook, stirring constantly, until thickened, about 5 minutes. Stir in cheese; cook, stirring constantly, until cheese is melted.

ONION SOUP WITH CHEESE
Makes 6 to 8 servings

2 pounds (900 g) onions
2 tablespoons (30 mL)
  butter or margarine
2 tablespoons (30 mL)
  olive oil
1 teaspoon (5 mL) salt
¼ teaspoon (1 mL) sugar
2 tablespoons (30 mL)
  all-purpose flour
7 cups (1750 mL) beef
  stock
½ cup (125 mL) dry red
  wine

1 bay leaf
¼ teaspoon (1 mL) dried
  thyme leaves
3 tablespoons (45 mL)
  cognac or brandy
2 ounces (60 g) Gruyère
  or Swiss cheese
6 to 8 slices dry French
  Bread, 1-inch (2.5
  cm) thick (see Index
  for page number)

1. Using slicing disc, slice onions.

2. Sauté onions in butter and oil in large saucepan, stirring occasionally, until soft, 10 to 15 minutes.

3. Stir in salt and sugar. Cook covered over medium heat, stirring frequently, until onions are tender and golden, 30 to 45 minutes. Sprinkle with flour; cook and stir 3 minutes.

4. Stir in beef stock, wine, bay leaf and thyme. Heat to boiling; reduce heat. Simmer partially covered 45 minutes. Stir in cognac.*

5. Using shredding disc, shred cheese.

6. Heat oven to 550°F (290°C) or broil. Pour soup into individual ovenproof bowls. Float bread slice on top. Sprinkle with shredded cheese. Broil until cheese is light brown and bubbling, 2 to 3 minutes.
   *Note: *Soup can be made up to this point 2 days in advance; refrigerate covered; heat until hot.*

STUFFED BREAST OF VEAL
Makes 6 servings

*1 breast of veal with
  pocket (about 4
  pounds or 1800 g)
1½ cups (375 mL) beef
  stock
¾ cup (180 mL) dry
  white wine
3 slices fresh bread,
  broken into pieces

¼ pound (115 g)
  mushrooms
2 onions
1 clove garlic
1 onion, cut into
  quarters
1 carrot, cut into
  1-inch (2.5 cm)
  pieces

2 ribs celery, cut into
    1-inch (2.5 cm)
    pieces
½ cup (125 mL)
    parsley sprigs
2 tablespoons (30 mL)
    butter or
    margarine
1 pound (450 g) lean
    pork, cut into
    1-inch (2.5 cm)
    cubes
2 ounces (60 g)
    pistachio nuts,
    shelled
2 eggs

2 tablespoons (30 mL)
    dried chives
¼ teaspoon (1 mL)
    dried rosemary
    leaves
⅛ teaspoon (0.5 mL)
    dried thyme leaves
½ teaspoon (2 mL) salt
⅛ teaspoon (0.5 mL)
    pepper
2 tablespoons (30 mL)
    olive oil
2 tablespoons (30 mL)
    butter or
    margarine
Water or beef stock

1. Enlarge pocket in larger side of breast with small knife. Be careful not to cut through meat. Push your hand around edges of cavity to enlarge it.

2. Boil 1½ cups (375 mL) beef stock and the wine in small saucepan until reduced to about 1½ cups (375 mL), 10 to 15 minutes.

3. Using steel blade, process bread to coarse crumbs.

4. Using slicing disc, slice mushrooms and whole onions separately; reserve.

5. Insert steel blade. Process garlic, quartered onion, the carrot, celery and parsley until finely chopped.

6. Sauté vegetable mixture in 2 tablespoons (30 mL) butter until tender, 10 to 15 minutes.

7. Using steel blade, process pork, ½ pound (225 g) at a time, until finely chopped.

8. Combine bread crumbs, cooked vegetable mixture, chopped pork, the pistachio nuts, eggs, chives, rosemary, thyme, salt and pepper in a large mixing bowl. Carefully fill pocket in meat with filling, distributing it evenly. Close opening with skewers.

9. Brown meat on both sides in oil and 2 tablespoons (30 mL) butter in roasting pan over medium-high heat, 3 to 5 minutes each side. Place sliced onions around meat. Add ½ cup (125 mL) of the wine mixture.

10. Heat oven to 350°F (180°C). Bake covered 30 minutes. Add remaining wine mixture; bake covered until meat is tender, 1 to 1½ hours. Remove meat from roasting pan. Let stand 15 minutes before carving.

11. Add enough water or beef stock to pan to measure 1 cup (250 mL) liquid. Heat mixture in roasting pan, stirring constantly, to boiling. Using steel blade, process mixture until smooth. Return to roasting pan. Add reserved mushrooms; simmer until mushrooms are soft, about 5 minutes.**

12. To serve, cut veal breast into thick slices, using ribs as guide. Sauce can be spooned over each portion or served separately.

    Notes: *Do not use a boned breast of veal.*

    ***If sauce is not as thick as desired, add 1 to 2 teaspoons (5 to 10 mL) cornstarch dissolved in 1 tablespoon (15 mL) cold water. Cook and stir over medium heat until slightly thickened.*

BRUSSELS SPROUTS POLONAISE
Makes 6 servings

3 slices fresh white
    bread, broken into
    pieces
1 small onion, cut into
    quarters

3 tablespoons (45 mL)
    butter or margarine
1½ quarts (1.5 L)
    Brussels sprouts
2 quarts (2 L) boiling
    salted water

1. Using steel blade, process bread to fine crumbs; reserve.

2. Using steel blade, process onion, using on/off technique, until finely chopped. Sauté onion in butter until tender, about 5 minutes. Add bread crumbs; cook until crumbs are golden.

3. Trim sprouts; cut an X in base of each sprout with sharp knife. Cook sprouts in boiling water until crisp-tender, 10 to 12 minutes. Drain.

4. Toss Brussels sprouts with bread crumb mixture. Serve immediately.

CHERRY AND PINEAPPLE CLAFOUTI
Makes 6 to 8 servings

*1 can (16 ounces or
    450 g) dark sweet
    cherries, pitted
*1 can (15 ounces or
    425 g) pineapple
    chunks
3 eggs
⅓ cup (80 mL)
    granulated sugar
½ cup (125 mL)
    all-purpose flour

1¼ cups (310 mL) milk
2 tablespoons (30 mL)
    kirsch or rum
1 tablespoon (15 mL)
    vanilla
⅛ teaspoon (0.5 mL)
    salt
Pinch ground
    nutmeg
Powdered sugar

1. Heat oven to 350°F (180°C). Drain cherries and pineapple; place on paper toweling.

2. Insert steel blade. Place eggs in bowl; process until foamy. Add remaining ingredients except fruit and powdered sugar. Process until blended and smooth.

3. Pour ¼ inch batter into buttered 9- or 10-inch (23 or 25 cm) quiche or pie pan. Spread cherries and pineapple over batter; pour remaining batter over top.

4. Bake until puffy and golden, 55 to 60 minutes. Let stand 15 to 20 minutes before cutting. Sprinkle generously with powdered sugar. Serve warm.

*Notes: *Other fresh or canned fruits, such as blueberries, peaches, pears,* *apples and plums, can be substituted for the cherries and pineapple. Fruit should measure 2½ to 3 cups (625 to 750 mL). If using fresh apples, slice with slicing disc and sauté in butter until light brown.*

Clafouti can be made in advance; heat at 300°F (150°C) until warm, about 10 minutes.

Elegant French Dinner Party

Onion-Mushroom Tart

Poached Salmon with Caper Hollandaise Sauce

Tomatoes with Herb Stuffing

French Chocolate Whiskey Cake

Neither heavy nor formal, this French dinner is sufficiently elegant for a party, yet not very demanding on the cook.

The key to its elegance is the main course of whole Poached Salmon draped in Caper Hollandaise Sauce. This dish can only be as good as the fish you use, so make sure the salmon is fresh and does not smell "fishy." The court bouillon, or fish-poaching liquid, couldn't be easier to prepare; vegetables are chopped in the food processor, combined with spices and herbs and simmered in white wine and vinegar diluted with water. If you don't have a fish poacher, you can poach the fish in any pan large enough to hold it. If you are using a fish poacher, you can ensure that the fish won't stick to the rack by lining the rack with cheesecloth.

The mystique of hollandaise-making is completely removed by the food processor. You don't have to worry about curdling or overcooking the egg yolks—the usual pitfalls of this sauce—when you blend everything quickly in the machine. Don't make this sauce in advance, if you can avoid it—it's far better freshly made and may thicken too much if left standing very long.

French dinners almost always begin with an interesting first course. So prepare a lovely golden Onion-Mushroom Tart for this fête. Make the pastry in the food processor and brush the pre-baked crust (pre-baking prevents sogginess) with mustard to give the custard filling a tangy accent.

There's a wonderful touch of intrigue in the rich dessert of French Chocolate Whiskey Cake. The secret lies in the mix of chocolate, whiskey and almonds—all easily blended into the batter in the food processor.

Complement the refinement of this menu with a dry white wine, a Pouilly-Fuissé from southern Burgundy.

ONION-MUSHROOM TART
Makes 6 to 8 servings

Tart Crust (recipe follows)
5 medium onions
3 tablespoons (45 mL) butter or margarine
½ teaspoon (2 mL) brown sugar
½ teaspoon (2 mL) dried tarragon leaves
½ teaspoon (2 mL) salt
⅛ teaspoon (0.5 mL) pepper

Pinch dried thyme leaves
¼ pound (115 g) mushrooms
Dijon-style mustard
3 eggs
1 cup (250 mL) heavy cream
¼ teaspoon (1 mL) salt
Pinch pepper
Pinch ground nutmeg

1. Make Tart Crust.

2. Using slicing disc, slice onions. Sauté onions in 2 tablespoons (30 mL) of the butter and the brown sugar until onions are tender and golden, 10 to 15 minutes. Stir in tarragon, ½ teaspoon (2 mL) salt, ⅛ teaspoon (0.5 mL) pepper and the thyme.

3. Using slicing disc, slice mushrooms. Sauté in remaining butter until all liquid has evaporated.

4. Heat oven to 375°F (190°C). Brush cooled Tart Crust with mustard. Spread onions in shell. Top with mushrooms.

5. Using plastic or steel blade, process eggs, cream, ¼ teaspoon (1 mL) salt, pinch pepper and the nutmeg until thoroughly blended. Pour over top of tart.

6. Bake until top is puffy and golden, 35 to 40 minutes.

Tart Crust

1¼ cups (310 mL)
all-purpose flour
½ cup (125 mL) frozen
butter or
margarine, cut into
8 pieces

⅛ teaspoon (0.5 mL)
salt
3 tablespoons (45 mL)
ice water

1. Insert steel blade. Place flour, butter and salt in bowl. Process until butter is mixed into dry ingredients. With machine running, add water through feed tube; process until dough forms ball.

2. Heat oven to 400°F (200°C). Roll dough on lightly floured surface to 11-inch (28 cm) circle. Ease pastry into 9-inch (23 cm) quiche or pie plate; trim edge and flute. Line shell with aluminum foil or parchment paper. Fill with pie weights, dried beans or rice.

3. Bake 10 minutes. Remove foil and weights. Bake 5 to 7 minutes longer, until shell is light brown. Cool on wire rack.

POACHED SALMON WITH CAPER HOLLANDAISE SAUCE
Makes 6 servings

2 onions, cut into
quarters
3 carrots, cut into 1-inch
(2.5 cm) pieces
1 rib celery, cut into
1-inch (2.5 cm)
pieces
8 cups (2 L) water
4 cups (1 L) dry white
wine
½ cup (125 mL) white
vinegar
1 bay leaf
6 peppercorns
3 parsley sprigs

1 teaspoon (5 mL) dried
thyme leaves
1 teaspoon (5 mL) dried
tarragon leaves
1 tablespoon (15 mL)
salt
1 whole salmon (3 to 4
pounds or 1350 to
1800 g), dressed
Caper Hollandaise
Sauce (recipe
follows)
Parsley sprigs
Lemon wedges

1. Using steel blade, process onions, carrots and celery until chopped.

2. In a fish poacher or any pan large enough to accommodate whole salmon, combine chopped vegetables, water, wine, vinegar, bay leaf, peppercorns, 3 parsley sprigs, the thyme, tarragon and salt. Heat to boiling; reduce heat. Simmer 30 minutes. Let stand until lukewarm.

3. Measure thickness of fish. Place fish on rack and lower into fish poacher. (If not using fish poacher, tie fish in cheesecloth; lower into pan.) Heat over medium heat until vegetable mixture is simmering; reduce heat to low. Simmer covered until fish is done, 10 minutes per inch of thickness.

4. While fish is simmering, make Caper Hollandaise Sauce.

5. When fish is done, carefully remove fish to serving platter. Cut away skin on top side of fish.

6. Spoon some sauce over top of fish. Garnish whole fish with parsley sprigs and lemon wedges. Serve remainder of sauce on the side.

Caper Hollandaise Sauce
Makes about 1 cup (250 mL)

½ cup (125 mL) butter
or margarine
3 egg yolks
2 tablespoons (30 mL)
lemon juice

⅛ teaspoon (0.5 mL) salt
Pinch pepper
2 tablespoons (30 mL)
drained capers

1. Heat butter in small saucepan until bubbly.

2. Using plastic or steel blade, process egg yolks, lemon juice, salt and pepper until thick and creamy, about 30 seconds.

3. With machine running, add hot butter in thin, steady stream through feed tube. Do not add milk residue left in bottom of butter. Process until butter is blended into sauce and sauce is slightly thickened. Stir capers into sauce.

4. To keep hollandaise warm until ready to serve, place in a pan of warm water.

TOMATOES WITH HERB STUFFING
Makes 6 servings

6 firm ripe tomatoes
Salt
Pepper
1 clove garlic
1 green onion, cut into
1-inch (2.5 cm)
pieces
½ cup (125 mL) parsley
sprigs

3 slices fresh white or
whole wheat bread
broken into pieces
½ teaspoon (2 mL)
dried basil leaves
¼ teaspoon (1 mL) salt
Pinch pepper
2½ tablespoons (40 mL)
olive oil

1. Cut slices from tops of tomatoes; discard seeds. Sprinkle insides lightly with salt and pepper; invert on paper toweling.

2. Heat oven to 400°F (200°C). Insert steel blade. With machine running, drop garlic through feed tube; process until minced. Add green onion and parsley to bowl; process until finely chopped. Add bread; process to fine crumbs. Add basil, ¼ teaspoon (1 mL) salt, pinch pepper and 2 tablespoons (30 mL) of the olive oil. Process briefly until blended.

3. Fill each tomato with bread crumb mixture. Place tomatoes in oiled baking dish. Sprinkle tops with re-

maining olive oil.* Bake until crumbs are light brown, 10 to 15 minutes.

*Note: *Stuffed tomatoes can be prepared to this point up to 3 hours in advance. Refrigerate covered. Bake at 400°F (200°C) 15 to 20 minutes.*

FRENCH CHOCOLATE WHISKEY CAKE

Makes 8 to 10 servings

⅓ cup (80 mL) dark raisins	6 eggs, separated
2 tablespoons (30 mL) whiskey	½ pound (225 g) semisweet chocolate, melted, cooled
1 slice fresh white bread, broken into pieces	2 teaspoons (10 mL) baking powder
6 ounces (170 g) blanched almonds	Pinch salt
¾ cup (180 mL) butter or margarine, room temperature	¼ teaspoon (1 mL) cream of tartar
¾ cup (180 mL) sugar	Chocolate Glaze (recipe follows)

1. Soak raisins in whiskey.

2. Using steel blade, process bread to fine crumbs; remove from bowl. Process almonds to fine powder; reserve.

3. Using steel blade, process butter until fluffy. With machine running, gradually add sugar through feed tube. Process until fluffy. Add egg yolks; process until blended. Drain whiskey from raisins. Add whiskey, melted chocolate, bread crumbs, almonds and baking powder to bowl; process until thoroughly blended. Transfer to large mixing bowl.

4. Heat oven to 350°F (180°C). Beat egg whites and salt with electric mixer until foamy. Add cream of tartar. Beat until stiff but not dry peaks form. Gently fold egg whites and raisins into chocolate mixture.

5. Butter 9-inch (23 cm) springform pan. Line bottom with waxed or parchment paper. Butter and flour paper. Pour batter into pan.

6. Bake until cake springs back when touched, 55 to 60 minutes. Cool on wire rack.

7. Make Chocolate Glaze.

8. When cake has cooled, remove sides of springform pan. Invert cake onto serving plate. Remove bottom of springform pan and peel off paper. Spread top and sides with glaze. Refrigerate until glaze is firm.

Note: Cake can be decorated with whole or chopped almonds, if desired.

Chocolate Glaze

Makes about ¾ cup (180 mL)

3 ounces (85 g) sweet baking chocolate, melted, cooled	¼ cup (60 mL) powdered sugar
3 tablespoons (45 mL) butter or margarine, room temperature	2 to 3 tablespoons (30 to 45 mL) whiskey

1. Using plastic or steel blade, process all ingredients until smooth.

India

Pappadams and Lamb Curry with Condiments (Peanuts, Kumquats, Bengal Chutney, Coconut and Green Onions)

Indian Curry Dinner

Lentil Soup

Lamb Curry

Pappadams

Bengal Chutney

Seasoned Rice

Spicy Eggs

Carrot Pudding

A kaleidoscope of colors, flavors and textures greets guests at an Indian Curry Dinner. This is a feast of Indian traditions, a brilliant marriage of various regional specialties.

The Lamb Curry takes center stage. In a country where most of the people will not eat beef or pork for religious reasons, lamb is the most frequently encountered meat, especially in the north. Currying, or stewing, is actually one of the fourteen different techniques of classical Indian cuisine, although in America the term "curry" has come to designate a packaged spice blend. The Indian term for such a spice mixture is "masala," and there is no single blend; the masala for each dish is carefully composed from a spectrum of spices (such as coriander, cumin, cardamom, ginger, turmeric and chili peppers). Like most northern Indian dishes, our Lamb Curry is cooked in Ghee, which is clarified butter. Make a supply of Ghee and store it tightly covered in the refrigerator for up to four months.

Curried dishes are always served with assorted condiments, and these are quickly prepared with the food processor. Another staple that adapts effortlessly is chutney—and you'll love the slightly-sweet piquancy of the Bengal Chutney in this menu.

Don't be frightened by this extensive menu—almost everything can be prepared a day in advance and reheated and garnished before serving. Leave the Seasoned Rice and Spicy Eggs for last. But plan to serve as many dishes as possible to capture all the excitement. Indians would drink tea with the meal, but beer offers perfect refreshment.

LENTIL SOUP
Makes 8 servings

1 quart (1 L) water	1 medium carrot, cut into 1-inch (2.5 cm) pieces
1 quart (1 L) chicken broth	1 medium onion, cut into eighths
2 cups (500 mL) dried lentils	1½ teaspoons (7 mL) curry powder
2 tablespoons (30 mL) Ghee (recipe follows) or butter or margarine	½ teaspoon (2 mL) ground coriander
½ cup (125 mL) packed fresh coriander leaves or parsley sprigs	¼ teaspoon (1 mL) ground cumin
1 clove garlic	⅛ teaspoon (0.5 mL) crushed red pepper flakes

1. Place water, broth and lentils in Dutch oven or large heavy saucepan. Heat to boiling; reduce heat. Simmer covered until lentils are tender, about 45 minutes.

2. Make Ghee.

3. Using steel blade, process coriander leaves until minced. Reserve for garnish.

4. Insert steel blade. With machine running, drop garlic through feed tube; process until minced. Place carrot and onion in bowl; process, using on/off technique, until coarsely chopped.

5. Heat Ghee in skillet; sauté garlic, carrot and onion until onion is tender, about 5 minutes. Stir in curry powder, ground coriander, cumin and red pepper flakes. Cook 1 minute. Stir into lentils. Simmer uncovered 20 minutes.

6. Remove half of lentil mixture from Dutch oven. Using steel blade, process 2 cups (500 mL) at a time until pureed. Return to Dutch oven; cook over medium heat 2 to 3 minutes. Serve in tureen or individual bowls; garnish with reserved coriander.

Ghee
Makes 1½ cups (375 mL)

1 pound (450 g) unsalted butter, cut into pieces

1. Heat butter in saucepan over medium heat, stirring constantly, until melted. Heat until butter foams; reduce heat. Simmer without stirring 30 minutes.

2. Line strainer with several layers of cheesecloth. Pour butter through strainer. (If any solids remain in the Ghee, strain until completely clear.) Ghee can be stored in refrigerator in a covered jar 3 to 4 months.

LAMB CURRY
Makes 6 to 8 servings

1 cup (250 mL) plain yogurt	½ teaspoon (2 mL) ground turmeric
1 teaspoon (5 mL) paprika	¼ teaspoon (1 mL) ground black pepper
1 teaspoon (5 mL) ground coriander	2½ pounds (125 g) boneless lamb, cut into 1-inch (2.5 cm) pieces
½ teaspoon (2 mL) ground cumin	
*½ teaspoon (2 mL) garam masala	1 small lime
½ teaspoon (2 mL) crushed red pepper flakes	1 small onion

¼ cup (60 mL) packed
    fresh coriander
    leaves or parsley
    sprigs
2 cloves garlic
1 slice fresh gingerroot,
    1-inch (2.5 cm)
    thick, pared, cut
    into chunks
2 medium onions, cut
    into quarters

¼ cup (60 mL) Ghee
    (see preceding
    recipe)
    or butter or
    margarine
½ cup (125 mL) chicken
    stock
½ cup (125 mL) water
Condiments (recipe
    follows)

1. Mix yogurt, paprika, ground coriander, cumin, garam masala, red pepper flakes, turmeric and pepper. Pour over lamb. Stir until lamb is coated with yogurt mixture. Refrigerate covered, stirring occasionally, 3 to 4 hours.

2. Using slicing disc, slice lime and 1 small onion; reserve for garnish.

3. Using steel blade, process coriander until minced; reserve for garnish.

4. Insert steel blade. With machine running, drop garlic and gingerroot through feed tube; process until minced. Add 2 medium onions; process, using on/off technique, until coarsely chopped.

5. Sauté onion mixture in Ghee in large saucepan until tender, about 5 minutes. Stir in lamb mixture, stock and water. Heat to boiling; reduce heat. Simmer covered until lamb is tender, about 1 hour.

6. Make Condiments.

7. Arrange lamb in deep platter. Garnish with reserved lime, onion and coriander. Serve with Condiments.
   *Note: *Garam masala is a mixture of ground spices; it can be purchased in Middle Eastern groceries or gourmet food stores.*

Condiments
Each Condiment makes ½ to ⅔ cup (125 to 160 mL)

⅔ cup (160 mL) peanuts
2 hard-cooked eggs, cut
    into halves
¼ small coconut
6 to 8 slices bacon
1 large banana
1 tablespoon (15 mL)
    lemon juice
1 small onion, cut into
    quarters

½ cup (125 mL) yogurt
6 to 8 green onions and
    tops
1 large avocado, peeled,
    pitted, cut into
    2-inch (5 cm) pieces
1 tablespoon (15 mL)
    lemon juice
1 jar (8 ounces or 225 g)
    preserved kumquats

Condiments are served with an Indian meal to add color and flavor contrast. Select 4 to 6 of the following:

1. PEANUTS: Insert steel blade. Using on/off technique, process until coarsely chopped.

2. EGGS: Insert steel blade. Using on/off technique, process until coarsely chopped.

3. COCONUT: See steps 1 and 2 of recipe for Grated Fresh Coconut (see Index for page number) to prepare fresh coconut. Shred coconut with shredding disc.

4. BACON: Cook bacon until crisp. Insert steel blade. Using on/off technique, process until crumbled.

5. BANANA: Slice with slicing disc. Mix with 1 tablespoon (15 mL) lemon juice.

6. ONION: Insert steel blade. Using on/off technique, process until coarsely chopped. Add yogurt; process just until blended.

7. GREEN ONIONS: Slice with slicing disc.

8. AVOCADO: Insert steel blade. Using on/off technique, process until coarsely chopped. Add 1 tablespoon (15 mL) lemon juice; process until blended.

9. KUMQUATS: Place in small serving bowl.

PAPPADAMS
Makes about 12

Vegetable oil

*1 package pappadams
    (about 12)

1. Heat 2 inches (5 cm) oil in skillet to 375 °F (190 °C). Fry bread in oil, one at a time, until brown, about 30 seconds on each side (see photo 1). Drain on paper toweling.

Photo 1. Fry pappadams, one at a time, until brown.

*Note: *Pappadams are a wafer-thin lentil bread and can be purchased at Indian groceries. They can be fried 24 hours before serving; store covered at room temperature.*

BENGAL CHUTNEY
Makes about 6 cups (1.5 L)

3 cloves garlic
1 medium onion, cut
    into quarters
3 pounds (1350 g) tart
    cooking apples
    (Granny Smith,
    Greening), pared,
    cored, cut into
    halves
1 small lemon
3 cups (750 mL)
    packed brown sugar

2 cups (500 mL) cider
    vinegar
1 cup (250 mL) golden
    raisins
1 tablespoon (15 mL)
    mustard seeds
2 teaspoons (10 mL)
    ground ginger
½ teaspoon (2 mL) salt
*¼ teaspoon (1 mL)
    crushed red pepper
    flakes

1. Insert steel blade. With machine running, drop garlic through feed tube. Add onion to bowl. Process, using on/off technique, until coarsely chopped. Using slicing disc, slice apples and lemon.

2. Place all ingredients in stainless steel or enamel Dutch oven. Heat to boiling; reduce heat. Simmer uncovered, stirring occasionally, until chutney has thickened and apples are tender, about 1½ hours. Cool. Chutney can be stored covered in refrigerator up to 3 months.

*Note: *If a hotter chutney is desired, increase measure of crushed red pepper flakes to ½ teaspoon (2 mL).*

SEASONED RICE
Makes 6 to 8 servings

⅓ cup (80 mL) salted
    cashews or peanuts
¼ cup (60 mL) loosely
    packed fresh or 2
    teaspoons dried
    coriander leaves
2 small onions
2 tablespoons (30 mL)
    Ghee (see Index
    for page number)
    or butter or
    margarine
1 teaspoon (5 mL)
    whole cumin seeds
3 whole cloves

2 whole cardamom
    seeds, crushed
¼ teaspoon (1 mL)
    ground turmeric
1 cinnamon stick, 3-
    inches (8 cm) long
1½ cups (375 mL)
    uncooked rice
3 cups (750 mL) water
1 teaspoon (5 mL) salt
½ cup (125 mL) frozen
    peas, thawed
2 hard-cooked eggs,
    cut into quarters
¼ cup (60 mL) dark
    raisins

1. Using steel blade, process nuts until coarsely chopped; reserve for garnish. Using steel blade, process fresh coriander until minced; reserve for garnish.

2. Using slicing disc, slice onions. Sauté onions in Ghee in large saucepan until tender, 3 to 4 minutes. Stir in cumin, cloves, cardamom, turmeric and cinnamon; cook and stir 1 minute.

3. Add rice; cook and stir 3 to 4 minutes. Stir in water and salt. Heat to boiling; reduce heat. Simmer covered until water is absorbed and rice is tender, about 20 minutes. Remove from heat and stir in peas. Let stand covered 10 minutes.

4. To serve, spoon rice onto serving platter. Sprinkle with reserved nuts and coriander. Arrange eggs and raisins around edge.

SPICY EGGS
Makes 6 servings

½ cup (125 mL) Grated
    Fresh Coconut
    (recipe follows) or
    dried unsweetened
    coconut
1 clove garlic
1 medium onion, cut
    into quarters
1 medium tomato,
    peeled, seeded, cut
    into quarters
2 tablespoons (30 mL)
    Ghee (see Index for
    page number) or
    butter or margarine

½ teaspoon (2 mL) salt
1 teaspoon (5 mL) curry
    powder
½ teaspoon (2 mL) chili
    powder
¼ teaspoon (1 mL)
    ground cinnamon
¼ teaspoon (1 mL)
    pepper
⅛ teaspoon (0.5 mL)
    ground cloves
¾ cup (180 mL) water
6 hard-cooked eggs, cut
    in half

1. Make Grated Fresh Coconut.

2. Insert steel blade. With machine running, drop garlic through feed tube; process until minced. Add onion and tomato to bowl; process, using on/off technique, until coarsely chopped.

3. Sauté garlic, onion and tomato in Ghee in skillet 2 to 3 minutes. Stir in salt and spices; cook and stir over medium heat 2 to 3 minutes.

4. Stir in coconut and water. Simmer uncovered 10 minutes. Add eggs; heat until hot.

Grated Fresh Coconut
Makes about 2½ cups (625 mL)

1 small coconut

1. Puncture eyes of coconut with ice pick; drain liquid and discard. Heat oven to 375°F (190°C). Bake coconut 15 minutes.

2. Crack coconut with hammer to open. Pare brown skin from coconut with a small paring knife or a vegetable peeler.

3. For grated coconut, break the coconut into chunks. Insert steel blade. With machine running, drop coconut chunks through feed tube; process until grated. Freeze extra grated coconut in plastic bags up to 4 months.

CARROT PUDDING
Makes 6 to 8 servings

½ cup (125 mL)
  unblanched whole
  almonds
1 pound (450 g)
  carrots, cut into
  1-inch (2.5 cm)
  pieces
1 cup (250 mL) milk
1 cup (250 mL)
  half-and-half
¾ cup (180 mL) packed
  light brown sugar

¼ cup (60 mL) butter or
  margarine, room
  temperature
2 tablespoons (30 mL)
  golden raisins
½ teaspoon (2 mL)
  ground cardamom
3 tablespoons (45 mL)
  slivered almonds,
  lightly toasted
Mint sprigs

1. Using steel blade, process whole almonds until finely ground; reserve. Using steel blade, process carrots, 1 cup (250 mL) at a time, until finely chopped. [T44]

2. Place carrots, milk and half-and-half in large saucepan. Heat to boiling; reduce heat. Simmer uncovered, stirring occasionally, until milk is absorbed and mixture is thick, about 1 hour.

3. Stir in reserved almonds, the sugar, butter, raisins and cardamom. Cook stirring frequently, over low heat, about 15 minutes.*

4. Spoon pudding into serving dish. Garnish with slivered almonds and the mint sprigs. Serve warm.
   *Note: *Carrot Pudding can be prepared up to this point 24 hours before serving. Store covered in refrigerator and heat in saucepan over low heat just before serving.*

Indian Vegetarian Supper

Deep-Fried Pastries

Mixed Vegetable Curry

Indian Bread

Spicy Eggplant in Yogurt

Mouth-watering meatless meals may be hard to imagine—until you've sampled the exquisite vegetarian cuisine that prevails in southern India. Due to the continued influence of Hinduism and Buddhism, vegetarian diets have been observed by Indians for hundreds of years.

You might consider the Deep-Fried Pastries to be an instant advertisement for vegetarian cookery and a superb preview of the rest of the menu. Both the flaky pastry and the shredded potato and carrot filling whiz through the food processor. You can roll out the dough and prepare the "turnovers" in advance (keeping them covered in the refrigerator), but leave the frying for later. The accompanying Coriander-Mint Chutney will store well in the refrigerator. The texture of this chutney requires that it be made with fresh herbs—and there is no real substitute for the irresistible fragrance of fresh mint and coriander leaves. In India, chutney-making approaches an art, and this hot-and-cool taste sensation offers abundant reason why.

Perhaps even more than the lamb version in the preceding menu, the Mixed Vegetable Curry testifies to the potential for harmony in spice blends, because the vegetables offer a more subtle counterpoint than the meat. Savor the mellow heat of the curry sauce in contrast to the cool, creamy Eggplant in Yogurt salad and you'll appreciate the scope of Indian food. Make the salad ahead of time and let the flavors fuse in the refrigerator. And be careful not to overcook the vegetables in the curry—they should be tender but not mushy.

Whole wheat Indian Bread offers suitable enrichment in this menu. Crisp, golden and delicious, the fried puffs are perfect for scooping up the vegetable dishes—and the practice is authentically Indian.

Serve this menu with assorted fresh fruit for dessert and tea, milk or beer.

DEEP-FRIED PASTRIES
Makes about 24

1½ cups (375 mL)
  all-purpose flour
1½ tablespoons (22 mL)
  frozen butter or
  margarine, cut into
  pieces
½ teaspoon (2 mL) salt
½ cup (125 mL) ice
  water
  Coriander-Mint
  Chutney (recipe
  follows)
1 clove garlic

1 slice fresh gingerroot,
  ½-inch (1.5 cm)
  thick, pared, cut
  into chunks
1 small onion, cut into
  quarters
1 tablespoon (15 mL)
  Ghee (see Index
  for page number)
  or butter or
  margarine
¾ teaspoon (4 mL)
  curry powder

½ teaspoon (2 mL)
  coriander seeds,
  crushed
½ teaspoon (2 mL) salt
½ teaspoon (2 mL)
  ground cumin

2 medium potatoes, cut
  into quarters, cooked
1 medium carrot,
  pared, cut into
  1-inch (2.5 cm)
  pieces, cooked
Vegetable oil

1. Insert steel blade. Place flour, butter and ½ teaspoon (2 mL) salt in bowl. Process, using on/off technique, until small particles form. With machine running, add water through feed tube; process until ball of dough forms. Place dough in lightly greased bowl; turn the dough to grease the top of the ball. Cover with damp towel and let stand at least 30 minutes. [T50]

2. Make Coriander-Mint Chutney.

3. Insert steel blade. With machine running, drop garlic and gingerroot through feed tube; process until minced. Add onion to bowl. Process, using on/off technique, until finely chopped. Sauté onion mixture in Ghee in skillet until tender, 2 to 3 minutes. Stir in curry, coriander, ½ teaspoon (2 mL) salt and cumin. Cook 1 minute. Using shredding disc, shred potatoes and carrot; stir into onion mixture. Cool.

4. Divide dough in half. Roll out each half ¹⁄₁₆-inch (2 mm) thick on lightly floured surface. Cut into 3-inch (8 cm) circles. Moisten edges with water. Place about 1 teaspoon (5 mL) filling on each circle. Fold dough in half and seal edges with tines of fork.

5. Heat 2 inches (5 cm) oil in saucepan or electric skillet to 375°F (190°C). Fry pastries, a few at a time, until golden, 3 to 4 minutes. Drain on paper toweling. Keep warm in oven while frying remaining pastries. Serve warm with Coriander-Mint Chutney.

Coriander-Mint Chutney
Makes about ½ cup (125 mL)

2 cloves garlic	½ cup (125 mL) packed
1 slice fresh gingerroot,	fresh mint leaves
½-inch (1.5 cm)	2 tablespoons (30 mL)
thick, pared	water
*3 hot green chilies,	1 tablespoon (15 mL)
stems removed, cut	lemon juice
into quarters	1 teaspoon (5 mL) salt
1 cup (250 mL) packed	1 teaspoon (5 mL) sugar
fresh coriander	⅛ teaspoon (0.5 mL)
leaves	ground cumin

1. Insert steel blade. With machine running, drop garlic and gingerroot through feed tube; process until minced. Add chilies to bowl; process, using on/off technique, until finely chopped.

2. Place remaining ingredients in bowl. Process until a thick paste is formed.
   *Note: *Wear rubber gloves when handling chilies; don't touch skin or eyes.*

MIXED VEGETABLE CURRY
Makes 4 to 6 servings

1 large clove garlic	1 teaspoon (5 mL)
1 slice fresh gingerroot,	ground coriander
¾-inch thick (2	½ teaspoon (2 mL)
cm), pared	ground cumin
1 medium onion, cut	¼ teaspoon (1 mL)
into quarters	ground turmeric
2 tablespoons (30 mL)	¼ teaspoon (1 mL)
vegetable oil	ground cinnamon

⅛ teaspoon (0.5 mL)	¾ pound (340 g)
ground red pepper	cabbage, cut into
½ pound (225 g) fresh	wedges
broccoli	1 cup (250 mL) frozen
2 large carrots	peas
½ cup (125 mL) water	1 tablespoon (15 mL)
1 teaspoon (5 mL) salt	lemon juice
1 large tomato, cut into	
eighths	

1. Insert steel blade. With machine running, drop garlic and gingerroot through feed tube; process until minced. Add onion to bowl; process, using on/off technique, until coarsely chopped.

2. Sauté onion mixture in oil in skillet 3 to 4 minutes. Stir in coriander, cumin, turmeric, cinnamon and red pepper; cook, stirring constantly, 2 to 3 minutes.

3. Trim stalks from broccoli; reserve tops. Using slicing disc, slice broccoli stalks and carrots. Add broccoli, stalks and tops, carrots, water and salt to skillet. Heat to boiling; reduce heat. Simmer covered until vegetables are almost tender, 8 to 10 minutes.

4. Using steel blade, process tomato, using on/off technique, until coarsely chopped. Add to skillet. Using slicing disc, slice cabbage. Add cabbage and peas to skillet. Simmer covered until vegetables are tender but not mushy, 5 to 8 minutes. Stir in lemon juice.

INDIAN BREAD
Makes 10 to 12

1 cup (250 mL)	½ teaspoon (2 mL) salt
all-purpose flour	½ to ¾ cup (125 to 180
1 cup (250 mL) whole	mL) water
wheat flour	Vegetable oil
1½ tablespoons (22 mL)	
Ghee (see Index	
for page number)	
or vegetable oil	

1. Insert steel blade. Place flours, Ghee and salt in bowl; process, using on/off technique, until small particles form.

2. With machine running, add water through feed tube until ball of dough forms. Place dough in greased bowl; turn the dough to grease the top of the ball. Cover with damp towel. Let stand 30 minutes.

3. Break off pieces of dough and shape into flattened balls, about 1½ inches (4 cm) in diameter. Roll out each piece of dough on lightly floured surface into a circle, about 4 inches (10 cm) in diameter. Place damp cloth over dough circles to prevent drying.

Deep-Fried Pastries and Coriander-Mint Chutney

4. Heat 2 inches (5 cm) oil in skillet to 360°F (185°C). Fry dough in hot oil, one piece at a time, pressing down with a perforated spoon or spatula until puffed golden on each side (see photo 2). Drain on paper toweling. Keep warm while frying remaining bread.
Note: Indian Bread can be made earlier in the day, wrapped in foil and reheated at 400°F (200°C) before serving.

Photo 2. Fry each piece of dough, pressing it down into oil, until puffed and brown on both sides.

SPICY EGGPLANT IN YOGURT
Makes 1½ cups (375 mL)

1 medium eggplant, about 1 pound (450 g)
¼ cup (60 mL) packed fresh or 1 teaspoon (5 mL) dried mint leaves
¼-inch (0.5 cm) piece fresh gingerroot, pared
1 small onion, cut into quarters

1 tablespoon (15 mL) vegetable oil
*1 teaspoon (5 mL) garam masala
½ teaspoon (2 mL) salt
⅛ teaspoon (0.5 mL) ground red pepper
1 cup (250 mL) unflavored yogurt
Mint sprig for garnish, if desired

1. Heat oven to 400°F (200°C). Make 6 to 8 incisions in eggplant with tip of sharp knife. Place in ungreased baking dish and bake until eggplant is soft, about 45 minutes. Remove from oven and cool slightly. Split eggplant in half and remove pulp; reserve.

2. Using steel blade, process fresh mint until chopped; remove from bowl and reserve.

3. Insert steel blade. With machine running, drop ginger through feed tube and process until minced. Add onion; process, using on/off technique, until finely chopped.

4. Sauté onion and ginger in oil in small skillet until soft and golden, 3 to 4 minutes. Stir in garam masala, salt and red pepper; cook 1 minute.

5. Using steel blade, process eggplant pulp, using on/off technique, until coarsely chopped.

6. Combine all ingredients except mint sprigs. Cover and refrigerate at least 1 hour. Garnish with mint sprigs, if desired.
*Note: *Garam masala is a mixture of ground spices; it can be purchased in Middle Eastern groceries or gourmet food stores.*

CHINA

Stuffed Clams, Egg Rolls, Shrimp Toast and Chicken Fried in Paper

Spicy Szechuanese-Style Chinese Dinner

Crab Won-Ton

Szechuan Bean Curd

Spicy Shrimp

Beef on Fried Noodles

Glazed Bananas

Szechuanese-style cooking—the most recent Chinese arrival on the American culinary scene—has taken the country's appetite by storm. This fascinating food from the agriculturally rich and heavily populated western part of China is known for its spiciness and diversity.

Hot bean paste and chili paste are the ingredients that make the dishes on this menu typically hot. But if you can't find these spicy blends, you can prepare the dishes anyway. For the initial hot taste of the Szechuan Bean Curd, the Spicy Shrimp and the Beef on Fried Noodles is merely the prelude to the intrinsic Szechuanese melodrama of sweet, sour, salty and aromatic sensations. Garlic, gingerroot, soy sauce, and green onions are the most important ingredients and these can be found anywhere. The bean thread noodles (also called cellophane noodles) are also widely available; their incomparable crispness comes from the fact that they are made neither from wheat nor flour but from ground mung beans.

This is a very easy, yet infinitely rewarding menu to serve. You can fill the Crab Won-Ton hours in advance, fry them close to the dinner hour and keep them warm in the oven. The shrimp and beef need to be marinated briefly in the common Chinese blend of egg white, cornstarch and seasoning, which both flavors and tenderizes the food. The Glazed Bananas should be a last-minute spectacular. It is not inappropriate to bring the syrup-coated fruit to the table in the wok and dip them into ice-water to crystallize the syrup in front of guests, who will be dazzled by the glistening drama.

Water is not recommended to soothe palates overheated by Szechuanese dishes, but a gentle Riesling white wine will prove quite agreeable.

CRAB WON-TON
Makes 30

1 clove garlic
8 ounces (225 g) cream cheese, cut into 3 pieces
½ pound (225 g) crabmeat
¼ teaspoon (1 mL) salt
⅛ teaspoon (0.5 mL) white pepper

Dash Worcestershire sauce
1 package won-ton wrappers
1 egg, slightly beaten
3 cups (750 mL) peanut oil

1. Insert steel blade. With machine running, drop garlic through feed tube; process until minced.

2. Add cream cheese to bowl; process, using on/off technique, until almost smooth.

3. Drain crabmeat; pick out all cartilage. Add crabmeat, salt, pepper and Worcestershire sauce to bowl; process until blended.

4. Place ½ teaspoonful (2 mL) of filling in center of each won-ton wrapper. Brush edges of wrappers with beaten egg. Fold each wrapper diagonally in half; fold pointed ends and pinch to seal (see photo 1).

5. Heat oil in wok or 8-inch (20 cm) skillet to 380°F (190°C). Fry won-tons, five at a time, until golden. Drain on paper toweling. Serve warm.

Photo 1. After folding filled won-ton wrapper diagonally in half, fold in the pointed ends and pinch to seal.

SZECHUAN BEAN CURD
Makes 4 servings

1 clove garlic
1 green onion, cut into 1½-inch (4 cm) pieces
½ pound (225 g) pork or beef, cut into 1-inch (2.5 cm) pieces

3 cups (750 mL) peanut oil
½ pound (225 g) bean curd (tofu), cut into ½-inch (1.5 cm) cubes

*1 tablespoon (15 mL) hot bean paste
2 tablespoons (30 mL) soy sauce
½ teaspoon (2 mL) salt
⅔ cup (160 mL) chicken stock
1 teaspoon (5 mL) sesame oil
2 tablespoons (30 mL) cornstarch
2 tablespoons (30 mL) cold water

1. Insert steel blade. With machine running, drop garlic and green onion through feed tube; process until minced.

2. Add pork to bowl; process, using on/off technique until minced.

3. Heat peanut oil in wok or 10-inch (25 cm) skillet to 380°F (190°C). Fry bean curd for 1 minute; drain.

4. Remove and discard all but 3 tablespoons (45 mL) oil from wok; heat oil remaining in wok. Add pork mixture; stir-fry until brown. Mix bean paste, soy sauce, salt, stock and sesame oil; stir into pork. Simmer, stirring occasionally, 1 minute. Stir in bean curd.

5. Mix cornstarch and water; stir into wok. Stir-fry until sauce thickens.

*Note: *Hot bean paste can be purchased at Oriental groceries. There is no substitute.*

SPICY SHRIMP
Makes 4 servings

1 tablespoon (15 mL) sherry
1 egg white
1 tablespoon (15 mL) cornstarch
1 pound (450 g) uncooked shrimp, shelled, deveined
1 slice gingerroot, ⅛-inch (0.5 cm) thick, pared
1 clove garlic
2 green onions and tops, cut into 1½-inch (4 cm) pieces
*2 teaspoons (10 mL) hot bean paste
5 tablespoons (75 mL) catsup
1 tablespoon (15 mL) soy sauce
1 teaspoon (5 mL) sugar
1½ teaspoons (7 mL) distilled white vinegar
½ teaspoon (2 mL) salt
½ cup (125 mL) cold chicken stock
2 tablespoons (30 mL) cornstarch
2 cups (500 mL) peanut oil
4 cups (1 L) hot cooked rice

1. Combine sherry, egg white, 1 tablespoon (15 mL) cornstarch and shrimp. Refrigerate 30 minutes.

2. Insert steel blade. With machine running, drop gingerroot, garlic and onions through feed tube; process until minced.

3. Combine bean paste, catsup, soy sauce, sugar, vinegar, salt, chicken stock and cornstarch in small bowl.

4. Heat oil in wok or 10-inch (25 cm) skillet to 380°F (190°C). Fry shrimp in oil just until they change color; drain on paper toweling.

5. Remove and discard all but 2 tablespoons (30 mL) of the oil from wok; heat remaining oil. Add gingerroot, garlic and onion. Stir-fry 30 seconds. Add bean paste mixture and shrimp. Stir-fry until thickened. Place in serving bowl and serve with rice.

*Note: *Hot bean paste can be purchased at Oriental groceries. There is no substitute.*

BEEF ON FRIED NOODLES
Makes 4 servings

1 pound (450 g) flank steak, slightly frozen
¼ teaspoon (1 mL) salt
1 egg white
2 teaspoons (10 mL) cornstarch
2 green onions and tops
½ cup (125 mL) bamboo shoots
½ green pepper
1 slice gingerroot, ⅛-inch (0.5 cm) thick, pared
1 clove garlic
*1 ounce (30 g) bean thread noodles
2 cups (500 mL) peanut oil
½ teaspoon (2 mL) sugar
2 teaspoons (10 mL) dry white wine
1 tablespoon (15 mL) cider vinegar
*1 teaspoon (5 mL) chili paste with garlic
1 tablespoon (15 mL) soy sauce

1. Using slicing disc, slice meat. Combine meat, salt, egg white and cornstarch; let stand at room temperature 20 minutes.

2. Using slicing disc, slice onions, bamboo shoots and green pepper.

3. Insert steel blade. With machine running, drop gingerroot and garlic through feed tube; process until minced.

4. Pull noodles apart. Heat oil in wok or 10-inch (25 cm) skillet to 380°F (190°C). Fry noodles 5 seconds on each side; drain on paper toweling and keep warm.

5. Add meat mixture to hot oil; fry until brown. Transfer to bowl.

6. Remove and discard all but 3 tablespoons (45 mL) oil from wok; heat remaining oil. Add gingerroot and garlic; stir-fry 30 seconds. Stir in onions, bamboo shoots and green pepper.

7. Mix sugar, wine, vinegar, chili paste and soy sauce and add to wok; stir-fry 30 seconds. Return meat to wok; stir-fry 1 minute. Serve over fried noodles.

*Note: *Bean thread noodles and chili paste can be purchased at Oriental groceries. There is no substitute for chili paste. If bean thread noodles are not available, serve beef over hot cooked rice.*

Crab Won-Ton and Beef on Fried Noodles

GLAZED BANANAS
Makes 4 servings

⅓ cup (80 mL) walnuts
½ cup (125 mL) cornstarch
3 firm bananas, cut into 3-inch (8 cm) pieces
2 eggs, beaten
3 cups (750 mL) peanut oil

1 cup (250 mL) sugar
¼ cup (60 mL) water
3 tablespoons (45 mL) peanut oil
Water
Ice cubes

1. Using steel blade, process walnuts until finely chopped.

2. Combine cornstarch and walnuts in small bowl.

3. Roll bananas in eggs and then in cornstarch mixture.

4. Heat 3 cups (750 mL) oil in skillet to 380 °F (190 °C). Fry bananas until golden. Drain on paper toweling.

5. Heat sugar, water and 3 tablespoons (45 mL) oil in saucepan to 260 °F (125 °C). Fill large bowl with water and ice cubes.

6. Quickly coat each banana with syrup and dip in bowl of ice and water. Place on oiled platter. Serve immediately.

Chinese Dinner of Many Flavors

Hot-and-Sour Soup

Open Shrimp Dumplings

Green Onion Bread

Sweet-and-Sour Pork

Pork Fried Rice

Orange-Flavored Beef

Almond Cookies

This menu highlights a selection of splendid textures, tastes and cooking techniques from the infinitely varied repertoire of Chinese cuisine.

Crisp, fried Green Onion Bread makes a surprise appearance at this meal. Many people don't realize that bread plays a part in Chinese meals; but it does in the northern regions, where the cold climate nurtures wheat better than rice. Make the dough in the food processor; then proceed, after it rises, to roll the circles into tubes, coil the tubes and roll out the coils again. It's really an easy process and the fried discs freeze very well.

Hot-and-Sour Soup is a Szechuan treat that will not suffer if the tiger lily buds and cloud ears are omitted; both are added for texture rather than taste. Bean curd, or tofu, is becoming available in more and more supermarkets, because it's a good protein alternative to meat. The Open Shrimp

Dumplings can be prepared ahead of time and steamed while the soup course is being savored.

Pork is featured twice on this menu—once in everyone's favorite Sweet-and-Sour Pork and again in Pork Fried Rice. This double billing is quite appropriate in the cuisine that is reputed to have developed more ways of cooking pork than any other in the world. Scarcer and more traditionally and more highly prized is beef; so it appears here in a memorable orange-flavored sauce.

You'll doubtless be delighted with the recipe for Almond Cookies. They are so easy to make with the food processor to chop the nuts and blend the dough that they could well replace ordinary sweets in your cookie jar.

Wan Fu is an interesting white wine, with an indescribable flavor, that has been developed especially to complement Chinese feasts such as this one.

HOT-AND-SOUR SOUP
Makes 10 to 12 servings

5 dried Chinese mushrooms
*1 tablespoon (15 mL) dried tiger lily buds
*1 tablespoon (15 mL) dried cloud ears
Hot water
2 green onions and tops
½ cup (125 mL) bamboo shoots

1 chicken breast, boned, slightly frozen
*½ cup (125 mL) bean curd (tofu)
4 cups (1 L) chicken stock
1 tablespoon (15 mL) soy sauce
½ teaspoon (2 mL) sugar
¾ teaspoon (4 mL) salt

2 large eggs, slightly beaten
2 tablespoons (30 mL) cornstarch
3 tablespoons (45 mL) cold water

3 tablespoons (45 mL) wine vinegar
½ teaspoon (2 mL) black pepper
2 teaspoons (10 mL) sesame oil

1. Remove stems from mushrooms; discard. Soak mushrooms, lily buds and cloud ears in hot water, 15 minutes; drain.

2. Using slicing disc, slice green onions. Reserve. Using slicing disc, slice mushrooms, lily buds, cloud ears, bamboo shoots and chicken.

3. Cut bean curd into ½-inch (1.5 cm) cubes.

4. Place chicken stock in 3-quart (3 L) saucepan. Stir in mushrooms, lily buds, cloud ears, bamboo shoots, chicken and bean curd. Heat to boiling; reduce heat. Simmer uncovered 15 minutes.

5. Stir in soy sauce, sugar and salt. Heat to boiling. Add eggs and cornstarch mixed with cold water. Turn off heat.

6. Mix vinegar, pepper and sesame oil; place in tureen.

7. Pour soup into tureen on top of vinegar mixture. Garnish with green onion.

> Note: *Tiger lily buds, cloud ears and bean curd can be purchased at Oriental groceries. There are no substitutes.*

OPEN SHRIMP DUMPLINGS
Makes 30

3 dried Chinese
   mushrooms
Hot water
1 pound (450 g) pork,
   cut into 1-inch (2.5
   cm) cubes
½ pound (225 g) cooked
   shrimp, shelled,
   deveined
½ teaspoon (2 mL)
   sugar
1 teaspoon (5 mL)
   sesame oil

¼ teaspoon (1 mL) salt
⅛ teaspoon (0.5 mL)
   pepper
1½ teaspoons (7 mL) soy
   sauce
1 teaspoon (5 mL)
   sherry
30 won-ton wrappers
   Water
2 tablespoons (130 mL)
   vegetable oil

Green Onion Bread and Hot-and-Sour Soup

1. Remove stems from mushrooms; discard. Soak mushrooms in hot water until soft, about 15 minutes. Drain.

2. Using steel blade, process pork, ½ pound (225 g) at a time, using on/off technique, until minced. Transfer to mixing bowl. Process mushrooms, shrimp, sugar, sesame oil, salt, pepper, soy sauce and sherry, using on/off technique, until minced. Stir into pork.

3. Cut corners off won-ton wrappers to form circles. Place 1½ tablespoons (7 mL) filling on each wrapper; bring up edges and pinch to form a rim (see photo 2).

4. Heat 1-inch (2.5 cm) water in bottom of wok or Dutch oven to boiling. Place dumplings in oiled bamboo steamer or on oiled rack in wok.* Cook covered over high heat 20 minutes. Add water if necessary to maintain water level. Serve hot.

   *Note: *Bamboo steamer should be supported in wok on a steaming rack. A steamer can be improvised by placing an ovenproof plate on an inverted soup bowl in Dutch oven or wok.*

Photo 2. To form dumpling, bring up edges of filled wrapper and pinch to form a rim.

GREEN ONION BREAD
Makes 2 (16 wedges)

2 cups (500 mL) all-purpose flour	Coarse salt
2 tablespoons (30 mL) baking powder	3 green onions and tops, cut into 1½-inch (4 cm) pieces
¾ cup (180 mL) boiling water	½ cup (125 mL) peanut oil
2 tablespoons (30 mL) vegetable shortening	

1. Insert steel blade. Place flour and baking powder in bowl. With machine running, add water through feed tube. Process until dough forms ball.

2. Place dough in a covered bowl. Let stand 2 hours. Dough will be sticky.

3. Divide dough in half. Knead each piece 1 minute on floured surface.

4. Roll out each piece into 10-inch (25 cm) circle. Coat surface of each circle with 1 tablespoon (15 mL) shortening. Sprinkle lightly with salt.

5. Using steel blade, process onions until minced. Sprinkle on dough.

6. Roll up each circle into a tube (see photo 3). Wind each tube into a 6-inch (15 cm) coil, starting at the center and coiling around until all dough is used.

7. Flatten each coil and roll out to a 10-inch (25 cm) circle (see photo 4).*

Photo 3. Roll up circle of dough-- coated with shortening and sprinkled with salt and onions-- into a tube.

Photo 4. After forming a coil with tube of dough, flatten coil and roll out to a 10-inch (25 cm) circle.

8. Heat oil in 12-inch (30 cm) skillet to 380 °F (190 °C). Fry breads, one at a time, 30 seconds and turn. Cook until golden. Drain on paper toweling. Cut into wedges and serve warm.**

> Notes: *Breads may be frozen, wrapped in aluminum foil or waxed paper, at this point. Defrost before frying.
>
> **For easier cutting, use kitchen shears.

SWEET-AND-SOUR PORK
Makes 4 servings

1 large green pepper, cut in half	2 cups (500 mL) peanut oil
1 tomato, cut in half	4 cups (1 L) cooked rice
2 cloves garlic	½ cup (125 mL) pineapple chunks, drained
½ cup (125 mL) all-purpose flour	
½ teaspoon (2 mL) salt	¼ cup (60 mL) sugar
½ teaspoon (2 mL) baking powder	¼ cup (60 mL) white wine vinegar
1 extra-large egg	2 tablespoons (30 mL) soy sauce
¼ cup (60 mL) water	
1¼ pounds (565 g) pork tenderloin, cut into 1-inch (2.5 cm) pieces	½ cup (125 mL) pineapple juice
	4 tablespoons (60 mL) catsup
¼ cup (60 mL) all-purpose flour	2 tablespoons (30 mL) cornstarch

1. Using slicing disc, slice green pepper and tomato; reserve.

2. Insert steel blade. With machine running, drop garlic through feed tube; process until minced. Add ½ cup (125 mL) flour, the salt, baking powder, egg and water to bowl; process, using on/off technique, until combined to form batter.

3. Coat pork with ¼ cup (60 mL) flour.

4. Heat oil in wok or 10-inch (25 cm) skillet to 380 °F (190 °C). Dip pork in batter, coating evenly. Fry pork, a few pieces at a time, until golden, about 3 minutes. Drain on paper toweling. Arrange pork on rice.

5. Combine reserved green pepper and tomato, the pineapple, sugar, vinegar, soy sauce, pineapple juice, catsup and cornstarch in a medium saucepan. Cook over medium heat, stirring frequently, until sauce thickens. Pour over pork.

PORK FRIED RICE
Makes 6 servings

1 carrot	2 eggs, beaten
3 green onions and tops, cut into 1½-inch (4 cm) pieces	3 cups (750 mL) cooked rice
1 cup (250 mL) cooked pork, cut into 1-inch (2.5 cm) pieces	2 tablespoons (30 mL) soy sauce
6 tablespoons (90 mL) oil	1 cup (250 mL) cooked peas

1. Using shredding disc, shred carrot.

2. Using steel blade, process green onions and pork separately until coarsely chopped.

3. Heat 2 tablespoons (30 mL) of the oil in wok or skillet; fry eggs. Reserve.

4. Heat remaining 4 tablespoons (60 mL) oil in wok. Add green onions; stir-fry until tender. Add rice, soy sauce, pork and carrot, stirring after each addition.

5. Add peas and eggs; stir-fry 1 minute.

ORANGE-FLAVORED BEEF
Makes 4 servings

2 teaspoons (10 mL) soy sauce	3 green onions and tops, cut into 1½-inch (4 cm) pieces
*1½ teaspoons (7 mL) oyster sauce	
2 teaspoons (10 mL) sherry	2 cups (500 mL) peanut oil
1 tablespoon (15 mL) cornstarch	1 teaspoon (5 mL) soy sauce
1 pound (450 g) flank steak, cut into ½-inch (1.5 cm) pieces	2 teaspoons (10 mL) white wine vinegar
3 teaspoons (15 mL) orange rind	1 teaspoon (5 mL) cornstarch
2 cloves garlic	2 teaspoons (10 mL) cold water
1 slice gingerroot, ⅛-inch (0.5 cm) thick, pared	4 cups (1 L) hot cooked rice

1. Mix 2 teaspoons (10 mL) soy sauce, the oyster sauce, sherry and 1 tablespoon (15 mL) cornstarch; add beef. Let stand at room temperature 20 minutes.

2. Insert steel blade. With machine running, drop orange rind, garlic, gingerroot and green onions through feed tube; process until minced.

3. Heat oil in wok or 10-inch (25 cm) skillet to 380 °F (190 °C). Add beef; fry until brown. Remove beef with slotted spoon. Let oil cool.

4. Remove and discard all but 3 tablespoons (45 mL) of the oil; heat remaining oil. Add green onion mixture to heated oil in wok; stir-fry 30 seconds.

5. Add beef to wok; stir-fry 30 seconds. Mix 1 teaspoon (5 mL) soy sauce, the vinegar, 1 teaspoon (5 mL) cornstarch and the water; add to wok. Stir-fry until thickened. Serve hot with rice.

> Note: *Oyster sauce can be purchased at Oriental groceries. There is no substitute.

ALMOND COOKIES
Makes about 3 dozen

1 cup (250 mL) whole
    blanched almonds
½ cup (125 mL) lard
½ cup (125 mL) butter
    or margarine
1 cup (250 mL) sugar
½ teaspoon (2 mL) salt

1 teaspoon (5 mL)
    almond extract
2 extra-large eggs,
    separated
2⅔ cups (660 mL)
    all-purpose flour

1. Using steel blade, chop ½ cup (125 mL) of the almonds.

2. Add lard, butter and sugar to bowl; process until mixed. Add salt, almond extract, egg yolks and flour; process until blended.

3. Refrigerate dough 2 hours.

4. Heat oven to 350°F (180°C). Shape dough into 1-inch (2.5 cm) balls. Place on ungreased cookie sheets. Flatten cookies with bottom of glass. Brush tops of cookies with beaten egg whites. Press one whole almond on top of each cookie. Bake until light brown, 15 to 20 minutes.

T44

Chinese Dim Sum Brunch

Egg Rolls

Shrimp Toast

Chicken Fried in Paper

Stuffed Clams

Stuffed Sweet Peppers

Egg Fu Yung

Noodles with Hot Sauce

Shrimp Balls

Fried Dumplings

Dim Sum literally means "something to dot the heart with" and the loving practice of serving a medley of many appetite-enchanting dishes began in the tea houses of Canton. The glorious array of seafood, meat, vegetable and dumpling dishes are customarily served around lunchtime. But you may want to serve this perfect buffet-table fare for late-night partying too.

Although Cantonese was the first of the fine great schools of Chinese cooking to achieve popularity here, it wasn't until the advent of the food processor that many Americans would undertake all of the mincing, chopping, cutting and slicing required for this kind of meal. However, machine-age preparation can be accomplished not only quickly, but also hours in advance. You can refrigerate all the ingredients and assemble the dishes for cooking just before guests are due to arrive. The super-efficient

heat conduction of the concave wok makes cooking a matter of minutes. And everything can be kept warm in a low oven—250 to 275°F (120 to 140°C). The Egg Rolls can even be frozen once they're rolled up, then thawed and deep-fried on the day of the party.

Chinese ingredients, including egg roll wrappers, dried mushrooms, canned water chestnuts, fresh bean sprouts, oyster sauce and sesame oil, can be purchased at many supermarkets. But if you can, do pay a visit to an Oriental grocery, for the marvelous array of exotic ingredients there will prove inspiring. If you can't find an ingredient for which there is no substitute, such as chili paste with garlic, prepare the dish without it. Any loss of flavor will not be easily detected.

Tea is, of course, the appropriate beverage for this menu filled with delightful surprises.

EGG ROLLS
Makes 20

Sweet Sauce (recipe
    follows)
5 dried Chinese
    mushrooms
Hot water
1 slice gingerroot,
    ⅛-inch (0.5 cm)
    thick, pared
1 teaspoon (5 mL)
    cornstarch
½ pound (225 g)
    uncooked shrimp,
    shelled, deveined

2 cloves garlic
2 green onions and
    tops, cut into
    2-inch (5 cm)
    pieces
2 carrots
1 cup (250 mL) water
    chestnuts
1 cup (250 mL)
    bamboo shoots
2 tablespoons (30 mL)
    peanut oil

1 tablespoon (15 mL)
    peanut oil
2 cups (500 mL) fresh
    or canned bean
    sprouts
½ teaspoon (2 mL)
    sugar
2 tablespoons (30 mL)
    soy sauce
¾ teaspoon (4 mL) salt

¼ teaspoon (1 mL)
    pepper
1 tablespoon (15 mL)
    cornstarch
2 tablespoons (30 mL)
    cold water
1 pound (450 g) egg
    roll wrappers
1 egg, slightly beaten
2 cups (500 mL) peanut
    oil

1. Make Sweet Sauce.

2. Remove stems from mushrooms; discard. Soak mushrooms in hot water until soft, about 15 minutes. Drain.

3. Insert steel blade. With machine running, drop gingerroot through feed tube; process until minced. Sprinkle gingerroot and 1 teaspoon (5 mL) cornstarch on shrimp.

4. Insert steel blade. With machine running, drop garlic and green onions through feed tube; process until minced.

5. Using shredding disc, shred carrots.

6. Using slicing disc, slice mushrooms, water chestnuts and bamboo shoots separately.

7. Heat 2 tablespoons (30 mL) oil in wok or 12-inch (30 cm) skillet. Stir-fry garlic and green onions until light brown, about 3 minutes. Add shrimp; stir-fry until shrimp turns pink. Remove and reserve.

8. Heat 1 tablespoon (15 mL) oil in wok. Add carrots, bean sprouts, mushrooms, water chestnuts and bamboo shoots; stir-fry 30 seconds after each addition.

9. Add shrimp mixture, sugar, soy sauce, salt and pepper to wok. Combine 1 tablespoon (15 mL) cornstarch and the cold water; add to wok. Stir-fry until sauce thickens. Remove from wok.

10. Place 2 tablespoons (30 mL) filling on each egg roll wrapper. Fold nearest corner over filling. Fold in 2 side corners and roll up, sealing last corner with egg (see photo 5). Place seam-sides down on lightly floured surface.

11. Heat 2 cups (500 mL) peanut oil in wok or skillet to 380°F (190°C). Deep-fry egg rolls, four at a time, until golden; drain on paper toweling. Keep warm in oven until frying is completed.

12. Serve Egg Rolls hot with Sweet Sauce.

Photo 5. Fold corner of egg roll wrapper over filling; then fold in 2 side corners and roll up, sealing last corner with egg.

Sweet Sauce
Makes 1 cup (250 mL)

1 cup (250 mL) apricot jam	3 tablespoons (45 mL) water
3 tablespoons (45 mL) white distilled vinegar	2 tablespoons (30 mL) minced pimiento

1. Using plastic or steel blade, mix all ingredients until blended. Heat to boiling in saucepan; reduce heat. Simmer 1 minute. Serve warm or cold.

SHRIMP TOAST
Makes 28 pieces

1 slice gingerroot, ⅛-inch (0.5 cm) thick, pared	1 tablespoon (15 mL) white wine
¾ pound (340 g) uncooked shrimp, shelled, deveined	1 egg ¼ teaspoon (1 mL) salt ⅛ teaspoon (0.5 mL) cornstarch
1 can (6 ounces or 170 g) water chestnuts	7 slices stale white bread 2 cups (500 mL) peanut oil
1 green onion, cut into 2-inch (5 cm) pieces	

1. Insert steel blade. With machine running, drop gingerroot through feed tube; process until minced.

2. Add shrimp, water chestnuts, green onion, wine, egg, salt and cornstarch to bowl. Process until minced.

3. Remove crusts from bread; cut bread into quarters. Spread shrimp mixture on bread.

4. Heat oil in wok or skillet to 380°F (190°C). Carefully place 4 pieces bread, shrimp sides down, in oil. Fry until golden. Turn; fry 15 seconds. Drain on paper toweling. Keep warm in oven until frying is completed.

CHICKEN FRIED IN PAPER
Makes 18

1 large chicken breast, boned, skinned, slightly frozen	½ pound (225 g) fresh or thawed frozen snow peas
1½ tablespoons (22 mL) soy sauce	2 tablespoons (30 mL) sesame oil
1 tablespoon (15 mL) sherry	1 egg, slightly beaten 2 cups (500 mL) peanut oil
¼ teaspoon (1 mL) ground cinnamon	

1. Using slicing disc, slice chicken. Mix chicken with soy sauce, sherry and cinnamon; marinate at room temperature 30 minutes. Drain.

2. Remove tough ends of snow peas.

3. Cut waxed paper into eighteen 5-inch (13 cm) squares. Lightly brush centers of paper with sesame oil. Divide chicken and snow peas on papers. Fold envelope style, moistening edges of paper with egg before folding. Fold bottom of paper up to 1½ inches (4 cm) from top, fold sides in ½ inch (1.5 cm), fold top down (see photo 6).

Photo 6. To enclose chicken and snow peas in waxed paper, fold bottom of paper up, fold sides in and then fold top down.

4. Heat peanut oil in wok or 12-inch (30 cm) skillet to 380 °F (190 °C). Carefully lower 4 to 6 envelopes into oil. Fry until chicken changes color, about 3 minutes. Turn and fry 1 minute; drain on paper toweling. Keep warm in oven until frying is completed.

5. Serve hot, allowing guests to open packets.

STUFFED CLAMS
Makes 24

1 slice gingerroot, ⅛-inch (0.5 cm) thick, pared	1 egg
2 green onions and tops, cut into 2-inch (5 cm) pieces	2 tablespoons (30 mL) dry white wine
	1½ tablespoons (22 mL) soy sauce
½ pound (225 g) pork, cut into 1-inch (2.5 cm) cubes	½ teaspoon (2 mL) salt
	¼ cup (60 mL) cornstarch
2 cans (6½ ounces or 185 g each) minced clams, drained	*24 clamshells
	Water
	**Oyster sauce

1. Insert steel blade. With machine running, drop gingerroot through feed tube; process until minced. Add green onions to bowl; process until minced.

2. Add pork to bowl; process, using on/off technique, until minced.

3. Transfer pork mixture to mixing bowl. Stir in clams, egg, wine, soy sauce, salt and cornstarch. Fill 24 clean clamshells with mixture.

4. Heat 1-inch (2.5 cm) water in bottom of wok or Dutch oven to boiling. Place clam shells in bamboo steamer in wok.*** Cook covered over high heat 20 minutes. Add water if necessary to maintain water level.

5. Serve hot with oyster sauce.

   Notes: *Twelve ramekins or custard cups can be used in place of the shells.

   **Oyster sauce is made from fresh oysters and can be purchased at Oriental food markets.

   ***Bamboo steamer should be supported in wok on a steaming rack. A steamer can be improvised by placing an ovenproof plate on an inverted soup bowl in Dutch oven or wok (see photos 7 and 8).

Photo 7. Place steaming rack in bottom of wok to support bamboo steamer.

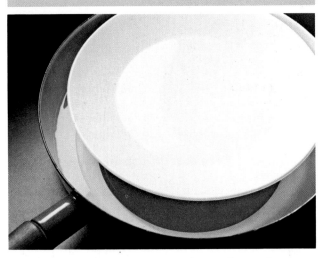

Photo 8. To improvise a steamer, place an inverted soup bowl in bottom of wok; position oven-proof plate on top.

STUFFED SWEET PEPPERS
Makes 12

1 slice gingerroot,
⅛-inch (0.5 cm)
thick, pared
6 ounces (170 g) pork,
cut into ½-inch
(1.5 cm) pieces
½ can (6 ounces or 170
g) water chestnuts
1 green onion, cut into
2-inch (5 cm)
pieces
2 tablespoons (30 mL)
sherry
2½ tablespoons (37 mL)
soy sauce

⅛ teaspoon (0.5 mL)
salt
3 red or green sweet
peppers, cut into
quarters
2 tablespoons (30 mL)
cornstarch
3 tablespoons (45 mL)
peanut oil
1 teaspoon (5 mL)
sugar
½ cup (125 mL) water

1. Insert steel blade. With machine running, drop gingerroot through feed tube; process until minced.

2. Add pork, water chestnuts, green onion, sherry, 1½ tablespoons (22 mL) of the soy sauce and the salt to bowl; process, using on/off technique, until minced.

3. Spoon mixture onto peppers; sprinkle with cornstarch.

4. Heat oil in wok or 12-inch (30 cm) skillet. Place peppers, meat sides down, in wok. Cook over medium heat 2 minutes.

5. Mix remaining soy sauce, the sugar and water. Add to wok; simmer covered until pork is cooked through, about 10 minutes.

6. Remove peppers carefully with spatula; place meat-sides up on serving plate.
Note: Peppers can be kept warm in oven until ready to serve.

EGG FU YUNG
Makes 20

3 dried Chinese
mushrooms
Hot water
½ pound (225 g) cooked
pork, cut into
1-inch (2.5 cm)
pieces
2 green onions and tops,
cut into 2-inch (5
cm) pieces
4 eggs, slightly beaten
1 cup (250 mL) fresh or
canned bean sprouts
1 cup (250 mL) beef
bouillon

2 tablespoons (30 mL)
soy sauce
½ teaspoon (2 mL) salt
5 tablespoons (75 mL)
peanut oil
1 teaspoon (5 mL)
cornstarch
1 tablespoon (15 mL)
cold water
2 tablespoons (30 mL)
fresh, cooked or
frozen, thawed peas

1. Remove stems from mushrooms; discard. Soak mushrooms in hot water until soft, about 15 minutes. Drain.

2. Using steel blade, process pork, using on/off technique, until coarsely chopped.

3. Using steel blade, process green onions, using on/off technique, until chopped. Using slicing disc, slice mushrooms.

4. Mix eggs, pork, onions, mushrooms, bean sprouts, ⅓ cup (80 mL) of the bouillon, 1 tablespoon (15 mL) of the soy sauce and the salt.

5. Heat oil in wok or 12-inch (30 cm) skillet. Pour egg mixture by tablespoons into skillet. Fry egg cakes until golden, about 3 minutes on each side.

6. Heat remaining stock and soy sauce in saucepan to boiling. Mix cornstarch and cold water; stir into stock. Boil, stirring constantly, until thickened. Stir in peas. Serve over egg cakes.

NOODLES WITH HOT SAUCE
Makes 12 appetizer servings

1 green onion, cut into
1½-inch (4 cm)
pieces
1 tablespoon (15 mL)
soy sauce
1 tablespoon (15 mL)
dry white wine
1 tablespoon (15 mL)
distilled white
vinegar
*1 teaspoon (5 mL) chili
paste with garlic
½ teaspoon (2 mL) sugar
1 teaspoon (5 mL) salt

½ cup (125 mL) chicken
stock
4 cups (1 L) cooked
medium egg noodles
1 large cucumber,
pared, seeded
1 boneless chicken
breast, boiled,
cooled, cut into
2-inch (5 cm) pieces
2 tablespoons (30 mL)
peanut oil
2 eggs, beaten

1. Using steel blade, process green onion, using on/off technique, until chopped.

2. Combine green onion, soy sauce, wine, vinegar, chili paste, sugar, salt and chicken stock. Toss with noodles; arrange on plate.

3. Using slicing disc, slice cucumber.

4. Using steel blade, process chicken, using on/off technique, until coarsely chopped.

5. Heat oil in wok or small skillet; fry eggs.

6. Arrange chicken on noodles; top with cucumber. Arrange eggs on top of cucumbers. Toss gently before serving.
*Note: *Chili paste with garlic can be purchased at Oriental stores. There is no substitute.*

SHRIMP BALLS
Makes 24

1 slice gingerroot,
⅛-inch (0.5 cm)
thick, pared
1 pound (450 g)
uncooked shrimp,
shelled, deveined
*3 tablespoons (45 mL)
fresh pork fat
½ can (6-ounce or 170 g
size) water chestnuts

¼ teaspoon (1 mL) salt
⅛ teaspoon (0.5 mL)
pepper
1 teaspoon (5 mL)
sesame oil
1 teaspoon (5 mL)
cornstarch
1 egg white
2 cups (500 mL) peanut
oil

1. Insert steel blade. With machine running, drop gingerroot through feed tube; process until minced.

2. Add shrimp, pork fat, water chestnuts, salt, pepper, sesame oil and cornstarch to bowl. Process, using on/off technique, until smooth.

3. Beat egg white with electric mixer until soft peaks form. Fold into shrimp mixture.

4. Heat oil in wok or 10-inch (25 cm) skillet to 380°F (190°C). Spoon shrimp mixture by teaspoonfuls into oil. Fry 6 at a time, turning once, until golden, about 3 minutes. Drain on paper toweling. Keep warm in oven until frying is completed.
    *Note: *If fat is not available from butcher, trim fat from pork chops or roast.*

FRIED DUMPLINGS
Makes 26 to 30 dumplings

2½ cups (625 mL)
all-purpose flour
½ teaspoon (2 mL)
sesame or
vegetable oil
1 cup (250 mL) boiling
water
¼ cup (60 mL) cold
water
3 green onions and
tops, cut into
2-inch (5 cm)
pieces
5 ounces (140 g) pork,
cut into ½-inch (1.5
cm) cubes

¼ cup (60 mL) bamboo
shoots, cut into
½-inch (1.5 cm)
pieces
1 teaspoon (5 mL) dry
white wine
⅛ teaspoon (0.5 mL)
pepper
4 tablespoons (60 mL)
peanut or vegetable
oil
4 tablespoons (60 mL)
cold water
2 cloves garlic
6 tablespoons (90 mL)
soy sauce
4 tablespoons (60 mL)
cider vinegar

1. Insert steel blade; place flour and sesame oil in bowl. With machine running, add boiling water. Add ¼ cup (60 mL) cold water, processing until ball of dough is formed.

2. Place dough in a bowl. Cover with a damp towel. Let stand 15 minutes.

3. Using steel blade, process green onions, pork and bamboo shoots, using on/off technique, until minced. Add wine and pepper; process until combined.

4. Roll dough ⅛-inch (0.5 cm) thick on a lightly floured surface. Cut circles with a 2½-inch (6.5 cm) cookie cutter.

5. Place ¾ teaspoon (4 mL) pork mixture on each circle. Fold circles in half; pinch edges to seal.

6. Heat peanut oil in wok or 12-inch (30 cm) skillet until hot.

7. Place half of dumplings in wok. Cook covered over medium heat 5 minutes. Sprinkle 2 tablespoons (30 mL) cold water over dumplings; cook covered until tops are soft and the bottoms are crisp, about 5 minutes. Remove dumplings from wok with slotted spoon; drain on paper toweling. Repeat with remaining dumplings.

8. Insert steel blade. With machine running, drop garlic through the feed tube; process until minced. Add soy sauce and vinegar; process until mixed. Serve with dumplings.

ITALY

Antipasto and Cold Sliced Veal with Tuna Sauce

Light, Lyrical Italian Dinner

Spinach Soup with Tiny Meatballs

Yellow and Green Noodles in Cream Sauce

Braised Veal with Lemon

Peas with Prosciutto

Chilled Zabaglione with Strawberries

Paglia e Fiena, or Yellow and Green Noodles, is one of the most beautiful dishes in the Italian repertoire. Its name, in Italian, means "straw and hay"—a poetic reference to the colors of the spinach-tinted and golden egg pasta. The homemade fettucine is much lighter than any comparable commercial product; the simple mushroom cream sauce is nothing more than a gracious compliment paid to the noodles. In this menu, the dish appears as a first course—following the soup and preceding the entree—as it would in Italy.

If you enjoy the freshest and most delicate pasta, you should own a pasta machine. In conjunction with the food processor, this inexpensive, mechanical device eliminates the efforts required to knead, roll out and cut the dough. The whole process takes only minutes, and truly the only trick lies in not overcooking the noodles. It should be noted, however, that some purists claim that noodles rolled out by hand have a less slippery texture and hold the sauce better. So if you don't wish to use a pasta machine, you are not alone and you will still appreciate the convenience of the food processor for mixing and kneading the dough. You can make the noodles and allow them to dry days ahead of your dinner party; store them uncovered and allow them to cook two or three minutes longer than undried pasta.

Braised Veal, scented with lemon, is the easy-to-make and appropriately light entree. Its subtle flavor is balanced by a side-dish of peas richly flavored with prosciutto, the dried Italian ham.

Chilled Zabaglione with Strawberries, a froth of Marsala wine and eggs that's much fluffier than most custards, adds a refreshing ending to the meal. Cortese, a marvelously light, dry white wine, will pick up the lyrical tone of the pasta and not overwhelm the veal; a good Frascati will provide similar pleasure.

SPINACH SOUP WITH TINY MEATBALLS
Makes 6 to 8 servings

4 pounds (1800 g) beef soup bones
2 quarts (2 L) water
1 can (6 ounces or 170 g) tomato paste
2½ teaspoons (12 mL) salt
⅛ teaspoon (0.5 mL) pepper
2 slices dry bread, broken into pieces
1 ounce (30 g) Parmesan cheese, cut into 1-inch (2.5 cm) cubes
¼ cup (60 mL) parsley sprigs
1 clove garlic
¾ pound (340 g) beef, cut into 1-inch (2.5 cm) cubes
1 egg
¼ teaspoon (1 mL) dried basil leaves
½ teaspoon (2 mL) salt
⅛ teaspoon (0.5 mL) pepper
¾ cup (180 mL) uncooked soup pasta
1 pound (450 g) fresh spinach, stems trimmed

1. Combine bones, water, tomato paste, 2½ teaspoons (12 mL) salt and ⅛ teaspoon (0.5 mL) pepper in large saucepan. Heat to boiling; reduce heat. Simmer covered 1 hour; remove bones.

2. Insert steel blade. Process bread to fine crumbs; remove from bowl. With machine running, drop Parmesan cheese through feed tube; process until finely grated. Remove from bowl. Process parsley until chopped.

3. Insert steel blade. With machine running, drop garlic through feed tube; process until minced.

4. Insert steel blade. Process meat, using on/off technique, until finely chopped. Add bread crumbs, Parmesan cheese, parsley, garlic, egg, basil, ½ teaspoon (2 mL) salt and ⅛ teaspoon (0.5 mL) pepper to bowl. Process, using on/off technique, until mixed.

5. Shape mixture into ¾-inch (2 cm) meatballs. Add meatballs to hot stock. Simmer covered, stirring occasionally, 15 minutes.

6. Add soup pasta to stock; cook uncovered until pasta is tender according to package directions.

7. Using steel blade, process spinach, 2 cups (500 mL) at a time, using on/off technique, until chopped. Add to soup during last 15 minutes of cooking time.

YELLOW AND GREEN NOODLES IN CREAM SAUCE
Makes 6 to 8 servings

Egg Pasta (recipe follows)
Spinach Pasta (recipe follows)
¼ pound (115 g) Parmesan cheese, cut into 1-inch (2.5 cm) cubes
¼ cup (60 mL) parsley sprigs
Flour
2 cloves garlic
8 tablespoons (125 mL) butter or margarine
½ pound (225 g) mushrooms
1 teaspoon (5 mL) dried basil leaves
1 cup (250 mL) whipping cream
6 quarts (6 L) water
2 tablespoons (30 mL) salt

1. Make Egg Pasta.

2. Make Spinach Pasta.

3. Insert steel blade. With machine running, drop Parmesan cheese through feed tube. Process until finely grated; reserve. Process parsley until chopped; reserve.

4. **To roll and cut pasta by hand:** Cut each ball of dough into 2 or 3 pieces. (It is easier to roll out smaller pieces of dough than 1 large one.) With rolling pin, roll out and stretch 1 piece of dough on floured surface to thickness of a dime (see photo 1 on page 74). (Keep other pieces of dough sealed in plastic wrap.) Flour dough as necessary to keep it from sticking. Repeat with remaining dough. Let dough dry on floured towel 10 minutes. Turn over and let dry 10 minutes longer. To cut into noodles, roll dough into a loose roll (see photo 2). Cut roll into ¼-inch-wide (0.5 cm) strips (see photo 3). Open up on a dry floured towel 10 minutes.

5. **To roll and cut pasta by machine:** Cut each ball of dough into 6 pieces. Pat each piece of dough into a rectangle about ⅛-inch (0.5 cm) thick. Lightly flour 1 piece of dough and run it through rollers set at thickest setting (see photo 4). (Keep other pieces of dough sealed in plastic wrap.) Fold into thirds and coat with flour; run it through again (see photo 5). Repeat procedure 6 to 8 times until dough is smooth. Reset rollers for next thinner setting; run dough through. Do not fold dough. Repeat using thinner setting each time until thinnest setting has been used. Repeat with remaining dough. Let dough dry on a floured towel 10 minutes. Turn over and let dry 10 minutes longer. Cut dough on noodle setting of pasta machine (see photo 6). Dry on floured towel 30 minutes.

6. While noodles are drying, sauté whole garlic cloves in 2 tablespoons (30 mL) of the butter in skillet until garlic is light brown, about 5 minutes. Remove garlic from skillet; discard garlic.

7. Using slicing disc, slice mushrooms. Add mushrooms to skillet; sauté until liquid is evaporated, about 8 minutes. Stir in basil and chopped parsley.

8. Combine remaining 6 tablespoons (90 mL) butter, the cream and half the Parmesan cheese in large saucepan. Simmer, stirring constantly, until cheese is melted and sauce is blended. Keep warm over low heat.

9. To cook noodles, heat 6 quarts (6 L) water to boiling. Add salt to water just before adding noodles. Add noodles; heat to boiling. Start checking for doneness. (Fresh pasta cooks very quickly. It will be done 15 to 30 seconds after water has returned to boiling.)

10. Drain noodles in a colander; quickly add to cream sauce. Add mushrooms. Toss briefly until noodles are coated with cream sauce. Turn into heated serving dish.

11. Serve immediately with remaining Parmesan cheese.
    Note: You may find that you have more noodles than you need for 6 first-course servings of pasta. To keep leftover uncooked noodles, let noodles dry thoroughly. Transfer to large platter or baking sheet. Store uncovered in cool dry cupboard. Cooking time will be increased by 2 or 3 minutes.

Egg Pasta

2 cups (500 mL) all-purpose flour
3 eggs
2 teaspoons (10 mL) olive oil
¼ teaspoon (1 mL) salt
1 to 2 tablespoons (15 to 30 mL) warm water
Flour

1. Insert steel blade. Place 2 cups (500 mL) flour, eggs, oil and salt in bowl; process until thoroughly blended, 3 to 5 seconds. With machine running, add 1 to 2 tablespoons (15 to 30 mL) warm water through feed tube; process until dough forms ball.

2. Once dough has formed ball, let dough spin around bowl 15 to 20 seconds.

3. Roll dough ball in flour. Cover with plastic wrap and let stand 30 minutes.

Spinach Pasta

5 ounces (140 g) frozen spinach or ½ pound (225 g) fresh spinach, stems trimmed
2 cups (500 mL) all-purpose flour
3 eggs
2 teaspoons (10 mL) olive oil
¼ teaspoon (1 mL) salt
Flour

1. If using frozen spinach, cook according to package directions. If using fresh spinach, rinse and cook covered with water clinging to leaves over medium heat about 10 minutes. Drain well. Cool.

2. Squeeze spinach as dry as possible. Insert steel blade. Process spinach until finely chopped. Add 2 cups (500 mL) flour, eggs, oil and salt to bowl. Process until dough forms ball. (You may need to add a little more flour or water to the dough, depending upon the spinach. The dough should form into ball but not be too sticky to the touch.)

3. Once dough has formed ball, let dough spin around bowl 15 to 20 seconds.

4. Roll dough ball in flour. Cover with plastic wrap and let stand 30 minutes.

BRAISED VEAL WITH LEMON
Makes 6 servings

2 pounds (900 g) veal shank or shoulder, cut into 1½-inch (4 cm) cubes	2 onions, cut into quarters
2 tablespoons (30 mL) butter or margarine	1½ cups (375 mL) dry sherry or white wine
2 tablespoons (30 mL) olive oil	1 teaspoon (5 mL) dried basil leaves
¼ cup (60 mL) parsley sprigs	½ teaspoon (2 mL) salt
1 clove garlic	¼ teaspoon (1 mL) pepper
	2 tablespoons (30 mL) lemon juice

1. Sauté veal in butter and oil in large skillet until light brown on all sides, about 5 minutes.

2. Using steel blade, process parsley until chopped; reserve.

3. Insert steel blade. With machine running, drop garlic through feed tube; process until minced. Add onions to bowl; process, using on/off technique, until chopped.

4. Remove meat from skillet; sauté garlic and onions in skillet until soft, about 5 minutes.

5. Add meat, sherry, basil, salt and pepper to skillet. Heat to boiling; reduce heat. Simmer covered until meat is tender, about 1 hour.

6. Just before serving, stir in lemon juice. Sprinkle with chopped parsley.

PEAS WITH PROSCIUTTO
Makes 6 servings

¼ cup (60 mL) parsley sprigs	2 packages (10 ounces or 285 g each) frozen peas, thawed
2 ounces (60 g) sliced prosciutto, cut into 2-inch (5 cm) pieces	¼ teaspoon (1 mL) salt
2 cloves garlic	⅛ teaspoon (0.5 mL) pepper
2 tablespoons (30 mL) olive oil	Water

1. Insert steel blade; process parsley and prosciutto separately until chopped.

2. Sauté garlic clove in olive oil in medium saucepan until light brown, 3 to 5 minutes. Remove garlic from pan; discard garlic.

3. Add chopped prosciutto to saucepan; sauté 1 minute. Add peas, parsley, salt and pepper. Cook covered over medium heat, stirring occasionally, until peas are tender, about 10 minutes. Add water, 2 tablespoons (30 mL) at a time, if necessary, to keep mixture from sticking.

CHILLED ZABAGLIONE WITH STRAWBERRIES
Makes 8 servings

8 egg yolks	1 cup (250 mL) whipping cream
⅔ cup (160 mL) sugar	1 pint (500 mL) strawberries
⅔ cup (160 mL) dry Marsala wine	

1. Insert steel or plastic blade. Process egg yolks and sugar until pale yellow and fluffy.

2. Cook egg yolk mixture in top of double boiler over simmering water, stirring constantly, until slightly thickened. Add wine gradually, stirring constantly, until mixture thickens to consistency of whipped cream.

3. Transfer egg yolk mixture to medium bowl; cool slightly. Whip cream with electric mixer; fold into egg yolk mixture.

4. Reserve 8 strawberries for garnish. Using slicing disc, slice remaining strawberries. Place sliced strawberries in bottoms of 8 stemmed glasses or bowls. Spoon yolk mixture over strawberries. Refrigerate until chilled, about 1 hour.

5. Garnish each serving with a reserved strawberry.

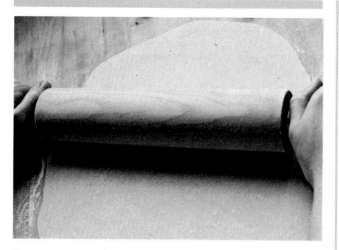

Photo 1. On floured surface, roll out and stretch 1 piece of dough to thickness of a dime.

Photo 4. Lightly flour 1 piece of dough and run it through rollers set at thickest setting.

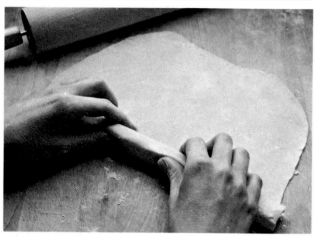

Photo 2. After dough has dried on a floured towel for 10 minutes on each side, roll dough into a loose roll.

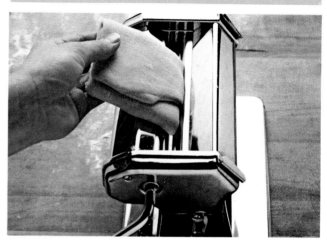

Photo 5. Fold dough into thirds and run it through rollers again. Repeat procedure at same setting 6 to 8 times until dough is smooth.

Photo 3. Cut roll of dough into 1/4-inch-wide (0.5 cm) strips. Open up strips and let noodles dry on a floured towel for 10 minutes.

Photo 6. After running unfolded dough through rollers using thinner setting each time until thinnest setting has been used, cut dough on noodle setting of machine.

Do-Ahead Italian Buffet

Antipasto

Cold Sliced Veal with Tuna Sauce

Lasagne Bolognese

Italian Bread

Cannoli

Many conveniences make this menu perfect for an informal party or a hearty family dinner. Every dish can be made in advance and refrigerated or frozen.

The Antipasto is a food-processor tour de force. It can be composed of virtually any fresh vegetables, meats and cheeses, sliced or julienned and attractively arranged on a platter with olives, anchovies, and hard-cooked eggs. As is customary, our Antipasto includes two marinated salads, as well. The whole platter doubles as both hors d'oeuvre and salad course on the buffet table.

Veal is the preferred meat of Italy and Vitello Tonnato, or Veal with Tuna Sauce, is a classic preparation. Besides presenting diners with the surprise flavors of the tuna, anchovies and capers in the sauce, this dish also offers the advantage of advance preparation.

Use either homemade or commercial pasta in the Lasagne Bolognese. There will of course be great differences of texture and flavor between the two, but the meaty Bolognese sauce turns the noodles into a treat regardless. Refer to this recipe when you want a quick homemade sauce for spaghetti, too. Similarly, you will want to bake the crusty loaves of Italian Bread for many occasions.

Complete this generous buffet with two wines—white Lacrima Christi with the veal and plenty of Chianti with the lasagne.

ANTIPASTO
Makes 8 servings

Marinated Carrot Slices (recipe follows)	1 package (10 ounces or 285 g) frozen artichoke hearts, cooked, drained
Pepper Salad (recipe follows)	12 cherry tomatoes
4 ounces (115 g) pepperoni	12 rolled anchovy fillets
1 cucumber	12 green olives
8 large fresh mushrooms	12 ripe olives
4 ounces (115 g) provolone cheese	4 hard-cooked eggs, cut into wedges
1 can (16 ounces or 450 g) whole beets, drained	12 pimiento strips, rolled
	12 slices prosciutto or other Italian ham, rolled
	Lettuce leaves
	Olive oil

1. Make Marinated Carrot Slices.

2. Make Pepper Salad.

3. Using slicing disc, separately slice pepperoni, cucumber, mushrooms, provolone cheese and beets.

4. Arrange all foods attractively on large lettuce-lined serving platter; sprinkle lightly with olive oil.

Marinated Carrot Slices
Makes about 1½ cups (375 mL)

4 large carrots	1 tablespoon (15 mL) olive oil
Water	¼ teaspoon (1 mL) dried oregano leaves
½ teaspoon (2 mL) salt	¼ teaspoon (1 mL) salt
2 teaspoons (10 mL) red wine vinegar	Pinch black pepper

1. Using slicing disc, slice carrots. Cover carrots with water in medium saucepan; stir in ½ teaspoon (2 mL) salt. Heat to boiling; boil 1 minute. Drain.

2. Mix carrots and remaining ingredients in small bowl. Refrigerate covered 4 hours or overnight.

Pepper Salad
Makes about 1 cup (250 mL)

1 small clove garlic	2 teaspoons (10 mL) red wine vinegar
2 large parsley sprigs	1 tablespoon (15 mL) olive oil
1 large green pepper	Pinch salt
¼ teaspoon (1 mL) dried basil leaves	Pinch pepper

1. Insert steel blade. With machine running, drop garlic through feed tube; process until minced. Add parsley to bowl. Process until finely chopped.

2. Using slicing disc, slice green pepper. Mix all ingredients in small bowl. Refrigerate covered 4 hours or overnight.

T52 T53

COLD SLICED VEAL WITH TUNA SAUCE
Makes 8 to 10 servings

2 carrots, cut into 1-inch (2.5 cm) pieces	1 egg yolk
2 onions, cut into quarters	¼ teaspoon (1 mL) salt
2 ribs celery, cut into 1-inch (2.5 cm) pieces	⅛ teaspoon (0.5 mL) pepper
4 parsley sprigs	6 tablespoons (90 mL) lemon juice
1 bay leaf	1¼ cups (310 mL) olive oil
½ teaspoon (2 mL) dried thyme leaves	5 tablespoons (75 mL) capers, drained
6 cups (1.5 L) water	1 can (7 ounces or 200 g) tuna in oil
2 cups (500 mL) dry white wine	1 can (2 ounces or 60 g) anchovy fillets
2½ to 3 pounds (1125 to 1350 g) boneless tied veal roast	Lemon slices
Water	Parsley sprigs
1 egg	Rolled anchovies with capers, if desired

1. Using steel blade, process carrots, onions, celery and parsley until finely chopped.

2. Combine chopped vegetables, bay leaf, thyme, 6 cups (1.5 L) water and the wine in Dutch oven. Heat to boiling. Add meat. (Add more water to cover, if necessary.) Heat to boiling; reduce heat. Simmer covered until meat is tender, about 1½ hours.

3. Let meat cool in broth. Refrigerate until cold.

4. Remove meat from broth; reserve ½ cup (125 mL) broth. Remove strings from roast. Cut veal into thin, uniform slices.

5. Using steel blade, process egg and egg yolk about 5 seconds. Add salt, pepper and 3 tablespoons (45 mL) of the lemon juice to bowl. Process 10 seconds, until thoroughly blended. With machine running, gradually add olive oil through feed tube. Process until mayonnaise is thick.

T36

6. Add 3 tablespoons (45 mL) of the capers, the tuna and anchovy fillets to mayonnaise. Process until mixture is smooth. With machine running, add remaining 3 tablespoons (45 mL) lemon juice and ¼ to ½ cup (60 to 125 mL) reserved veal broth through feed tube to get consistency of heavy cream.

7. Spread thin layer of tuna sauce in bottom of glass dish. Overlap half the veal slices on top of sauce. Spoon tuna sauce over veal. Arrange another layer

veal slices and top with remaining tuna sauce. (Completely cover veal with sauce.)

8. Cover tightly with plastic wrap. Refrigerate 24 hours before serving.

9. Just before serving, transfer veal and sauce to serving platter; sprinkle with remaining 2 tablespoons (30 mL) capers. Garnish with lemon slices, parsley sprigs and anchovies.

LASAGNE BOLOGNESE
Makes 8 servings

¼ pound (115 g) Parmesan cheese, cut into 1-inch (2.5 cm) cubes	1 cup (250 mL) dry white wine
2 onions, cut into quarters	1 can (28 ounces or 800 g) tomatoes, undrained
1 carrot, cut into 1-inch (2.5 cm) pieces	¼ cup (60 mL) tomato paste
1 rib celery, cut into 1-inch (2.5 cm) pieces	1 teaspoon (5 mL) salt
½ cup (125 mL) parsley sprigs	⅛ teaspoon (0.5 mL) pepper
¼ cup (60 mL) butter or margarine	Egg Pasta (see Index for page number)
¼ pound (115 g) prosciutto or other Italian ham, cut into 1-inch (2.5 cm) pieces	½ pound (225 g) chicken livers, cut into pieces
1 pound (450 g) beef, cut into 1-inch (2.5 cm) cubes	2 tablespoons (30 mL) butter or margarine
½ pound (225 g) pork, cut into 1-inch (2.5 cm) cubes	White Sauce (recipe follows)
2 tablespoons (30 mL) olive oil	Flour
	6 quarts (6 L) water
	2 tablespoons (30 mL) salt
	Cold water
	1 pound (450 g) ricotta cheese

1. Insert steel blade. With machine running, drop Parmesan cheese through feed tube; process until finely grated. Reserve.

2. Using steel blade, process onions, carrot, celery and parsley until finely chopped.

3. Sauté chopped vegetables in ¼ cup (60 mL) butter in saucepan until soft, about 10 minutes.

4. Using steel blade, process prosciutto, beef (½ pound at a time) and pork separately, using on/off technique, until finely chopped. Add chopped meats and olive oil to saucepan. Cook over medium heat until brown, about 10 minutes. Add wine. Cook uncovered until juices are almost evaporated.

5. Using steel blade, process tomatoes, using on/off technique, until finely chopped. Add tomatoes, tomato paste, 1 teaspoon (5 mL) salt and the pepper to saucepan. Simmer uncovered until most of liquid is evaporated, 1 to 1½ hours.

6. While sauce is cooking, make Egg Pasta.

7. Sauté chicken livers in 2 tablespoons (30 mL) butter in skillet until no longer pink, about 10 minutes. Stir into meat sauce.

8. Make White Sauce.

9. **To roll pasta by hand:** Cut dough into 2 or 3 pieces. With a rolling pin, roll out and stretch 1 piece of dough on floured surface to thickness of a dime (keep other pieces of dough sealed in plastic wrap). Flour dough as necessary to keep it from sticking. Cut dough into rectangular strips, 13 × 4½ inches (33 × 11 cm). Repeat with remaining dough.

10. **To roll pasta by machine:** Cut dough into 6 pieces. With fingers, shape each piece of dough into rectangle about ⅛-inch (0.5 cm) thick. Lightly flour 1 piece of dough and run it through rollers set at thickest setting (keep other pieces of dough sealed in plastic wrap). Fold dough into thirds and coat with flour; run it through again. Repeat procedure 6 to 8 times until dough is smooth. Reset rollers for next thinner setting; run dough through rollers again; do not fold dough. Repeat on each thinner setting until dough is not quite paper thin (usually next to the thinnest setting). Cut dough into rectangular strips, 13 × 4½ inches (33 × 11 cm). Repeat with remaining dough.

11. Heat 6 quarts (6 L) water to boiling. Just before adding pasta, add 2 tablespoons (30 mL) salt. Add 4 strips pasta. Heat to boiling. Cook pasta about 10 seconds. Remove with slotted spoon. Dip pasta in bowl of cold water. Place flat on damp towel; dry tops thoroughly. Repeat with remaining pasta.

12. Heat oven to 450°F (230°C). To assemble, spread about 1 cup (250 mL) White Sauce in buttered 13 × 9-inch (33 × 21 cm) baking dish. Place 1 layer pasta over bottom of pan. Spread with about ⅓ meat mixture. Place dollops of ricotta cheese over meat sauce; sprinkle with ⅓ of the Parmesan cheese. Repeat layers with remaining pasta, meat sauce and cheeses. Pour White Sauce over all.

13. Bake until crust is light golden, 10 to 15 minutes. If necessary, broil lasagne 1 minute to brown. (Do not bake any longer than 15 minutes or lasagne will be overcooked.)

White Sauce

6 tablespoons (90 mL) butter or margarine	3 cups (750 mL) milk
4½ tablespoons (67 mL) all-purpose flour	¼ teaspoon (1 mL) salt
	⅛ teaspoon (0.5 mL) ground nutmeg

1. Melt butter in saucepan; stir in flour to make a smooth paste. Cook, stirring constantly, 2 to 3 minutes.

2. Remove pan from heat; stir in milk gradually. Stir in salt and nutmeg. Heat to boiling. Cook, stirring constantly, until thickened, 3 to 5 minutes. Cover with plastic wrap.

ITALIAN BREAD
Makes 2 loaves

1 package active dry yeast	Pinch sugar
2 cups (500 mL) lukewarm water (105 to 115°F or 40 to 45°C)	1½ teaspoons (7 mL) salt
	4½ to 5 cups (1125 to 1250 mL) all-purpose flour
	Cornmeal

1. Combine yeast and warm water in 1-quart (1 L) measuring cup. Stir to dissolve yeast. Sprinkle with pinch of sugar; let stand 3 to 5 minutes. Add salt; stir until salt is dissolved.

2. Insert steel blade. Place 2 cups (500 mL) flour in bowl. With machine running, add half the yeast mixture through feed tube; process a few seconds until blended. Add ¼ to ½ cup (60 to 125 mL) more flour, ¼ cup (60 mL) at a time, processing until dough forms smooth, slightly sticky ball. Let ball of dough spin around bowl 20 to 30 seconds. Turn dough onto lightly floured board. Knead for 1 minute (see photo 7 on page 78). Shape into smooth ball.

3. Repeat step 2 with remaining flour and yeast mixture.

4. Place each ball of dough in a greased bowl; turn the dough to grease the top of the ball. Let rise covered in warm place until doubled, about 2 hours.

5. Punch down dough. Let rise until doubled, about 45 minutes.

6. Shape each ball of dough into long, wide loaf on lightly floured surface (see photo 8). Place on greased baking sheet lightly sprinkled with cornmeal.

7. Let rise covered in warm place 30 minutes. Score surface of dough with diagonal cuts (see photo 9). Let rise 30 minutes.

8. Heat oven to 400°F (200°C). Bake until golden and bread sounds hollow when tapped, about 50 minutes.

Note: Italian Bread freezes very well. Let loaves cool. Wrap cool loaves tightly and freeze. To thaw, unwrap and place on baking sheet in cold oven. Heat at 400°F (200°C) until hot, about 20 minutes.

Photo 7. On lightly floured surface, knead bread dough for 1 minute; then shape into a smooth ball.

Photo 8. After 2 risings, shape each ball of dough into a long, wide loaf on lightly floured surface. Place on baking sheet that is greased and lightly sprinkled with cornmeal.

Photo 9. Score surface of dough on top of each loaf with 2 or 3 diagonal cuts.

CANNOLI
Makes about 16

2 cups (500 mL) all-purpose flour	¼ cup (60 mL) plus 2 tablespoons (30 mL) white wine
¼ teaspoon (1 mL) salt	
2 tablespoons (30 mL) granulated sugar	Cannoli Filling (recipe follows)
¼ teaspoon (1 mL) ground cinnamon	1 egg white, slightly beaten
2 tablespoons (30 mL) butter or margarine, cut into pieces	Vegetable oil
	Chopped pistachio nuts
1 egg	Powdered sugar

1. Insert steel blade. Place flour, salt, granulated sugar, cinnamon and butter in bowl; process until butter is coarsely cut into dry ingredients.

2. With machine running, add egg and ¼ cup (60 mL) wine through feed tube; process until dough forms ball. (Add additional wine drop by drop if necessary.)

3. Lightly flour ball of dough; cover with plastic wrap. Let stand 15 minutes.

4. Make Cannoli Filling.

5. Divide dough into 4 pieces. Roll out on lightly floured surface to thickness of a dime; cut into 4- to 5-inch (10 to 13 cm) circles.

6. Wrap circles of dough around cannoli tubes (see photo 10). Seal edges with egg white.

7. Heat about 2 inches (5 cm) of vegetable oil in skillet to 400°F (200°C). Fry Cannoli until light brown, about 2 minutes (see photo 11). Drain on paper toweling. Let cool slightly; remove from tubes. Repeat with remaining pastry. Cool completely. *

Photo 10. Wrap 4- to 5-inch (10 to 13 cm) circle of dough around cannoli tube. Seal overlapping edges with egg white.

Photo 11. Fry Cannoli in about 2 inches (5 cm) of hot vegetable oil until light brown, approximately 2 minutes.

8. Up to 1 hour before serving, fill each shell with Cannoli Filling; dip ends into chopped pistachio nuts. Sprinkle Cannoli with powdered sugar.

*Note: *Cannoli shells can be fried early in the day; store unwrapped at room temperature until ready to use.*

Cannoli Filling

3 ounces (90 g) semisweet chocolate
1 pound (450 g) ricotta cheese
¾ cup (180 mL) sugar
1 teaspoon (5 mL) vanilla

1. Using shredding disc, shred chocolate squares.

2. Using steel blade, process ricotta cheese, sugar and vanilla until blended. Add shredded chocolate; process only until blended. Refrigerate until ready to use.

Italian Holiday Dinner

Stuffed Mushroom Caps

Shrimp Soup with Pasta

Cheese Ravioli with Pesto

Stuffed Flank Steak

Green Beans Parmesan

Semisweet Chocolate Tortoni

To feast Italian-style, prepare a multi-course dinner that celebrates the abundant ingredients and rich culinary imagination of Italy.

The pasta course is truly memorable—tender, fluffy cheese-filled ravioli tossed with a heavenly variation of Genoa's classic Pesto sauce. If you've never made ravioli before, you'll discover that the preparation is neither difficult nor too time-consuming. And the incomparable flavor makes it worth every minute! You don't have to knead the dough when you mix it in the food processor, and you don't need any special equipment to cut the ravioli. If you do have a pasta machine, you can use it to roll and stretch; otherwise, use a rolling pin. In Genoa, the pesto is made from fresh basil leaves and ground in a mortar and pestle; we've substituted more-readily available fresh parsley, spinach, and dried basil and chopped them in seconds in the food processor.

Another dinner delight, Semisweet

Chocolate Tortoni, is a legacy derived from the famous frozen dessert invented in 18th-century Naples by Signor Tortoni. Shredded chocolate and homemade macaroons, ground in the food processor, distinguish our version.

Many parts of this dinner, such as the ravioli, pesto and tortoni, can be prepared at least a day in advance. You can make the Stuffed Mushroom Caps and refrigerate them, covered, early in the day; then bake them just before serving. Similarly, the stuffing for the Stuffed Flank Steak can be made and refrigerated hours in advance; but don't stuff the meat until you're ready to cook it.

This is a special-occasion menu. To serve it in style, you might begin with a Campari aperitif with the Stuffed Mushroom Caps; then enjoy a soft Valpolicella wine with dinner.

STUFFED MUSHROOM CAPS
Makes 6 servings

12 large mushrooms (about 1 pound or 450 g)
2 ounces (60 g) Parmesan cheese, cut into 1-inch (2.5 cm) cubes
1 slice fresh white bread, broken into pieces

⅓ cup (80 mL) walnuts
2 ounces (60 g) sliced mortadella, prosciutto or other ham, cut into 2-inch (5 cm) pieces
2 cloves garlic
¼ cup (60 mL) parsley sprigs

1 teaspoon (5 mL) dried basil leaves
½ teaspoon (2 mL) salt

⅛ teaspoon (0.5 mL) pepper
3 to 4 tablespoons (45 to 60 mL) olive oil

1. Carefully remove stems from mushroom caps. Using steel blade, process stems until finely chopped; reserve.

2. Insert steel blade. With machine running, drop Parmesan cheese through feed tube; process until finely grated. Remove from bowl. Process bread, walnuts and mortadella until finely chopped.

3. Insert steel blade. With machine running, drop garlic through feed tube; process until minced. Add parsley to bowl; process until chopped. Add chopped mushroom stems, Parmesan cheese, bread crumb mixture, basil, salt, pepper and 1 to 2 tablespoons (15 to 30 mL) of the olive oil to bowl; process, using on/off technique, until combined.

4. Heat oven to 375°F (190°C). Fill mushroom caps with mixture. Arrange in baking dish lightly coated with olive oil. Sprinkle each mushroom cap with a few drops of the remaining olive oil.

5. Bake uncovered until hot and golden, 15 to 20 minutes.

SHRIMP SOUP WITH PASTA
Makes 6 servings

1 clove garlic	¼ cup (60 mL) tomato paste
2 onions, cut into quarters	1 teaspoon (5 mL) dried basil leaves
2 carrots, cut into 1-inch (2.5 cm) pieces	½ teaspoon (2 mL) dried oregano leaves
2 ribs celery, cut into 1-inch (2.5 cm) pieces	½ cup (125 mL) uncooked soup pasta
¼ cup (60 mL) parsley sprigs	¼ teaspoon (1 mL) salt
2 tablespoons (30 mL) butter or margarine	⅛ teaspoon (0.5 mL) pepper
2 tablespoons (30 mL) olive oil	1 pound (450 g) shrimp in shells
5 cups (1250 mL) chicken stock	⅓ cup (80 mL) Marsala wine
1 cup (250 mL) dry sherry or white wine	

1. Insert steel blade. With machine running, drop garlic through feed tube; process until minced. Add onions, carrots, celery and parsley to bowl; process, using on/off technique, until coarsely chopped.

2. Sauté chopped vegetables in butter and olive oil in large saucepan until soft, about 10 minutes.

3. Add chicken stock, sherry, tomato paste, basil, oregano, pasta, salt and pepper. Heat to boiling; reduce heat. Simmer covered 15 minutes. Add shrimp; simmer covered until shrimp turns pink, about 5 minutes.

4. Remove shrimp from soup; shell shrimp. Return shrimp and add Marsala to soup. Heat until hot.

CHEESE RAVIOLI WITH PESTO
Makes 6 Servings (about 45 ravioli)

Egg Pasta (see Index for page number)	⅛ teaspoon (0.5 mL) salt
2 ounces (60 g) Parmesan cheese, cut into 1-inch (2.5 cm) cubes	Flour
	Pesto (recipe follows)
	6 quarts (6 L) water
1 pound (450 g) ricotta cheese	2 tablespoons (30 mL) salt
2 egg yolks	Grated Parmesan cheese (optional)
¼ teaspoon (1 mL) ground nutmeg	

1. Make Egg Pasta.

2. Insert steel blade. With machine running, drop 2 ounces (60 g) Parmesan cheese through feed tube; process until finely grated.

3. Add ricotta cheese, egg yolks, nutmeg and ⅛ teaspoon (0.5 mL) salt to bowl; process, using on/off technique, until combined.

4. **To roll pasta by hand:** Cut dough into 2 pieces. With a rolling pin, roll out and stretch 1 piece of dough on floured surface to thickness of a dime (keep other piece of dough sealed in plastic wrap). Flour dough as necessary to keep it from sticking.

5. **To roll pasta by machine:** Cut dough into 6 pieces. With fingers, shape each piece of dough into rectangle about ⅛-inch (0.5 cm) thick. Lightly flour 1 piece of dough and run it through rollers set at thickest setting (keep other pieces of dough sealed in plastic wrap). Fold dough into thirds and coat with flour; run it through again. Repeat procedure 6 to 8 times until dough is smooth. Reset rollers for next thinner setting; run dough through rollers again; do not fold dough. Repeat on each thinner setting until dough is not quite paper thin (usually next to the thinnest setting).

6. Place 1 heaping teaspoon (5 mL) cheese filling at 2-inch (5 cm) intervals on sheet of pasta (see photo 12). Cover with second sheet of pasta. Gently press down around mounds of filling (see photo 13). Using fluted pastry wheel, cut into 2-inch (5 cm) squares (see photo 14). Or, using a round cookie cutter, cut dough into 2-inch (5 cm) circles. Seal edges with tines of fork. Repeat with remaining dough if pasta machine was used.

7. Place ravioli on dry towel. Let dry 1 hour. Turn ravioli over; let dry 1 hour.

8. Make Pesto.

9. Heat 6 quarts (6 L) water to boiling. Just before adding ravioli, add 2 tablespoons (30 mL) salt. Drop

Photo 12. Place cheese filling at 2-inch (5 cm) intervals on sheet of pasta dough.

Photo 13. Cover with second sheet of dough and gently press down all around mounds of filling.

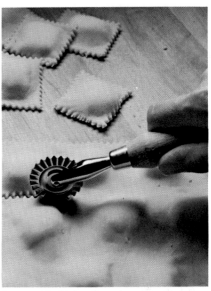

Photo 14. Using fluted pastry wheel, cut between mounds of filling to form 2-inch (5 cm) squares.

Cheese Ravioli with Pesto

ravioli into boiling water. Heat to boiling; cook uncovered *al dente,* 3 to 5 minutes.

10. Remove ravioli with slotted spoon; drain. Place on heated serving platter. Add Pesto and toss gently.

11. Sprinkle with grated Parmesan cheese. Serve immediately.

> *Notes: Cooking time will vary depending upon the length of time the ravioli was dried. Check ravioli frequently as they are cooking.*
>
> *Uncooked ravioli freeze well. Place dried ravioli on lightly floured cookie sheet. Freeze several hours until firm. Transfer to plastic bag and seal tightly. To cook, drop frozen ravioli into boiling, salted water. Cook until tender, 5 to 10 minutes.*

Pesto
Makes 2 cups (500 mL)

2 ounces (60 g) Parmesan cheese, cut into 1-inch (2.5 cm) cubes	1 tablespoon (15 mL) dried basil leaves
½ ounce (15 g) Romano cheese, cut into 1-inch (2.5 cm) cubes	2 tablespoons (30 mL) pine nuts
2 cloves garlic	4 tablespoons (60 mL) butter or margarine, room temperature
2 cups (500 mL) parsley sprigs	1 teaspoon (5 mL) salt
1 cup (250 mL) fresh spinach, stems trimmed	¼ teaspoon (1 mL) pepper
	1 cup (250 mL) olive oil

1. Insert steel blade. With machine running, drop cheeses through feed tube; process until finely grated. Add garlic, parsley, spinach, basil, pine nuts, butter, salt, pepper and ½ cup (125 mL) of the olive oil to bowl; process until finely chopped.

2. With machine running, gradually add remaining olive oil through feed tube; process until smooth.

> *Notes: The traditional pesto from Genoa is made with fresh basil leaves. If fresh basil is available, use 2 cups (500 mL) fresh basil leaves in place of the parsley and spinach; omit dried basil.*
>
> *Pesto freezes very well. Or, if covered with ½ inch (1.5 cm) olive oil, it will keep in the refrigerator up to 4 weeks.*
>
> *Pesto is used principally as a sauce for pasta. If you have some left over, try stirring a tablespoon (15 mL) of Pesto into a bowl of hot soup.*

STUFFED FLANK STEAK
Makes 6 to 8 servings

2 slices fresh bread, broken into pieces	1 tablespoon (15 mL) butter or margarine
2 ounces (60 g) Parmesan cheese, cut into 1-inch (2.5 cm) cubes	1 tablespoon (15 mL) vegetable oil
½ cup (125 mL) parsley sprigs	1 carrot, cut into 1-inch (2.5 cm) pieces
1 clove garlic	1 onion, cut into quarters
2 onions, cut into quarters	1 rib celery, cut into 1-inch (2.5 cm) pieces
1 tablespoon (15 mL) butter or margarine	3 tablespoons (45 mL) warm cognac
1 pound (450 g) pork or veal, cut into 1-inch (2.5 cm) cubes	1 cup (250 mL) red wine
¼ pound (115 g) prosciutto or other ham, cut into 1-inch (2.5 cm) cubes	1 cup (250 mL) beef stock
1 egg	3 tablespoons (45 mL) tomato paste
⅛ teaspoon (0.5 mL) dried oregano leaves	1 bay leaf
1 teaspoon (5 mL) salt	⅛ teaspoon (0.5 mL) dried thyme leaves
⅛ teaspoon (0.5 mL) pepper	¼ teaspoon (1 mL) dried basil leaves
1 flank steak (about 2½ pounds or 1125 g)	½ teaspoon (2 mL) salt
	⅛ teaspoon (0.5 mL) pepper
	Parsley sprigs

1. Using steel blade, process bread to fine crumbs; remove from bowl. With machine running, drop Parmesan cheese through feed tube; process until finely grated; remove from bowl. Process ½ cup (125 mL) parsley until chopped.

2. Insert steel blade. With machine running, drop garlic through feed tube; process until minced. Add 2 onions to bowl; process, using on/off technique, until chopped.

3. Sauté garlic and onion in 1 tablespoon (15 mL) butter until soft, about 5 minutes.

4. Using steel blade, process pork, ½ pound (225 g) at a time, using on/off technique, until finely chopped. Process prosciutto until chopped.

5. Combine bread crumbs, Parmesan cheese, parsley, onion mixture, pork, prosciutto, egg, oregano, 1 teaspoon (5 mL) salt and ⅛ teaspoon (0.5 mL) pepper in large mixing bowl.

6. Place flank steak flat on counter. Cut into steak from the side with small sharp knife to make pocket for stuffing. Pocket should extend across width of steak and along length of steak to within about 1 inch (2.5 cm) of other 3 edges. Be careful not to cut through top or bottom of steak.

7. Fill cavity evenly with stuffing. Bring cut edges together. Skewer edges securely.

8. Brown flank steak in 1 tablespoon (15 mL) butter and the oil in large skillet or Dutch oven. Remove meat.

9. Using steel blade, process carrot, 1 onion and the celery until finely chopped. Sauté chopped vegetables in pan drippings until soft, 10 to 15 minutes.

10. Add warm cognac to vegetables. Ignite and shake pan until flames burn out. Stir in wine, stock, tomato paste, bay leaf, thyme, basil, ½ teaspoon (2 mL) salt and ⅛ teaspoon (0.5 mL) pepper. Add meat.

11. Heat to boiling; reduce heat. Simmer covered until meat is tender, 1½ to 2 hours.* Remove meat from sauce. Using steel blade, process sauce until smooth.

12. To serve, cut meat into ½-inch (1.5 cm) slices. Pour a little sauce over top. Garnish with parsley sprigs. Serve remaining sauce on the side.

*Note: *Stuffed Flank Steak can also be baked covered at 350°F (180°C) for same amount of time.*

GREEN BEANS PARMESAN
Makes 6 servings

2 ounces (60 g) Parmesan cheese, cut into 1-inch (2.5 cm) cubes	2 pounds (900 g) green beans, ends trimmed, cut into 2-inch (5 cm) pieces
1 clove garlic	¼ cup (60 mL) water
1 onion, cut into quarters	1 teaspoon (5 mL) dried basil leaves
2 small green peppers, cut into 1-inch (2.5 cm) pieces	1 teaspoon (5 mL) salt
¼ cup (60 mL) olive oil	⅛ teaspoon (0.5 mL) pepper

1. Insert steel blade. With machine running, drop Parmesan cheese through feed tube; process until finely grated. Reserve.

2. Insert steel blade. With machine running, drop garlic through feed tube; process until minced. Add onion to bowl; process, using on/off technique, until chopped.

3. Using steel blade, process green peppers, using on/off technique, until finely chopped.

4. Sauté garlic, onion and green peppers in olive oil 5 minutes.

5. Add green beans, water, basil, salt and pepper to vegetables. Cook covered over medium heat until green beans are tender, about 15 to 20 minutes. Drain.

6. Stir half the Parmesan cheese into beans. Spoon vegetables into serving dish. Sprinkle with remaining Parmesan cheese.

SEMISWEET CHOCOLATE TORTONI
Makes 6 to 8 servings

Macaroons (recipe follows)	⅔ cup (160 mL) powdered sugar
2 ounces (60 g) semisweet chocolate	1 teaspoon (5 mL) vanilla
2 cups (500 mL) whipping cream	1 tablespoon (15 mL) rum, sweet sherry or almond liqueur
2 egg whites	

1. Make Macaroons.

2. Using steel blade, process enough Macaroons (about 15) to make 1 cup (250 mL) crumbs; reserve.

3. Using shredding disc, shred chocolate; reserve.

4. Whip cream with electric mixer until stiff. Place in large bowl. Beat egg whites with electric mixer until stiff but not dry peaks form. Fold egg whites, powdered sugar, vanilla, rum and ½ cup (125 mL) of the Macaroon crumbs into whipped cream.

5. Sprinkle ¼ cup (60 mL) of the crumbs in bottom of 5- to 6-cup (1250 mL to 1.5 L) soufflé dish or glass bowl. Spoon half the cream mixture into dish. Sprinkle with all but 1 tablespoon (15 mL) shredded chocolate. Spoon remaining cream mixture into dish. Top with remaining chocolate and crumbs.

6. Cover dish with plastic wrap. Freeze until firm, about 4 hours.

7. Let stand at room temperature about 30 minutes before serving.

Macaroons
Makes about 3 dozen

6 ounces (170 g) blanched almonds	1 cup (250 mL) sugar
3 egg whites	½ teaspoon (2 mL) almond extract
Pinch salt	

1. Using steel blade, process almonds until finely ground.

2. Beat egg whites and salt with electric mixer until soft peaks are formed. Gradually beat in sugar. Beat until stiff but not dry peaks form. Fold in almonds and almond extract.

3. Heat oven to 350°F (180°C). Place dough by teaspoons on greased and floured baking sheets.

4. Bake until light brown, 15 to 20 minutes. Remove from baking sheets with spatula; let cool on wire racks.

Note: Extra Macaroons can be stored at room temperature in airtight container.

Homestyle Italian Supper

Minestrone

Cannelloni with Tomato-Meat Sauce

Chicken Marsala

Zucchini with Walnuts

Sicilian Cake

Measure out this menu according to the number of people you wish to serve. For six guests, make the complete dinner. To serve fewer, you may wish to make the Minestrone and either the Cannelloni with Tomato-Meat Sauce or the Chicken Marsala.

The soup is a superb food-processor recipe for any occasion—hot lunches, light suppers or big dinners. The machine takes care of all vegetable preparation; so the satisfying mélange virtually cooks itself.

Since the stuffed Cannelloni are blanketed in a hearty sauce, you could use packaged tube pasta; but of course it offers no substitute for the flavor and texture of homemade pasta. There is no excuse for using anything but good, aged Parmesan cheese, freshly grated, in all the Italian pasta recipes; the food processor reduces the cubes of cheese to grated texture in no time and the flavor adds an incomparable dimension to all the sauces. The best cheese is imported Parmigiano Reggiano, the original Parmesan cheese, which is aged for years before it comes to market.

If you're always looking for new ways to prepare chicken and zucchini, two staples on any budget-minded shopper's list, then you'll doubly appreciate the recipes for Chicken Marsala and Zucchini with Walnuts. Marsala wine, which takes its name from the town in Sicily, is one of the most pleasant and distinctive flavor enrichers of southern Italian cooking. Use the dry version in this dish and serve the chicken with a good Soave, if you wish. Also from Sicily is the rich cake layered with a chocolate-ricotta cheese filling. Make this glazed and fruit-decorated dessert with sweet Marsala and serve it with glasses of this festive wine for special occasions.

MINESTRONE
Makes 8 servings

2 ounces (60 g) Parmesan cheese, cut into 1-inch (2.5 cm) cubes	1 can (16 ounces or 450 g) tomatoes, undrained
1 clove garlic	¼ small head cabbage, cut into wedges
¼ cup (60 mL) parsley sprigs	2 small zucchini
1 onion, cut into quarters	2 carrots
1 leek, trimmed, cut into 1-inch (2.5 cm) pieces	2 teaspoons (10 mL) dried basil leaves
2 ribs celery, cut into 1-inch (2.5 cm) pieces	½ teaspoon (2 mL) dried oregano leaves
3 tablespoons (45 mL) olive oil	6 cups (1.5 L) water
2 potatoes, pared, cut into 1-inch (2.5 cm) cubes	1 tablespoon (15 mL) salt
1 small turnip, pared, cut into 1-inch (2.5 cm) cubes	½ teaspoon (2 mL) pepper
	1 bay leaf
	1 can (16 ounces or 450 g) white beans, drained
	¾ cup (180 mL) uncooked soup pasta

1. Insert steel blade. With machine running, drop Parmesan cheese through feed tube; process until finely grated. Reserve.

2. Insert steel blade. With machine running, drop garlic through feed tube; process until minced. Add parsley, onion, leek and celery to bowl; process, using on/off technique, until coarsely chopped. Sauté these processed vegetables in olive oil in large saucepan until light brown, 10 minutes.

3. Using steel blade, process potatoes, turnip and tomatoes, using on/off technique, until coarsely chopped; add to saucepan.

4. Using shredding disc, shred cabbage.

5. Using slicing disc, slice zucchini and carrots.

6. Add cabbage, zucchini, carrots, basil, oregano, water, salt, pepper and bay leaf to saucepan.* Cook uncovered over low heat 45 minutes.

7. Add beans and pasta; cook uncovered until pasta is tender according to package directions.

8. Top each serving with a generous portion of grated Parmesan cheese.

*Notes: *For a thicker, heartier soup, add 1 can (6 ounces or 170 g) tomato paste at this point.*

One tablespoon (15 mL) of Pesto (see Index for page number) stirred into each portion is a delicious addition.

Soup is better if made 1 to 2 days in advance. Heat until hot.

Chicken Marsala

CANNELLONI WITH TOMATO-MEAT SAUCE
Makes about 16 cannelloni

Tomato-Meat Sauce
  (recipe follows)
Egg Pasta (see Index
  for page number)
Flour
6 quarts (6 L) water
2 tablespoons (30 mL)
  salt
Cold water
4 ounces (115 g)
  Parmesan cheese,
  cut into 1-inch (2.5
  cm) cubes

*3 pounds (1350 g)
  fresh spinach
15 ounces (425 g)
  ricotta cheese
3 eggs
⅛ teaspoon (0.5 mL)
  ground nutmeg
½ teaspoon (2 mL) salt
¼ teaspoon (1 mL)
  pepper

1. Make Tomato-Meat Sauce.

2. Make Egg Pasta.

3. **To roll pasta by hand:** Cut dough into 2 or 3 pieces. With a rolling pin, roll out and stretch 1 piece of dough on floured surface to thickness of a dime. (Keep other pieces of dough sealed in plastic wrap.) Flour dough as necessary to keep it from sticking. Cut dough into 4 × 5-inch (10 × 13 cm) rectangles. Repeat with remaining dough.

4. **To roll pasta by machine:** Cut dough into 6 pieces. With fingers, shape each piece dough into rectangle about ⅛-inch (0.5 cm) thick. Lightly flour 1 piece of dough and run it through rollers set at thickest setting (keep other pieces of dough sealed in plastic wrap). Fold dough into thirds and coat with flour; run it through again. Repeat procedure 6 to 8 times until dough is smooth. Reset rollers for next thinner setting; run dough through rollers again; do not fold dough. Repeat on each thinner setting until dough is not quite paper thin (usually next to the thinnest setting). Cut dough into 4 × 5-inch (10 × 13 cm) rectangles. Repeat with remaining dough.

5. Heat 6 quarts (6 L) water to boiling; add 2 tablespoons (30 mL) salt. Cook pasta, 4 pieces at a time, until they float to the surface, 15 to 20 seconds. Remove immediately with slotted spoon; dip into bowl of cold water. Lay pasta flat on layers of lightly dampened toweling.

6. Insert steel blade. With machine running, drop Parmesan cheese through feed tube; process to fine powder. Reserve.

7. Rinse spinach; remove stems. Cook spinach in water clinging to leaves in Dutch oven until tender, 10 to 15 minutes.

8. Drain spinach well.

9. Using steel blade, process spinach until finely chopped. Add ½ cup (125 mL) grated Parmesan cheese, the ricotta, eggs, nutmeg, ½ teaspoon (2 mL) salt and the pepper to bowl; process until combined.

10. Heat oven to 350 °F (180 °C). Spread each piece pasta with about 3 tablespoons (45 mL) filling. Roll lengthwise.

11. Place cannelloni seam-side down in well-greased 14 × 9-inch (35 × 23 cm) baking pan. Do not overlap cannelloni (you may need two baking pans).

12. Spread Tomato-Meat Sauce over cannelloni. Sprinkle with remaining grated cheese.

13. Bake uncovered until bubbly, 15 to 20 minutes. Let stand 10 minutes before serving.

*Note: *4 packages (10 ounces or 285 g each) frozen spinach can be used. Cook according to package directions.*

Tomato-Meat Sauce
Makes about 3 cups (750 mL)

1 onion, quartered
2 tablespoons (30 mL)
  olive oil
1 pound (450 g) round
  steak, cut into
  1-inch (2.5 cm) pieces
1 can (28 ounces or 800
  g) whole tomatoes,
  undrained

1 can (6 ounces or 170
  g) tomato paste
1 bay leaf
1 teaspoon (5 mL) dried
  basil leaves
1 teaspoon (5 mL) salt
¼ teaspoon (1 mL)
  pepper

1. Insert steel blade. Process onion, using on/off technique, until chopped. Sauté in olive oil in large skillet until tender, about 5 minutes.

2. Using steel blade, process meat, 1 cup (250 mL) at a time, until chopped. Add to onions; cook until brown, 10 to 15 minutes.

3. Using steel blade, process tomatoes with juice until finely chopped. Add tomatoes and remaining ingredients to skillet. Simmer uncovered until thickened, 1 to 1½ hours.

CHICKEN MARSALA
Makes 6 servings

¼ cup (60 mL)
  all-purpose flour
½ teaspoon (2 mL) salt
¼ teaspoon (1 mL)
  pepper
2 chickens (2½ pounds
  or 1125 g each), cut
  into serving pieces
2 tablespoons (30 mL)
  butter or margarine
2 tablespoons (30 mL)
  olive oil
¼ cup (60 mL) parsley
  sprigs
1 clove garlic
1 onion, cut into quarters
1 rib celery, cut into
  1-inch (2.5 cm) pieces

1 carrot, cut into 1-inch
  (2.5 cm) pieces
1 can (16 ounces or
  450 g) tomatoes,
  drained
1 cup (250 mL) chicken
  stock
¾ cup (180 mL) Marsala
  wine
½ teaspoon (2 mL) dried
  rosemary leaves
1 bay leaf
1 teaspoon (5 mL) salt
¼ teaspoon (1 mL)
  pepper
½ pound (225 g)
  mushrooms

1. Mix flour, ½ teaspoon (2 mL) salt and ¼ teaspoon (1 mL) pepper. Coat chicken pieces with flour mixture; shake off excess flour.

2. Sauté chicken in butter and olive oil in large skillet or Dutch oven until light brown on both sides, about 15 minutes. Remove from skillet.

3. Using steel blade, process parsley until chopped; reserve.

4. With machine running, drop garlic through feed tube; process garlic until minced. Add onion, celery and carrot to bowl; process until finely chopped. Add these processed vegetables to skillet; sauté until tender, 10 minutes.

5. Using steel blade, process tomatoes, using on/off technique, until chopped. Add tomatoes, chicken, chicken stock, wine, rosemary, bay leaf, 1 teaspoon (5 mL) salt and ¼ teaspoon (1 mL) pepper to skillet. Simmer covered 30 minutes.

6. Using slicing disc, slice mushrooms; add to skillet. Cook covered until chicken is tender, 10 to 15 minutes.

7. Before serving, sprinkle with chopped parsley.

ZUCCHINI WITH WALNUTS
Makes 6 servings

½ cup (125 mL) walnuts	2 tablespoons (30 mL)
1 clove garlic	lemon juice
3 tablespoons (45 mL)	½ teaspoon (2 mL) salt
olive oil	¼ teaspoon (1 mL)
2 pounds (900 g) zucchini	pepper

1. Insert steel blade. Process walnuts, using on/off technique, until coarsely chopped; reserve.

2. Sauté garlic clove in olive oil in large skillet until golden. Remove garlic from skillet; discard garlic.

3. Using slicing disc, slice zucchini. Add zucchini to skillet; sauté until tender and light brown, about 10 minutes.

4. Just before serving, toss zucchini with lemon juice, walnuts, salt and pepper.

SICILIAN CAKE
Makes 10 to 12 servings

6 eggs, separated	¼ teaspoon (1 mL) salt
1 cup (250 mL) sugar	Ricotta Filling
1 tablespoon (15 mL)	(recipe follows)
lemon juice	*9 tablespoons (135 mL)
Rind of 1 lemon, cut	rum, Marsala wine
into small pieces	or brandy
1¼ cups (310 mL)	Almond Glaze (recipe
all-purpose flour	follows)
1½ teaspoons (7 mL)	Whole almonds
baking powder	Candied cherries

1. Using steel blade, process egg yolks 2 to 3 seconds. With machine running, gradually add sugar, lemon juice and lemon rind through feed tube; process until mixture is thick and lemon colored.

2. Add flour, baking powder and salt to bowl; process only until flour is partially incorporated into batter, 2 to 3 seconds. Remove mixture to large mixing bowl.

3. Heat oven to 375 °F (190 °C). Beat egg whites with electric mixer until stiff but not dry peaks form. Stir ¼ egg whites into batter; fold remaining egg whites into batter. Pour into buttered and floured 9-inch (23 cm) springform pan.

4. Bake until cake springs back when lightly touched, 35 to 40 minutes. Cool in pan on wire rack.

5. Make Ricotta Filling.

6. To assemble, cut cooled cake into 3 layers. Sprinkle each layer with 3 tablespoons (45 mL) rum. Spread bottom layer with half the Ricotta Filling. Top with middle layer; spread with remaining Ricotta Filling. Top with last layer.

7. Cover tightly with plastic wrap; refrigerate several hours or overnight.

8. Make Almond Glaze.

9. Place cake on rack. Cover top and side of cake with Almond Glaze. Decorate with whole almonds and candied cherries. Refrigerate until ready to serve.
*Note: *Any liqueur can be used.*

Ricotta Filling

2 ounces (60 g)	1½ pounds (675 g)
semisweet	ricotta cheese
chocolate, broken	¾ cup (180 mL) sugar
into pieces	1 teaspoon (5 mL)
	vanilla

1. Using metal blade, process chocolate until finely grated.

2. Using steel blade, process ricotta cheese, sugar and vanilla until thoroughly blended. Add chocolate; process only until chocolate is blended into cheese mixture, 2 to 3 seconds.

Almond Glaze
Makes ½ to ¾ cup (125 to 180 mL)

1½ cups (375 mL)	1 tablespoon (15 mL)
powdered sugar	lemon juice
1 egg white	1½ teaspoons (7 mL)
	almond extract

1. Using plastic or steel blade, process all ingredients until thoroughly blended and thick enough to spread.

Korea, Japan & Indonesia

Sukiyaki

Indonesian Rijsttafel Buffet

Yellow Rice

Skewered Meat with Peanut Sauce

Curried Chicken

Corn Fritters

Spicy Baked Fish

Vegetable Salad

Shrimp and Green Beans

Fresh Mango Ice with Sliced Kiwi

Indonesia, formerly the Dutch East Indies, is a nation of thousands of islands strung along the equator like precious jewels. The cuisine of the Spice Islands, as Marco Polo called them, is as unique as the mixed Chinese, Indian and Dutch heritage of the people. The islands have always been a rich source of aromatic spices, such as cloves, nutmeg, mace and pepper.

Rice is the staple of all Indonesian meals. And the word Rijsttafel is the Dutch term for rice table. Not unlike a Scandinavian smörgåsbord, the rice table consists of a sumptuous array of dishes—both spicy and bland and soft and crisp—surrounding a mound of yellow, turmeric-tinted rice. Dutch colonists adopted this Indonesian invention, named it and often expanded it into an opulent entertainment with fifty to sixty dishes—each carried into the dining room by a different servant.

Our Rijsttafel Buffet disdains such ostentation in favor of a superb sampling of great dishes for eight guests (servings indicated following each recipe apply to the dish when it is prepared by itself). Many recipes can be prepared in advance; which is not only convenient but also gives the spices time to merge and develop best flavor. Indonesians prefer that food be served at room temperature—making this buffet very easy on the host or hostess. Guests heap their plates with rice and select toppings and accompaniments from the colorful array of other foods. Most of the ingredients are cut into bite-size pieces; so no knives are required. Tea is the beverage of Indonesia, but Dutch beer is also an appropriate thirst-quencher.

Coconut milk is an essential ingredient in Indonesian cooking. It enhances the spice mixtures with its delicate sweet overtones. Make it with freshly grated coconut if at all possible; the flavor is far superior to canned coconut and the food processor accomplishes the grating in no time. Peanut Sauce is another common enhancement and it too is easily processed by machine. The availability of kiwi fruit and fresh mangoes depends on the season; so use substitutes, as indicated in the dessert recipe, when you can't find the fresh tropical fruit. Try to use fresh coriander leaves, where indicated; the dry leaves are relatively flavorless. And do look for the dried shrimp chips in the oriental section of a supermarket; when fried, these chips add the loveliest pastel color and ethereal texture to the buffet table.

The saté, or Skewered Meat with Peanut Sauce, is probably the most popular meat dish of the islands. Curried Chicken demonstrates the strong influence Indian cooking has had there. And the Spicy Baked Fish is a wonderful tribute to the enchantment of the South Seas.

YELLOW RICE
Makes about 6 cups (1.5 L)

*4 cups (1 L) Coconut Milk (recipe follows)
2 cups (500 mL) uncooked white rice
1 teaspoon (5 mL) salt
½ teaspoon (2 mL) ground coriander
½ teaspoon (2 mL) ground turmeric
2 small onions
Vegetable oil
½ small cucumber, ends trimmed

1. Make Coconut Milk.

2. Heat Coconut Milk in large saucepan to boiling. Stir in rice, salt, coriander and turmeric. Reduce heat and simmer covered until rice is tender, 15 to 20 minutes.

3. Using thin or regular slicing disc, slice onions. Pat dry on paper toweling.

4. Heat 1 inch (2.5 cm) oil in wok or small saucepan until hot. Fry onions until golden. Drain on paper toweling.

5. Using thin or regular slicing disc, slice cucumber.

6. Arrange rice in bowl. Garnish with fried onions and cucumber slices.

*Note: *Canned or frozen coconut milk can be purchased in Oriental groceries and at many gourmet food stores. It can be substituted for fresh Coconut Milk.*

Coconut Milk
Makes about 5 cups (1250 mL)

*2 small coconuts
5 cups (1250 mL) boiling water

1. Heat oven to 375 °F (190 °C). Puncture eyes of coconuts with ice pick; drain liquid and discard. Bake coconuts 15 minutes.

2. Crack coconuts with hammer to open. Pare brown skin from coconuts with small paring knife or vegetable peeler. Break the coconuts into small chunks.

3. Insert steel blade. With machine running, drop coconut chunks through feed tube. Process until

grated. Add 1 cup (250 mL) boiling water. Process 30 seconds.

4. Transfer mixture to mixing bowl. Stir in remaining water. Let stand until cool.

5. Strain through cheesecloth, reserving liquid. Store liquid covered in refrigerator up to 2 days.

*Note: *Unsweetened dried coconut can be substituted for the fresh. Place equal amounts of dried coconut and boiling water in a bowl. Cool and strain as directed above.*

SKEWERED MEAT WITH PEANUT SAUCE
Makes 6 servings

Peanut Sauce (recipe follows)	2 tablespoons (30 mL) dry sherry
2 cloves garlic	1 tablespoon (15 mL) vegetable oil
1½ pounds (675 g) boneless beef sirloin, pork tenderloin or chicken breasts, slightly frozen	1 tablespoon (15 mL) brown sugar
½ cup (125 mL) soy sauce	½ teaspoon (2 mL) ground ginger

1. Make Peanut Sauce.

2. Insert steel blade. With machine running, drop garlic through feed tube; process until minced.

3. Using slicing disc, slice meat. Thread 4 to 5 pieces of meat close together on bamboo skewers. Arrange the skewers in a shallow baking dish.

4. Combine garlic, soy sauce, sherry, oil, brown sugar and ginger. Pour over meat. Let meat stand at least 1 hour or refrigerate overnight.

5. Remove meat from the marinade. Broil meat or grill over charcoal, turning occasionally, until brown, about 5 minutes. Serve with Peanut Sauce.

Peanut Sauce
Makes about 1¾ cups (430 mL)

*1½ cups (375 mL) Coconut Milk (see Index for page number)	1½ teaspoons (7 mL) crushed red pepper flakes
1 cup (250 mL) salted blanched peanuts	1 teaspoon (5 mL) ground coriander
4 cloves garlic	2 tablespoons (30 mL) brown sugar
1 slice gingerroot, ½-inch (1.5 cm) thick, pared	2 tablespoons (30 mL) soy sauce
1 small onion, cut into quarters	2 teaspoons (10 mL) lemon juice

1. Make Coconut Milk.

2. Using steel blade, process peanuts 45 seconds. Remove from bowl.

3. Insert steel blade. With machine running, drop garlic and gingerroot through feed tube; process until minced. Add onion and process, using on/off technique, until finely chopped.

4. Combine onion mixture, red pepper and coriander in small skillet. Cook, stirring constantly, over low heat 2 to 3 minutes. Add peanuts, brown sugar, soy sauce and lemon juice. Gradually stir in Coconut Milk. Cook over medium heat until thickened, about 15 minutes. Serve warm or at room temperature.

*Notes: *Canned or frozen coconut milk can be purchased in Oriental groceries and at many gourmet food stores. It can be substituted for fresh Coconut Milk.*

Peanut Sauce can be prepared 2 to 3 days in advance. Store covered in refrigerator. Heat slightly before serving.

CURRIED CHICKEN
Makes 4 servings

*1½ cups (375 mL) Coconut Milk (see Index for page number)	2½ teaspoons (12 mL) ground coriander
2 cloves garlic	2½ teaspoons (12 mL) curry powder
1 slice gingerroot, ¾-inch (2 cm) thick, pared	¾ teaspoon (4 mL) caraway seeds
3 small onions	⅛ teaspoon (0.5 mL) ground red pepper
2 tablespoons (30 mL) vegetable oil	1 teaspoon (5 mL) salt
1 frying chicken (2½ to 3 pounds or 1125 to 1350 g), cut into eight pieces	Fresh coriander or parsley sprigs
	1 lime, cut into wedges

1. Make Coconut Milk.

2. Insert steel blade. With machine running, drop garlic and gingerroot through feed tube; process until minced.

3. Using thin or regular slicing disc, slice onions.

4. Heat oil in wok or large skillet. Cook chicken in oil until brown, about 15 minutes; remove from wok. Stir-fry garlic mixture and onions in wok, 2 to 3 minutes. Stir in ground coriander, curry powder, caraway seeds and red pepper. Cook, stirring constantly, about 1 minute.

5. Return chicken to wok. Add Coconut Milk and salt. Heat to boiling; reduce heat. Simmer uncovered until chicken is tender, about 30 minutes.

6. Arrange on serving platter. Garnish with coriander sprigs and lime wedges.

*Notes: *Canned or frozen coconut milk can be purchased in Oriental groceries and at many gourmet food stores. It can be substituted for fresh Coconut Milk.*

Curried Chicken can be prepared 24 hours in advance. Store covered in refrigerator. Heat before serving.

CORN FRITTERS
Makes about 16

2 tablespoons (30 mL) fresh coriander leaves	Vegetable oil
1 large clove garlic	1 can (12 ounces or 340 g) corn, drained
8 whole blanched almonds	1 tablespoon (15 mL) all-purpose flour
4 green onions and tops, cut into 1-inch (2.5 cm) pieces	¾ teaspoon (4 mL) salt
1 rib celery, cut into 1-inch (2.5 cm) pieces	¼ teaspoon (1 mL) freshly ground black pepper

1. Using steel blade, process fresh coriander until minced. With machine running, drop garlic and almonds through feed tube; process until minced. Add onions and celery. Process, using on/off technique, until minced.

2. Heat 1 inch (2.5 cm) oil in wok or skillet to 365 °F (185 °C). Combine all ingredients. Drop mixture by tablespoonfuls into hot oil. Fry until golden, 2 to 3 minutes. Drain on paper toweling. Keep warm in oven while frying remaining fritters.

SPICY BAKED FISH
Makes 8 servings

2 limes or small lemons	½ teaspoon (2 mL) ground turmeric
¼ cup (60 mL) fresh or 2 teaspoons (10 mL) dry coriander leaves	½ teaspoon (2 mL) salt
1 slice gingerroot, 1-inch (2.5 cm) thick, pared	2 whole red snapper, sea bass or whitefish, (1½ to 2 pounds or 675 to 900 g each), dressed
3 green onions and tops, cut into 1-inch (2.5 cm) pieces	2 tablespoons (30 mL) soy sauce
¼ cup (60 mL) melted butter or margarine	2 tablespoons (30 mL) dry sherry
1 teaspoon (5 mL) crushed red pepper flakes	

1. Using thin or regular slicing disc, slice limes; reserve.

2. Using steel blade, process fresh coriander until minced. With machine running, drop gingerroot through feed tube; process until minced. Add green onions to bowl. Process until minced. Combine with butter, red pepper, turmeric and salt and coriander, if using dried.

3. Heat oven to 400 °F (200 °C). Cut about 3 diagonal slashes through skin on each side of fish. Arrange fish on aluminum foil in shallow baking dish. Brush fish inside and out with butter mixture. Mix soy sauce and sherry. Pour over fish.

4. Bake fish, basting occasionally, until fish flakes easily with fork, 20 to 30 minutes. Arrange fish whole on serving platter or cut into serving pieces. Garnish with lime slices.

VEGETABLE SALAD
Makes 8 servings

Peanut Sauce (see Index for page number)	½ pound (225 g) green beans, cut into 2-inch (5 cm) pieces, or pea pods
Fried Shrimp Chips (recipe follows)	1 small head cauliflower, separated into flowerets
1 small cucumber	
6 radishes	½ pound (225 g) fresh spinach, stems trimmed, torn into pieces
2 small red potatoes, cooked, pared	
1 small sweet potato, cooked, pared	¼ pound (115 g) fresh or canned bean sprouts
2 large carrots	2 hard-cooked eggs, sliced
½ pound (225 g) cabbage, cut into wedges	

1. Make Peanut Sauce.

2. Make Fried Shrimp Chips.

3. Using thin or regular slicing disc, slice cucumber and radishes separately. Using regular slicing disc, slice potatoes, carrots and cabbage separately.

4. Cook carrots, cabbage, green beans and cauliflower in boiling water until crisp-tender; drain. Toss cooked vegetables with spinach and bean sprouts. Arrange vegetables in large serving dish.

5. Garnish with sliced cucumber, radishes, potatoes, eggs and Fried Shrimp Chips. Serve with Peanut Sauce.

Spicy Baked Fish, Vegetable Salad and Peanut Sauce

Fried Shrimp Chips
Makes 8 servings

Vegetable oil
*1 package (8 ounces or
  225 g) shrimp chips

1. Heat 1 to 2 inches (2.5 to 5 cm) oil in skillet to 350°F (180°C). Fry chips in oil, a few at a time, until expanded 3 to 4 times their original size. Drain on paper toweling.

   *Notes: *Shrimp Chips can be purchased in Oriental groceries and gourmet food shops.*

   Shrimp Chips can be fried 24 hours in advance. Cool; store in airtight container.

SHRIMP AND GREEN BEANS
Makes 6 servings

*1½ cups (375 mL)
  Coconut Milk (see
  Index for page
  number)
¼ cup (60 mL) fresh
  or 2 teaspoons (10
  mL) dry coriander
  leaves
3 cloves garlic
2 medium onions, cut
  into quarters
6 green onions and
  tops
3 tablespoons (45 mL)
  vegetable oil
1 pound (450 g)
  uncooked medium
  shrimp, shelled,
  deveined

¾ pound (340 g) fresh
  green beans,
  trimmed, or 1
  package (10
  ounces or 285 g)
  frozen green
  beans, slightly
  thawed, cut on
  the diagonal into
  1-inch (2.5 cm)
  pieces
2 teaspoons (10 mL)
  paprika
1½ teaspoons (7 mL)
  crushed red
  pepper flakes
1 teaspoon (5 mL)
  ground cumin
½ teaspoon (2 mL)
  salt
1 teaspoon (5 mL)
  brown sugar
1 teaspoon (5 mL)
  lemon juice

1. Make Coconut Milk.

2. Using steel blade, process fresh coriander until minced; reserve.

3. Insert steel blade. With machine running, drop garlic through feed tube; process until minced. Add onion quarters and process, using on/off technique, until coarsely chopped.

4. Using medium slicing disc, slice green onions.

5. Heat oil in wok or large skillet. Stir-fry shrimp until pink, about 2 minutes. Remove from wok with slotted spoon.

6. Add green beans to wok. Stir-fry 3 to 4 minutes. Add onion mixture. Stir-fry 2 to 3 minutes. Stir in remaining ingredients except coriander and shrimp. Stir-fry over medium heat until beans are almost tender, 8 to 10 minutes. Add shrimp and stir-fry 2 to 3 minutes longer.

7. Spoon into serving bowl. Sprinkle with coriander.

   *Note: *Canned or frozen coconut milk can be purchased in Oriental groceries and at many gourmet food stores. It can be substituted for fresh Coconut Milk.*

FRESH MANGO ICE WITH SLICED KIWI
Makes 4 to 6 servings (about 3½ cups or 875 mL)

*2 large ripe mangoes,
  peeled, cut into
  1-inch (2.5 cm)
  chunks
½ cup (125 mL) water
⅓ cup (80 mL) sugar

1 teaspoon (5 mL)
  grated lime rind
3 tablespoons (45 mL)
  fresh lime juice
**3 kiwi fruit, peeled
Mint sprigs

1. Using steel blade, process mangoes, 1 cup (250 mL) at a time, until smooth. You should have about 2 cups (500 mL) pureed mango.

2. Add remaining ingredients except kiwi and mint sprigs to bowl. Process 15 seconds. Pour mixture into shallow pan. Cover and freeze until solid, about 12 hours.

3. Remove mixture from freezer and break into chunks. Using steel blade, process half the mixture at a time until smooth. Place in bowl or plastic container. Cover and freeze at least 12 hours.

4. Using slicing disc, slice kiwi. Place a few slices in bottom of individual serving bowls. Top with scoops of mango ice. Garnish each serving with mint sprig.

   *Notes: *Canned mangoes can be substituted for the fresh.*

   ***Melon can be substituted for the kiwi.*

Savory Dinner from Korea

Grilled Meat on Skewers

Korean Fried Rice and Vegetables

Pickled Cabbage

Korean Fruit Salad

Virtually unknown outside its native land until recent decades, Korean food has attracted a rapidly growing group of devotees. Although related by ingredients to Chinese and Japanese cuisines, Korean cookery has a bold spicy nature all its own. Yet the abundant uses of beef and broiling and barbecueing techniques give it a sense of familiarity.

If there is a national dish, it is Bulgogi, or grilled meat. Marinated in a blend of sesame seeds, garlic, gingerroot, green onions, soy sauce, sherry, sesame oil, sugar and red pepper, the beef is very easy to prepare and offers a tantalizing alternative to run-of-the-mill outdoor grill fare. It can be broiled indoors as well and can be refrigerated in the marinade overnight.

As popular as beef is the omnipresent hot Korean relish, Kim Chee, or Pickled Cabbage. Make it as hot as you like and prepare it days in advance. For Koreans, the fall harvest is not complete until the vegetables have been sliced, spiced and salted to fill pickle crocks for winter.

Rice is always served with Korean dinners and Korean Fried Rice and Vegetables highlights the tradition. A sauce of ground sesame seeds, green onions and garlic gives this dish a somewhat richer and more exciting texture than the usually-encountered Chinese version.

Although desserts are not an essential adjunct to Oriental meals, you can satisfy the American sweet tooth and still remain true to this cuisine with a Korean Fruit Salad. Use any seasonal fruit you wish; the cinnamon, orange and lime flavored syrup will flatter winter citrus or summer peaches, strawberries and cherries.

This is an extremely easy menu to prepare; and it's even easier to serve, since Koreans usually present the meat, rice and vegetable courses together. Cold beer and the nutty, barley-flavored tea available at Korean groceries would be appropriate beverages.

GRILLED MEAT ON SKEWERS
Makes 4 servings

1¼ pounds (565 g) boneless sirloin, slightly frozen
*1 tablespoon (15 mL) toasted sesame seeds
1 large clove garlic
1 slice fresh gingerroot, ½-inch (1.5 cm) thick, pared
4 green onions and tops, cut into 1-inch (2.5 cm) pieces

¼ cup (60 mL) soy sauce
1 tablespoon (15 mL) dry sherry
1 tablespoon (15 mL) sesame oil
2 teaspoons (10 mL) sugar
½ teaspoon (2 mL) crushed red pepper flakes

1. Using slicing disc, slice beef; place in medium bowl.

2. Insert steel blade. Place sesame seeds in bowl. With machine running, drop garlic and gingerroot through feed tube; process until minced. Add onions to bowl; process, using on/off technique, until minced.

3. Combine onion mixture with remaining ingredients. Pour over meat; stir. Let stand at room temperature 30 minutes.

4. Thread meat on wooden skewers. Broil, basting with remaining marinade, until meat is brown, about 2 minutes on each side.

*Note: *To toast sesame seeds, cook in small skillet over medium heat until brown.*

KOREAN FRIED RICE AND VEGETABLES
Makes 4 servings

*1 tablespoon (15 mL) toasted sesame seeds
2 cloves garlic
6 green onions and tops, cut into 1-inch (2.5 cm) pieces
2 carrots
1 medium zucchini or yellow squash
¼ pound (115 g) mushrooms
4 to 6 ounces (115 to 170 g) boneless chicken breast or pork tenderloin, slightly frozen

2 to 3 tablespoons (30 to 45 mL) vegetable oil
½ pound (225 g) fresh or canned bean sprouts, rinsed, drained
2½ cups (625 mL) cups cooked rice
3 to 4 tablespoons (45 to 60 mL) soy sauce
Salt

1. Insert steel blade. Place sesame seeds in bowl. With machine running, drop garlic through feed tube; process until minced. Add onions to bowl; process, using on/off technique, until minced.

2. Using slicing disc, slice carrots and zucchini. Make matchstick pieces by packing slices into feed tube from bottom, perpendicular to slicing disc, and slicing again.

3. Using slicing disc, separately slice mushrooms and chicken.

4. Heat 2 tablespoons (30 mL) oil in wok or large skillet. Stir-fry chicken in oil over medium heat until tender, about 2 minutes. Remove from wok.

5. Add carrots to wok. Stir-fry 1 minute. Add zucchini. Stir-fry about 2 minutes, adding remaining oil if necessary. Add mushrooms. Stir-fry 2 minutes. Add bean sprouts. Stir-fry 1 minute.

6. Stir in onion mixture, rice, chicken and soy sauce. Stir-fry until hot. Season to taste with salt. Arrange on serving dish.

*Note: *To toast sesame seeds, cook in small skillet over medium heat until brown.*

PICKLED CABBAGE
Makes about 1 quart (1 L)

*2 pounds (900 g) Chinese cabbage, stalk trimmed	4 green onions and tops, cut into 1-inch (2.5 cm) lengths
2 tablespoons (30 mL) salt	1 teaspoon (5 mL) sugar
2 cloves garlic	1 teaspoon (5 mL) salt
1 slice fresh gingerroot, 1-inch (2.5 cm) thick, pared	**½ teaspoon (2 mL) ground red pepper

1. Using slicing disc, slice cabbage. Place in large bowl and sprinkle with 2 tablespoons (30 mL) salt. Let stand at room temperature 3 to 4 hours. Rinse with cold water and drain.

2. Insert steel blade. With machine running, drop garlic and gingerroot through feed tube; process until minced. Add onions to bowl; process, using on/off technique, until chopped.

3. Mix cabbage and onion mixture; stir in sugar, 1 teaspoon (5 mL) salt and the pepper. Refrigerate tightly covered 3 to 4 days. Serve as a relish.

*Notes: *Chinese cabbage can be purchased in Oriental groceries. Regular cabbage can be substituted.*

***If a hotter version of this recipe is desired, double or triple the amount of red pepper.*

KOREAN FRUIT SALAD
Makes 4 servings

½ cup (125 mL) orange juice	½ small pineapple, pared, cut into wedges
½ cup (125 mL) water	1 pint (500 mL) strawberries, hulled
¼ cup (60 mL) sugar	¼ cup (60 mL) toasted pine nuts or slivered almonds
½ teaspoon (2 mL) ground cinnamon	
1 tablespoon (15 mL) lime juice	
2 pears, unpared, cored	

1. Heat juice, water, sugar and cinnamon in small saucepan to boiling; reduce heat. Simmer uncovered 5 minutes. Cool slightly. Stir in lime juice.

2. Using slicing disc, slice pears, pineapple and strawberries. Combine fruit and syrup. Refrigerate covered until cold. Serve in individual bowls. Sprinkle with nuts.

Note: Other fruits such as peaches, oranges, cherries and bananas can be used.

Grilled Meat on Skewers and Korean Fried Rice and Vegetables

Japanese Tempura Dinner

Clear Soup with Chicken Balls

Tempura

Japanese Marinated Vegetables

Seafood is a mainstay of Japanese cooking. And although Americans may be put off by the exquisite renderings of raw fish in Sashimi and Sushi, nobody can resist the crisp, fried Tempura, which puts all other fried food to shame with its remarkable delicacy.

The Tempura batter is simplicity itself, but the water must be ice cold and the seafood and vegetables should be, too. Don't overbeat the batter or attempt to fry too many pieces of food at one time. You can use virtually any white fish fillet, such as flounder, sole or whitefish. You'll find the Japanese ingredients in many supermarkets. Mirin, or sweet Japanese rice wine, has a lighter taste than sweet sherry, although the latter can be substituted. You can use any white radish instead of the large Japanese daikon, but you

will miss the unique flavor. The same is true of dashi, the Japanese dried fish broth, which comes in foil packets ready for re-hydration in boiling water.

Soups are an indispensable element of Japanese cooking and they can be served either before or with the entree. Traditionally covered lacquer bowls keep them warm throughout the meal; you eat the solid ingredients first and then drink the broth from the bowl like a beverage. Warm sake may be drunk with the meal as well and tea served afterward.

As with most Japanese dinners, vegetables are used more lavishly than meat or fish in this one. The chilled salad of Japanese Marinated Vegetables offsets the hot main course with its delightful piquancy. Serve melon or another fresh fruit for dessert.

CLEAR SOUP WITH CHICKEN BALLS
Makes 4 servings

1 piece carrot, 2-inches (5 cm) long
1 slice fresh gingerroot, ½-inch (1.5 cm) thick, pared
1 green onion, cut into 1-inch (2.5 cm) pieces
¼ pound (115 g) boneless chicken breast, cut into 1-inch (2.5 cm) pieces

2 teaspoons (10 mL) soy sauce
6 cups (1.5 L) water
*4 cups (1 L) instant dashi or canned chicken broth
1 teaspoon (5 mL) sake or dry sherry
4 watercress sprigs

1. Using thin or regular slicing disc, slice carrot. If desired, cut carrot slices into fancy shapes with hors d'oeuvre cutters.

2. Insert steel blade. With machine running, drop gingerroot through feed tube; process until minced. Add onion to bowl. Process, using on/off technique, until minced. Add chicken and 1 teaspoon (5 mL) of the soy sauce to bowl. Process, using on/off technique, until chicken is minced.

3. Heat water in large saucepan to simmering. Shape chicken mixture into 1-inch (2.5 cm) balls. Drop chicken balls and carrots into simmering water. Cook uncovered 2½ minutes. Remove from water with slotted spoon.

4. Heat dashi in saucepan until hot. Stir in remaining soy sauce and the sake. Pour into individual soup bowls. Place 2 or 3 chicken balls in soup bowls. Float 2 carrot slices and a watercress sprig on top.

*Note: *Dashi is Japanese fish stock. It can be purchased in foil packets at Oriental groceries; prepare according to package directions.*

TEMPURA
Makes 4 servings

2 small sweet potatoes, pared
1 small eggplant (about 8 ounces or 225 g), pared, cut into wedges
2 small green or red peppers
1 slice fresh gingerroot, 1-inch (2.5 cm) thick, pared
2 ounces (60 g) daikon (Japanese radish) or white radishes, cut into 1-inch (2.5 cm) pieces

12 large uncooked shrimp in shells
½ pound (225 g) scallops or boneless fish fillets, cut into chunks
16 mushrooms
Tempura Sauce (recipe follows)
Vegetable oil
1 egg yolk
1 cup (250 mL) ice water
1 cup (250 mL) all-purpose flour

1. Using slicing disc, slice potatoes, eggplant and peppers.

2. Insert steel blade. With machine running, drop gingerroot through feed tube; process until minced. Remove from bowl. Using steel blade, process daikon until minced; remove from bowl. Place ginger and daikon in separate small bowls; refrigerate covered.

3. Shell shrimp, leaving tails intact; remove vein (see photo 1). To butterfly shrimp, slash open nearly all the way to tail and flatten with back of knife (see photo 2). Slice scallops if large.

Photo 1. After shelling, remove vein from shrimp.

Photo 2. Slash open underside; flatten with back of knife.

4. Arrange sliced vegetables, mushrooms and seafood on serving platter. Refrigerate covered until serving time.

5. Make Tempura Sauce.

6. Heat 2 inches (5 cm) oil in wok or electric skillet to 375 °F (190 °C). Beat egg yolk with water. Stir quickly into flour. (Batter will be slightly lumpy.)

7. With tongs or chopsticks, dip vegetables and seafood, one piece at a time, into batter to coat lightly. Fry a few pieces at a time until light brown. Drain on paper toweling. Keep warm in oven while preparing remaining pieces.

8. Serve each guest an assortment of seafood and vegetables with an individual bowl of the Tempura Sauce. Pass ginger and daikon.

Tempura Sauce
Makes 1½ cups (375 mL)

*1 cup (250 mL) instant dashi or beef broth
¼ cup (60 mL) soy sauce
¼ cup (60 mL) mirin (Japanese sweet rice wine) or sweet sherry

1. Heat all ingredients in small saucepan until hot. Spoon into individual serving bowls.

Note: *Dashi is Japanese fish stock. It can be purchased in foil packets at Oriental groceries; prepare according to package directions.

JAPANESE MARINATED VEGETABLES
Makes 4 servings

¼ cup (60 mL) water
3 tablespoons (45 mL) cider vinegar
1 tablespoon (15 mL) sugar
1 teaspoon (5 mL) salt
1 small cucumber
2 ribs celery
3 small turnips, pared
3 large carrots

1. Heat water, vinegar, sugar and salt in small saucepan to boiling. Cool.

2. Pare cucumber lengthwise, leaving a few strips of green. Using thin or regular slicing disc, slice cucumber and celery. Remove from bowl. Slice turnips and carrots. Make matchstick pieces by packing turnip and carrot slices into feed tube from bottom, perpendicular to slicing disc; slice again.

3. Pour vinegar mixture over vegetables in large bowl. Refrigerate covered at least 24 hours.

Japanese Sukiyaki Party

Sukiyaki

Cucumber and Crab Salad

Fruit-and-Nut Cake

The harmony of Japanese cooking cannot be challenged by any other cuisine. It is an art that has been developed over centuries; yet with fresh ingredients and simple recipes, it is amazingly easy to imitate at American tables.

There are many dimensions to this unique harmony. First, the food must be presented with an eye for color and textural contrast. Second, food must be served at the correct temperature, so that none of the intrinsic beauty of any ingredient is diminished. Third, the table should be set to enhance the visual still life of the food. You can create a Japanese atmosphere in your home by arranging cushions on the floor around a low coffee table. Keep table decorations to a minimum; the food is sufficient adornment. Pass hot towels for guests to refresh themselves before eating and use chopsticks rather than silverware.

Begin the meal with warm sake, the fermented rice liquor from Japan. There is an etiquette to serving sake that's as charming as the miniature cups into which it's traditionally poured: The host or hostess pours the first cup for the guest seated beside them and that guest pours for the next person. It is considered rude to serve yourself.

Quite the contrary is true of the main course, Sukiyaki. Typical of nabe ryari, or tableside cooking, Sukiyaki is prepared over a portable brazier or in an electric skillet and guests help themselves to the varied ingredients, dipping each into a beaten egg.

The Sukiyaki ingredients and the delicate Cucumber and Crab Salad should be brought to the table together, making this one meal where the host or hostess has no reason to remain hidden in the kitchen. Conclude the meal with tea and a simple delicious Japanese Fruit-and-Nut Cake.

SUKIYAKI
Makes 4 servings

1¼ pounds (565 g) beef
    tenderloin or
    boneless sirloin,
    slightly frozen
4 carrots
2 small onions
6 ounces (170 g)
    mushrooms
6 green onions and
    tops, cut
    diagonally into
    3-inch (8 cm) pieces
½ pound (225 g) fresh
    spinach, stems
    trimmed

¼ pound (115 g) fresh
    or frozen pea
    pods, thawed
*½ pound (225 g) fresh
    or canned bean
    thread noodles
    (shirataki), rinsed
*¼ pound (115 g) fresh
    or canned soybean
    curd (tofu), cut
    into chunks
Warashita Sauce
    (recipe follows)
4 eggs, if desired
1 small piece beef suet

1. Using slicing disc, slice meat, carrots, onions and mushrooms separately. Arrange meat, carrots, onions, mushrooms, green onions, spinach, pea pods, noodles and bean curd in separate mounds on large platter or tray.

2. Make Warashita Sauce.

3. Lightly beat each egg and place in individual serving bowls.

4. Heat electric skillet to 400°F (200°C). (If using nonelectric skillet, heat until hot.) Rub suet in skillet until the bottom is well coated. Remove suet and discard. Place half the beef in the pan. Brown on both sides and push to one side. Add half the carrots; cook and stir about 2 minutes. Pour in about half the Warashita Sauce.

5. Add half the remaining vegetables to skillet. Cook until vegetables are crisp-tender. Add half the noodles and bean curd; cook until hot, about 2 minutes.

6. Allow guests to serve themselves from skillet. Dip cooked food into beaten egg.

7. Repeat cooking procedure with remaining ingredients.

*Note: *Bean thread noodles and soybean curd can be purchased at Oriental groceries. There are no substitutes; if unavailable, omit from recipe.*

Warashita Sauce

¾ cup (180 mL) beef
    broth
½ cup (125 mL) soy
    sauce

¼ cup (60 mL) mirin
    (Japanese sweet rice
    wine) or sweet
    sherry
3 tablespoons (45 mL)
    sugar

1. Mix ingredients in small pitcher or bowl.

CUCUMBER AND CRAB SALAD
Makes 4 servings

3 small cucumbers
2 teaspoons (10 mL) salt
1 slice fresh
    gingerroot, ½-inch
    (1.5 cm) thick,
    pared
¼ cup (60 mL) rice wine
    or white distilled
    vinegar

2 tablespoons (30 mL)
    sugar
2 to 3 teaspoons (10 to
    15 mL) soy sauce
¾ cup (180 mL) cooked
    crabmeat or tiny
    shrimp

1. Pare cucumbers lengthwise, leaving a few strips of green. Using thin or regular slicing disc, slice cucumber. Remove from bowl and sprinkle with salt. Let stand at room temperature about 1 hour.

2. Using thin or regular slicing disc, slice gingerroot. Mix gingerroot, wine, sugar, and soy sauce in medium bowl. Let stand 1 hour. Remove gingerroot slices; discard.

3. Rinse and drain cucumbers, squeezing out excess moisture. Place in bowl with wine dressing. Refrigerate covered 1 to 2 hours. To serve, place in individual bowls. Top with crabmeat.

FRUIT-AND-NUT CAKE
Makes 6 servings

½ cup (125 mL) walnuts
1 small banana, cut
    into chunks
½ cup (125 mL) crushed
    pineapple, drained
1½ cups (375 mL)
    all-purpose flour
¾ cup (180 mL) packed
    brown sugar

½ cup (125 mL) butter
    or margarine,
    melted
1 egg
1 teaspoon (5 mL)
    baking soda
½ teaspoon (2 mL) salt
½ teaspoon (2 mL)
    ground ginger

1. Heat oven to 325°F (160°C). Using steel blade, process nuts and banana, using on/off technique, until coarsely chopped.

2. Add remaining ingredients to bowl. Process, using on/off technique, until mixture is thoroughly blended and dry ingredients are no longer visible. Spread batter in greased 10¾ × 7-inch (27 × 18 cm) baking pan.

3. Bake until golden and cake springs back when lightly touched, 25 to 30 minutes. Cool on wire rack. Cut into squares or bars.

SPAIN & PORTUGAL

Paella

Exciting Taste of Portugal

Seafood Chowder

Braised Pork with Lemon Pilaf

Portuguese Sweet Bread

Chocolate-Cheese Tarts

Although Portugal was once a part of Spain, it is divided from the rest of the Iberian peninsula by rugged mountains and its cuisine is quite different.

There is, of course, much fish and shellfish to be had along Portugal's Atlantic coastline; so a steaming chowder, laden with diverse fruits of the sea, is an appropriate first course for this menu.

Portugal's extensive coast was also the point of departure for many of the sailors and explorers who first traveled around Africa to Asia and, in the other direction, to the New World. Therefore, Portuguese cooking, more so than any other European food, features exotic spices and chilies as well as other travel booty, such as chocolate, sugar and tomatoes. Obviously these ingredients are much easier for us to obtain than they were for Vasco da Gama or Magellan, and we reap the benefits in Portuguese food, not only of the appeal of these flavorings but also of the refinement in their use that has been developed by generations of Portuguese cooks.

The subtle blends achieved in the small country are exemplified in the popular entree, Braised Pork with Lemon Pilaf. The Portuguese Sweet Bread and Chocolate-Cheese Tarts remind us of another historical fact: sugar was quite rare in Europe until Portuguese planters began to cultivate it in Brazil. Today, nobody uses the commodity with as much élan as the Portuguese. You can bake the coiled bread and freeze it, if you wish. The tarts should be fresh and redolent of cinnamon and almonds.

This superb dinner deserves a rich, exciting red wine, like that of Portugal's Dão region.

SEAFOOD CHOWDER
Makes 6 servings

¼ cup (60 mL) parsley sprigs
2 cloves garlic
2 onions, cut into quarters
2 tablespoons (30 mL) olive oil
1 can (28 ounces or 800 g) tomatoes, drained
2 potatoes, pared
2 carrots
6 cups (1.5 L) water
⅛ teaspoon (0.5 mL) ground cinnamon
⅛ teaspoon (0.5 mL) dried thyme leaves

1 bay leaf
1½ teaspoons (7 mL) salt
⅛ teaspoon (0.5 mL) pepper
1½ pounds (675 g) halibut, haddock or other firm white fish, cut into serving pieces
½ pound (225 g) shrimp, shelled, deveined
½ pound (225 g) scallops, rinsed
6 hard-shelled clams, rinsed
½ cup (125 mL) water

1. Using steel blade, process parsley until chopped; reserve.

2. Insert steel blade. With machine running, drop garlic through feed tube; process until minced. Add onions to bowl; process, using on/off technique, until chopped. Sauté garlic and onions in olive oil in large saucepan until tender, about 5 minutes.

3. Using steel blade, process tomatoes until coarsely chopped. Add tomatoes to saucepan; heat to boiling.

4. Using slicing disc, slice potatoes and carrots. Add potatoes, carrots, 6 cups (1.5 L) water, the cinnamon, thyme, bay leaf, salt and pepper to saucepan. Heat to boiling; reduce heat. Simmer covered 20 minutes.

5. Add halibut, shrimp and scallops to saucepan; simmer covered 10 minutes.

6. Place clams in ½ cup (125 mL) water in small saucepan. Heat to boiling; reduce heat. Simmer covered until clams open, 5 to 10 minutes. Discard clams that have not opened. Add clams to chowder.* Simmer covered 5 minutes.

7. Ladle chowder into individual bowls; sprinkle each serving with chopped parsley.

*Note: *Clams can be removed from shells, if desired.*

BRAISED PORK WITH LEMON PILAF
Makes 6 servings

3 pounds (1350 g) pork, cut into 1-inch (2.5 cm) cubes
2 tablespoons (30 mL) lard or olive oil
¼ cup (60 mL) fresh or 1 tablespoon (15 mL) dried coriander leaves
2 cloves garlic
3 small onions
3 carrots

1 can (16 ounces or 450 g) tomatoes, drained
1 cup (250 mL) dry white wine
1 bay leaf
1½ teaspoons (7 mL) ground cumin
1 teaspoon (5 mL) salt
¼ teaspoon (1 mL) pepper
Lemon Pilaf (recipe follows)
1 small lemon

1. Sauté pork in lard in large skillet or Dutch oven until light brown on all sides, about 10 minutes.

2. Using steel blade, process fresh coriander until chopped; reserve.

3. Insert steel blade. With machine running, drop garlic through feed tube; process until minced.

4. Using slicing disc, slice onions. Add garlic and onions to skillet; cook until onions are tender, 5 minutes. Using slicing disc, slice carrots; add to skillet.

5. Using steel blade, process tomatoes, using on/off technique, until chopped. Add chopped tomatoes, wine, bay leaf, cumin, salt and pepper to pork mixture.

6. Heat to boiling; reduce heat. Simmer covered until meat is tender, 45 to 60 minutes. Cook uncovered until mixture thickens slightly, about 15 minutes.

7. Make Lemon Pilaf.

8. Using slicing disc, slice lemon. Cut 7 or 8 lemon slices into quarters. Add to skillet.

9. To serve, mound Lemon Pilaf onto heated serving platter; top with braised pork and sprinkle with coriander.

Lemon Pilaf
Makes 6 to 8 servings

¼ cup (60 mL) fresh or 1 tablespoon (15 mL) dried coriander leaves	2 cups (500 mL) uncooked rice
1 large onion, cut into eighths	4½ cups (1125 mL) chicken stock
½ cup (125 mL) butter or margarine	Grated rind of 1 lemon
	Pinch cayenne pepper

1. Using steel blade, process fresh coriander until chopped; reserve.

2. Using steel blade, process onion, using on/off technique, until chopped. Sauté onion in butter in medium saucepan until light brown, about 10 minutes.

3. Add rice to saucepan; stir until rice is coated with butter. Cook 2 to 3 minutes.

4. Stir in chicken stock, lemon rind, cayenne and coriander. Heat to boiling; reduce heat. Simmer covered until rice is tender, 20 to 30 minutes.

PORTUGUESE SWEET BREAD
Makes two 9-inch (23 cm) loaves

2 packages active dry yeast	¼ cup (60 mL) warm water (105 to 115°F or 40 to 45°C)
¾ cup (180 mL) milk, scalded	3 eggs
⅔ cup (160 mL) sugar	5½ to 6 cups (1375 mL to 1.5 L) all-purpose flour
½ cup (125 mL) butter or margarine	1 egg, slightly beaten
½ teaspoon (2 mL) salt	

1. Combine yeast and warm water. Stir until dissolved.

2. Combine milk, sugar, butter and salt in 1-quart (1 L) measuring cup; stir until salt is dissolved and butter is melted. Cool to lukewarm.

3. Using steel or plastic blade, process 3 eggs until foamy. Add eggs and yeast mixture to cooled milk mixture.

4. Insert steel blade. Place 2 cups (500 mL) of the flour in bowl. With machine running, add half the liquid mixture through feed tube; process until blended, 5 seconds. Add about ¾ cup (180 mL) more flour, ¼ cup (60 mL) at a time, processing until dough forms slightly sticky smooth ball. Let dough spin around bowl 20 to 30 seconds. Turn ball of dough onto lightly floured surface; knead briefly into smooth ball.

5. Place dough in greased bowl; turn the dough to grease the top of the ball.

6. Repeat steps 4 and 5 with remaining flour and liquid mixture.

7. Let stand covered in warm place until doubled, about 1 hour.

8. Punch down dough. Roll each piece of dough into long rope, about 1½ inches (4 cm) in diameter. Shape each rope of dough into a coil in a buttered 9-inch (23 cm) cake pan, starting at the center and coiling around until all dough is used.

9. Let stand covered in warm place until doubled, about 40 minutes.

10. Heat oven to 350°F (180°C). Brush each loaf with beaten egg. Bake until golden and bread sounds hollow when tapped, about 1 hour. Remove from pans; cool on wire racks.

CHOCOLATE-CHEESE TARTS
Makes 24

Rich Tart Crust (recipe follows)	½ cup (125 mL) sugar
3 ounces (85 g) blanched almonds	3 egg yolks
8 ounces (225 g) cream cheese, room temperature, cut into 2 pieces	1 teaspoon (5 mL) ground cinnamon
	Pinch salt
½ cup (125 mL) cottage cheese	4 ounces (115 g) semisweet chocolate, melted and cooled

1. Make Rich Tart Crust .

2. Heat oven to 400°F (200°C). Roll out dough to ⅛-inch (0.5 cm) thickness on lightly floured surface. Cut into 3½- to 4-inch (9 to 10 cm) circles with cookie cutter. Fit circles into muffin cups or individual tart tins.

3. Bake 8 minutes; cool.

4. Using steel blade, process almonds until coarsely chopped; reserve.

5. Using steel or plastic blade, process cream cheese, cottage cheese and sugar until smooth. Add egg yolks, cinnamon, salt and chocolate to bowl; process until blended.

6. Heat oven to 350°F (180°C). Spoon filling into cooked shells up to ¼ inch (0.5 cm) from top; sprinkle with chopped almonds.

7. Bake until filling is set, 25 to 30 minutes. Let tarts stand 5 minutes. Remove from tins; cool on wire rack.

Rich Tart Crust

1½ cups (375 mL) all-purpose flour	6 tablespoons (90 mL) lard, frozen, cut into pieces
3 tablespoons (45 mL) sugar	1 egg
Pinch salt	1 tablespoon (15 mL) ice water

1. Insert steel blade. Place flour, sugar, salt and lard in bowl; process until lard is mixed into dry ingredients. With machine running, add egg and ice water through feed tube; process until dough forms ball.

2. Cover with plastic wrap; refrigerate 1 hour.

Classic Spanish Dinner

Meat Turnovers

Gazpacho

Chicken in Wine Sauce with Raisins

Green Beans with Pine Nuts

Flan

Few appetizers anywhere in the world are as savory as empanaditas, or Spanish Meat Turnovers. The pastry should be made partially with lard for maximum flakiness and make sure all the shortening is frozen before processing so that it does not get absorbed to the point of toughening the dough. Cumin, coriander and cayenne give the wine-spiked meat filling an intriguingly complex flavor. You can either bake or deep-fry these turnovers and serve them hot or cold.

Follow the pastries with another classic, cold Gazpacho. The food processor is ideally suited to all the chopping required for this spicy, refreshing blend.

It is not uncommon in all cuisines influenced by the Persian cooking techniques introduced by Arab invaders to find a light sweetness in meat and poultry dishes. Chicken in Wine Sauce exemplifies this kind of cooking.

The golden raisins contribute a haunting counterpoint to the chicken flavor. You could serve either a dry white wine from the town of Valdepeñas with this dish or a slightly sweeter white wine from Tarragona.

The Spanish custards are probably another part of the Persian legacy. None of them is better known around the world than Flan, which is a remarkable amalgam of caramel, egg custard, rum, cinnamon and vanilla. The important cooking trick with Flan is not to let the oven get so hot that the water bath begins to boil. If necessary, turn down your oven and let the Flan bake longer until set. The increased baking time will not affect the creamy texture, but too much heat might turn it grainy.

MEAT TURNOVERS
Makes about 3 dozen

Turnover Pastry (recipe follows)
¼ cup (60 mL) fresh or 1 tablespoon (15 mL) dried coriander leaves
1 clove garlic
1 onion, cut into quarters
1 small green pepper, cut into 1-inch (2.5 cm) pieces
2 tablespoons (30 mL) olive oil

1 pound (450 g) beef, cut into 1-inch (2.5 cm) cubes
½ cup (125 mL) tomato sauce
½ cup (125 mL) red wine
¼ teaspoon (1 mL) ground cumin
¼ teaspoon (1 mL) dried oregano leaves
½ teaspoon (2 mL) salt
¼ teaspoon (1 mL) black pepper
Pinch sugar

Pinch cayenne pepper
*1 chorizo, cut into 1-inch (2.5 cm) pieces

Cold water
¼ cup (60 mL) whipping cream

1. Make Turnover Pastry.

2. Using steel blade, process fresh coriander until chopped.

3. Insert steel blade. With machine running, drop garlic through feed tube; process until minced. Add onion and green pepper to bowl; process until chopped. Sauté garlic, onion and green pepper in olive oil in large skillet until onion is tender, about 5 minutes.

4. Using steel blade, process meat, ½ pound at a time, using on/off technique, until finely chopped. Add meat to skillet; cook until brown, about 5 minutes.

5. Add tomato sauce, wine, cumin, oregano, salt, black pepper, sugar, cayenne pepper and coriander to skillet. Heat to boiling; reduce heat. Simmer uncovered until liquid has evaporated, about 30 minutes.

6. Using steel blade, process chorizo until finely chopped. Cook in separate skillet until brown; drain well on paper toweling. Add to meat mixture; cool.

7. Heat oven to 375°F (190°C). Roll pastry on lightly floured surface. Cut into 3- to 3½-inch (8 to 9 cm) circles with cookie cutter. Place about 1 teaspoon (5 mL) filling on each circle; brush edge with cold water. Fold dough in half; seal with tines of a fork. Brush tops with cream.

8. Bake until light brown, 20 to 25 minutes.** Serve warm or cold.

*Notes: *Chorizo is a Spanish garlic-seasoned pork sausage; it can be purchased at specialty food stores or Spanish groceries.*

***Turnovers can also be deep-fried at 375°F (190°C) until golden; omit whipping cream. Drain on paper toweling before serving. Serve warm or cold.*

Turnover Pastry

2 cups (500 mL) all-purpose flour
2 teaspoons (10 mL) baking powder
1 teaspoon (5 mL) salt
1 teaspoon (5 mL) sugar
¼ cup (60 mL) lard, frozen, cut into pieces
¼ cup (60 mL) frozen butter or margarine, cut into pieces
1 egg
3 to 4 tablespoons (45 to 60 mL) dry white wine or sherry

1. Using steel blade, process flour, baking powder, salt, sugar, lard and butter until lard and butter are mixed into dry ingredients.

2. With machine running, add egg and 3 tablespoons (45 mL) wine through the feed tube; process until dough forms into ball. Add additional wine drop by drop as needed.

3. Refrigerate covered 1 hour.

GAZPACHO
Makes 6 to 8 servings

4 slices dry bread, broken into pieces
1 clove garlic
1 small onion, cut into quarters
1 small green pepper, cut into 1-inch (2.5 cm) pieces
1 cucumber, pared, seeded, cut into 1-inch (2.5 cm) pieces
6 large tomatoes, peeled, cut into quarters
¼ cup (60 mL) olive oil
2 tablespoons (30 mL) wine vinegar
1 teaspoon (5 mL) paprika
1 teaspoon (5 mL) sugar
1½ teaspoons (7 mL) salt
¼ teaspoon (1 mL) pepper
Dash red pepper sauce
Pinch ground cumin
2 to 3 cups (500 to 750 mL) cold chicken stock
2 hard-cooked eggs, cut into halves
1 green pepper, cut into 1-inch (2.5 cm) pieces
1 cucumber, pared, seeded, cut into 1-inch (2.5 cm) pieces
2 tomatoes, seeded, cut into 1-inch (2.5 cm) pieces
Toasted croutons

1. Using steel blade, process bread to fine crumbs; reserve.

2. Using steel blade, process garlic, onion, small green pepper, 1 cucumber, 6 tomatoes, the olive oil and vinegar until smooth. Transfer mixture to large bowl.

3. Stir in paprika, sugar, salt, pepper, red pepper sauce, cumin and bread crumbs until blended.

4. Stir in 2 to 3 cups (500 to 750 mL) chicken stock, depending upon desired consistency. Refrigerate covered several hours or overnight.

5. Using steel blade, process hard-cooked eggs, 1 green pepper, 1 cucumber and 2 tomatoes separately, using on/off technique, until coarsely chopped. Arrange in individual bowls.

6. Ladle soup into chilled cups. Top each cup with toasted croutons. Let guests add selection of chopped egg or vegetables to soup.

CHICKEN IN WINE SAUCE WITH RAISINS
Makes 6 servings

2 chickens (2½ pounds or 1125 g each), cut into serving pieces
3 tablespoons (45 mL) butter or margarine
3 tablespoons (45 mL) olive oil
2 onions, cut into quarters
½ pound (225 g) mushrooms
2 tablespoons (30 mL) all-purpose flour
1 cup (250 mL) dry white wine
1 cup (250 mL) chicken stock
2 tablespoons (30 mL) lemon juice
1 bay leaf
Pinch dried thyme leaves
½ teaspoon (2 mL) salt
¼ teaspoon (1 mL) pepper
¾ cup (180 mL) golden raisins

1. Sauté chicken in butter and olive oil in large skillet until light brown on all sides, about 10 minutes. Remove from skillet.

2. Using steel blade, process onions, using on/off technique, until chopped. Sauté in pan drippings until tender, 5 minutes.

3. Using slicing disc, slice mushrooms. Add to onions; sauté 2 to 3 minutes.

4. Stir in flour; cook 2 minutes. Remove from heat; stir in wine and chicken stock. Heat to boiling; reduce heat. Simmer, stirring constantly, until thickened and smooth.

5. Add chicken, lemon juice, bay leaf, thyme, salt, pepper and raisins.

6. Simmer covered until chicken is tender, 30 to 40 minutes.

GREEN BEANS WITH PINE NUTS
Makes 6 servings

½ cup (125 mL) pine nuts
4 tablespoons (60 mL) olive oil
*1 piece chorizo, 2-inches (5 cm) long, cut into quarters
2 cloves garlic
1 onion, cut into quarters

1 small green pepper, cut into 1-inch (2.5 cm) pieces
2 pounds (900 g) green beans, trimmed, cut into 2-inch (5 cm) pieces
½ teaspoon (2 mL) salt
¼ teaspoon (1 mL) pepper

1. Sauté pine nuts in 1 tablespoon (15 mL) of the olive oil in small skillet until light brown. Remove from skillet.

2. Using steel blade, process chorizo until chopped. Cook in separate small skillet until brown; drain on paper toweling.

3. Insert steel blade. With machine running, drop garlic through feed tube; process until minced. Add onion and green pepper to bowl; process, using on/off technique, until chopped.

4. Sauté garlic, onion and green pepper in remaining olive oil in large saucepan, about 5 minutes.

5. Add green beans, salt and pepper to saucepan; cook covered over medium heat, stirring frequently, until beans are tender, 15 to 20 minutes.

6. When beans are tender, add cooked chorizo and pine nuts; heat until hot.

*Note: *Chorizo is a Spanish garlic-seasoned pork sausage; it can be purchased at specialty food stores or Spanish groceries.*

FLAN
Makes 6 servings

1¼ cups (310 mL) sugar
3 cups (750 mL) milk
2 sticks cinnamon (about 2-inches or 5 cm long each)
1 teaspoon (5 mL) vanilla

3 tablespoons (45 mL) dark rum
4 whole eggs
2 egg yolks
Boiling water

1. Heat ½ cup (125 mL) of the sugar in a heavy saucepan or skillet over low heat until sugar melts. Do not stir. Tilt pan back and forth frequently until syrup turns light brown. Pour immediately into 1½-quart (1.5 L) baking dish or mold. Tilt to coat bottom of dish.

2. Heat milk and cinnamon sticks in saucepan just to boiling. Remove from heat; discard cinnamon sticks. Stir in vanilla and rum.

3. Heat oven to 350°F (180°C). Using steel blade, process eggs and egg yolks for several seconds. With machine running, gradually add remaining ¾ cup (180 mL) sugar through feed tube; process until thick and pale yellow.

4. With machine running, add 2 cups (500 mL) of the hot milk through feed tube; process until mixed. Strain mixture through a fine sieve. Stir in remaining 1 cup (250 mL) milk.

5. Pour custard into prepared baking dish. Place dish in large shallow baking pan. Set on middle rack of oven. Pour boiling water into baking pan to come halfway up sides of custard dish (see photo 1).

Photo 1. Place custard dish in shallow baking pan; set pan on oven rack; pour boiling water into pan to come halfway up sides of custard dish.

6. Bake until knife inserted halfway between edge and center comes out clean, 40 to 45 minutes. Remove dish from water. Let stand until cool. Refrigerate until custard is cold, at least 3 hours.

7. To unmold, run sharp knife around edges of flan. Place serving plate upside down over dish and invert. Pour any extra caramel remaining in the dish over flan.

Spanish Paella Party

Guacamole

Garlic Soup

Paella

Almond Roll with Rum Custard

Paella, in all its myriad variations, comes from the east coast of Spain, a land of rice, saffron, seafood, tomatoes, sweet and hot peppers and the spicy smoked sausage called chorizo. Like so many other great one-pot meals, this one began with the local staple, rice, and took on whatever embellishments people could find close at hand. You might interpret this as license to vary the meats, seafood and vegetables in your Paella any way you wish. The dish takes its name from the flat, two-handled pan, the paellera, in which it is traditionally prepared and not from any specific mix of ingredients. You can prepare our Paella through the next to last step in the recipe early in the day, refrigerate it and let it come to room temperature again; but do not add the seafood until shortly before serving time and be sure not to overcook it.

Garlic Soup is a Mediterranean classic and a food-processor natural. This, too, can be prepared up to the final baking stage, refrigerated in advance and baked just before serving. But leave the Guacamole for last-minute preparation; it will not keep in the refrigerator. The avocados for this delicious dip must be ripe and buttery; use the dark-skinned California variety rather than the more watery Florida-grown product, if possible. And be sure to use the on/off technique when processing; the Guacamole should retain the rich flavor of some chunks of avocado.

The Almond Roll with Rum Custard must be made in advance. It combines the marvelous flavors of almonds, cinnamon and rum in a truly elegant confection that's well worth every minute it takes to prepare.

A red wine from the Rioja district of Spain, which can be compared favorably with many French red wines, is the perfect beverage for this party.

GUACAMOLE
Makes 2 cups (500 mL)

1 clove garlic	Pinch cayenne pepper
½ small onion, cut in half	1 tablespoon (15 mL) olive oil
2 large avocados, peeled, pitted, cut into 2-inch (5 cm) pieces	1 tablespoon (15 mL) wine vinegar
	2 tomatoes, cut into 2-inch (5 cm) pieces
½ teaspoon (2 mL) salt	Tortilla chips

1. Insert steel blade. With machine running, drop garlic through feed tube; process until minced. Add onion; process, using on/off technique, until chopped.

2. Add avocados, salt, cayenne pepper, olive oil and vinegar to bowl. Process, using on/off technique, until coarsely chopped.

3. Add tomatoes to bowl; process, using on/off technique, until coarsely chopped and mixed.

4. Serve as a dip with tortilla chips.
   Note: Guacamole should be chunky; be sure to use on/off technique. Guacamole can also be served as a salad on a bed of lettuce.

GARLIC SOUP
Makes 6 servings

½ loaf stale French bread, broken into pieces	*5 cups (1250 mL) chicken stock
4 large cloves garlic	1 teaspoon (5 mL) paprika
1 onion, cut into quarters	1 bay leaf
¼ cup (60 mL) olive oil	Pinch cayenne pepper
	2 eggs

1. Using steel blade, process bread to coarse crumbs. Remove from bowl; measure 3 cups (750 mL).

2. Insert steel blade. With machine running, drop garlic through feed tube; process until minced. Add onion to bowl; process, using on/off technique, until chopped.

3. Sauté garlic and onion in oil in large ovenproof saucepan until onion is tender, about 5 minutes. Stir in bread crumbs; cook until golden, 5 to 8 minutes.

4. Stir chicken stock, paprika, bay leaf and cayenne pepper into saucepan. Heat to boiling; reduce heat. Simmer covered for 20 minutes.

5. Heat oven to 400°F (200°C). Using steel blade, process mixture, 2 cups (500 mL) at a time, until smooth. Return to saucepan; heat until hot.

6. Using steel or plastic blade, process eggs until lightly beaten. Gently spoon eggs over top of soup.

7. Bake until eggs are cooked and puffy, 10 to 15 minutes. Serve immediately.
   *Note: *More stock can be added if soup is too thick.*

PAELLA
Makes 6 servings

1 frying chicken (2½ to 3 pounds or 1125 to 1350 g), cut into serving pieces
¼ cup (60 mL) olive oil
4 thick boneless pork chops (about 1 pound or 450 g), cut into 1-inch (2.5 cm) cubes
*1 chorizo (about 6 inches or 15 cm long), cut into 1-inch (2.5 cm) pieces
2 cloves garlic
1 large onion, cut into eighths
1 green pepper, cut into 1-inch (2.5 cm) pieces
2 tomatoes, peeled, seeded, cut into quarters
¼ cup (60 mL) olive oil
3 cups (750 mL) uncooked rice
6½ cups (1625 mL) chicken stock
½ to 1 teaspoon (2 to 5 mL) salt
½ teaspoon (2 mL) pepper
¼ teaspoon (1 mL) saffron threads or powder
12 hard-shelled clams, washed
12 uncooked jumbo shrimp (about 1 pound or 450 g), shelled, deveined
12 large scallops (about 1 pound or 450 g)
1 cup (250 mL) frozen peas, thawed
6 lemon wedges

1. Sauté chicken in ¼ cup (60 mL) olive oil in large skillet until light brown. Remove from skillet.

2. Sauté pork in skillet until light brown. Remove from skillet. Discard fat.

3. Cook chorizo in skillet until light brown. Drain on paper toweling.

4. Insert steel blade. With machine running, drop garlic through feed tube; process until minced. Add onion to bowl; process, using on/off technique, until chopped.

5. Using steel blade, process green pepper and tomatoes until chopped.

6. Sauté garlic, onion, green pepper, and tomatoes in ¼ cup (60 mL) olive oil in large ovenproof skillet, stirring occasionally, until most of the liquid has evaporated (mixture should be fairly thick).

7. Heat oven to 400 °F (200 °C). Add rice, chicken stock, salt, pepper and saffron to skillet; heat to boiling. Place chicken, pork and chorizo on top of mixture; cover with aluminum foil. Bake 20 minutes.

8. Arrange clams, shrimp and scallops on top of rice; scatter peas over all. Bake covered until rice is tender, 10 to 15 minutes. Garnish with lemon wedges.

*Note: *Chorizo is a Spanish garlic-seasoned pork sausage; it can be purchased at specialty food stores or Spanish groceries. Any smoked pork sausage can be substituted.*

ALMOND ROLL WITH RUM CUSTARD
Makes 10 to 12 servings

Rum Custard (recipe follows)
3 ounces (85 g) blanched whole almonds
5 eggs, separated
⅔ cup (160 mL) granulated sugar
Rind of 1 lemon, cut into pieces
2 tablespoons (30 mL) dark rum
½ cup (125 mL) all-purpose flour
¼ teaspoon (1 mL) cream of tartar
Powdered sugar
Toasted sliced almonds, if desired

1. Make Rum Custard.

2. Using steel blade, process almonds until ground; reserve.

3. Using steel blade, process egg yolks until blended. With machine running, gradually add granulated sugar and lemon rind through feed tube; process until mixture is thick and lemon colored.

4. Add rum and flour to bowl; process just until flour is blended into mixture, 2 to 3 seconds. Transfer to large mixing bowl.

5. Beat egg whites with electric mixer until foamy. Add cream of tartar; beat until stiff but not dry peaks form.

6. Stir ¼ of the egg whites into egg yolk mixture. Spread remaining egg whites over top of mixture; sprinkle with ground almonds. Gently fold ingredients until blended.

7. Heat oven to 400 °F (200 °C). Butter a 15 × 10-inch (38 × 25 cm) baking pan and line it with waxed paper. Butter and flour waxed paper. Pour batter into pan and spread mixture evenly. Bake until cake springs back when touched, 10 to 12 minutes. Let stand 2 to 3 minutes.

8. Turn cake onto clean dry dish towel. Peel off waxed paper. Roll up cake with towel, beginning from narrow edge (see photo 2 on page 108). Let stand until cool.*

9. Unroll cake and remove dish towel. Remove cinnamon stick from custard. Spread cake with custard (see photo 3) and roll up again.** Sprinkle generously with powdered sugar. Garnish with toasted almonds, if desired. Refrigerate at least 2 hours before serving.

*Notes: *Cake can be made up to this point 1 day in advance; keep rolled and tightly wrapped in refrigerator.*

***If more rum flavor is desired, sprinkle cake roll with 3 to 4 tablespoons (45 to 60 mL) rum before spreading with custard.*

Photo 2. Place cake on dish towel, peel off waxed paper and roll up cake and towel together.

Photo 3. After cake has cooled, unroll and remove dish towel. Spread cake with custard filling and roll up again.

Rum Custard

2 cups (500 mL) milk	3 tablespoons (45 mL) dark rum
1 stick cinnamon (about 2-inches or 5 cm long)	1 teaspoon (5 mL) vanilla
3 egg yolks	Pinch salt
⅓ cup (80 mL) sugar	Pinch ground nutmeg
¼ cup (60 mL) cornstarch	2 tablespoons (30 mL) butter or margarine

1. Heat milk and cinnamon stick just to boiling; remove from heat. Remove cinnamon stick and reserve.

2. Using steel blade, process egg yolks until blended. With machine running, gradually add sugar and cornstarch through feed tube; process until mixture is thick and lemon colored.

3. With machine running, gradually add hot milk through feed tube. Return mixture to saucepan; cook over low heat, stirring constantly, until smooth and thickened. Remove from heat; stir in remaining ingredients and the cinnamon stick. Refrigerate until cold.

Almond Roll with Rum Custard

SCANDINAVIA

Danish Fish Mousse, Danish Liver Paste and Lucia Buns

Danish Liver Paste

Norwegian Veal

Beef à la Lindstrom

Danish Fish Mousse

Red Cabbage with Apples

Marinated Herring

Sweet-and-Sour Mackerel

Pancakes with Lingonberry Sauce

Lucia Buns

Chilled Cherry Soup

Scandinavian Smörgåsbord

The ingredients of Scandinavian cooking are necessarily more limited than those of countries with kinder climates. But Scandinavians traditionally compensate with imagination and generosity. A Swedish Smörgåsbord, or "bread and butter" table always holds a procession of herring preparations, followed by cold and then hot dishes. We have expanded on the Swedish custom by filling our buffet table with specialties from all of Scandinavia.

Sweden is represented on the menu with Beef à la Lindstrom, a tribute to that country's love of beef, as well as Lucia Buns, Pancakes with Lingonberry Sauce and Chilled Cherry Soup. The latter two are served as desserts; the pancakes should be eaten crisp and hot off the stove with a dollop of the tangy sauce. Lucia Buns are the swirled, saffron-flavored sweet baked to celebrate St. Lucia's Day, December 13. But the buns puff up so majestically and their flavor is so delicious that

they should be served more often. It's well worth doubling the recipe and stacking the dough coils on a baking sheet, for the larger quantity makes a beautiful centerpiece and any leftovers can be frozen.

From Norway came two simple gifts of the sea—Sweet-and-Sour Mackerel and Marinated Herring. Denmark is appropriately represented by the richer and more sophisticated Liver Paste and Fish Mousse. There is a paucity of leafy greens throughout the northern countries, so a sweet-and-sour Red Cabbage is often served. You may wish to fill out your menu with any seasonal vegetables as well as assorted breads and cheeses.

Every Smörgåsbord must have its Skoal, or toast, of icy aquavit. Danish Cherry Herring liqueur would go well with dessert and beer is never inappropriate with the main courses. Coffee is the indispensable accompaniment for Scandinavian desserts and the always-welcome symbol of hospitality.

DANISH LIVER PASTE
Makes 8 to 12 servings

½ pound (225 g) calf's liver, cut into 1½-inch (4 cm) pieces
½ pound (225 g) beef liver, cut into 1½-inch (4 cm) pieces
¼ pound (115 g) pork fat, cut into 1½-inch (4 cm) pieces
1 medium onion, cut into quarters
4 anchovy fillets
½ cup (125 mL) whipping cream
3 tablespoons (45 mL) vermouth
2 eggs, slightly beaten
3 tablespoons (45 mL) all-purpose flour
½ teaspoon (2 mL) salt
¼ teaspoon (1 mL) pepper
8 slices bacon
Hot water
Dill pickles
Tomatoes

1. Using steel blade, process livers, 1 cup (250 mL) at a time, using on/off technique, until minced. Transfer to large mixing bowl.

2. Using steel blade, process pork fat, onion and anchovy fillets until minced. Add cream, vermouth, eggs, flour, salt and pepper; process until mixed. Add to liver; mix well.

3. Heat oven to 350°F (180°C). Line terrine or loaf pan, 11 x 4½ x 3 inches (28 x 11 x 8 cm), with bacon. Add liver mixture and press into pan. Fold bacon over top.

4. Place terrine in roasting pan; fill half-way with hot water. Bake uncovered 1½ hours. Drain off fat.

5. Serve warm or cold; cut into slices and serve from pan with pickles and tomatoes.*

*Notes: *Danish Liver Paste may be garnished with decorative shapes cut from pimientos.*

Danish Liver Paste can be made up to 3 days in advance. Refrigerate covered.

NORWEGIAN VEAL
Makes 8 servings

1 medium onion, cut into quarters
¼ cup (60 mL) butter or margarine
2 tablespoons (30 mL) vegetable oil
1½ pounds (675 g) veal scallops
½ pound (225 g) Norwegian goat cheese (Gjetost)
1 cup (250 mL) sour cream
¼ teaspoon (1 mL) salt
⅛ teaspoon (0.5 mL) pepper

1. Using steel blade, chop onion. Sauté in butter and oil in large skillet 3 minutes.

2. Add veal to skillet; cook until browned, about 2 minutes on each side.

3. Using steel blade, process cheese until grated. Mix with sour cream.

4. Heat cheese and sour cream in small saucepan, stirring constantly, until cheese melts. Stir in salt and pepper.

5. Pour sauce over veal; simmer uncovered 2 minutes.

BEEF À LA LINDSTROM
Makes 8 servings

1½ pounds (675 g) round steak, cut into 1-inch (2.5 cm) cubes	2 egg yolks
	⅓ cup (80 mL) cream
	1 tablespoon (15 mL) capers, drained
1 large potato, pared, cooked	¾ teaspoon (4 mL) salt
¾ cup (180 mL) pickled beets, drained	⅛ teaspoon (0.5 mL) pepper
1 medium onion, cut into quarters	¼ cup (60 mL) butter or margarine
	1 cup (250 mL) beef consommé

1. Using steel blade, process steak, ½ pound (225 g) at a time, using on/off technique, until minced. Transfer to large mixing bowl.

2. Using steel blade, process potato, beets and onion, using on/off technique, until minced. Stir into meat.

3. Combine egg yolks, cream, capers, salt and pepper; stir into meat mixture.

4. Shape meat mixture into 16 patties. Heat butter in large skillet; add patties. Cook over medium heat until done in center, about 4 minutes on each side. Transfer to serving dish.

5. Add consommé to skillet; heat to boiling. Pour over meat and serve.

DANISH FISH MOUSSE
Makes 8 to 10 servings

1½ pounds (675 g) haddock, cod or pike fillets, cut into pieces	3 tablespoons (45 mL) dry bread crumbs
	Hot water
1 tablespoon (15 mL) salt	1 tablespoon (15 mL) white distilled vinegar
½ teaspoon (2 mL) white pepper	2 tablespoons (30 mL) sugar
⅛ teaspoon (0.5 mL) ground nutmeg	6 tablespoons (90 mL) Dijon-style mustard
1½ tablespoons (22 mL) cornstarch	2 tablespoons (30 mL) fresh or 2 teaspoons (10 mL) dry dillweed
1½ cups (375 mL) milk	
1½ cups (375 mL) whipping cream	½ cup (125 mL) vegetable oil
1 tablespoon (15 mL) butter or margarine	

1. Using steel blade, process fish, using on/off technique, until pureed.

2. Add salt, pepper, nutmeg and cornstarch to bowl. With machine running, pour milk and cream in slow steady stream through feed tube.

3. Heat oven to 350°F (180°C). Butter an 8-cup (2 L) mold with 1 tablespoon (15 mL) butter; sprinkle with bread crumbs. Pour filling into mold; cover with aluminum foil. Place mold in deep baking dish; fill half-way with hot water. Bake until knife inserted into center comes out clean, about 1 hour. Place under broiler 2 to 3 minutes to brown top.

4. Insert steel blade. Place vinegar, sugar, mustard and dillweed in bowl. With machine running, pour oil in slow steady stream through feed tube; process until combined. Refrigerate until serving time.

5. Serve hot with sauce.

RED CABBAGE WITH APPLES
Makes 8 to 10 servings

1 head red cabbage (4 pounds or 1800 g), cut into wedges	½ teaspoon (2 mL) ground nutmeg
	3 tablespoons (45 mL) white distilled vinegar
2 apples, pared, cored, cut into halves	
6 tablespoons (90 mL) butter or margarine	5 tablespoons (75 mL) brown sugar
¼ teaspoon (1 mL) salt	½ cup (125 mL) dark raisins
⅛ teaspoon (0.5 mL) pepper	

1. Using slicing disc, slice cabbage and apples.

2. Heat butter in Dutch oven. Add cabbage; sprinkle with salt, pepper, nutmeg, vinegar and sugar. Stir in raisins and apples. Cook over medium heat, stirring occasionally, 15 minutes.

3. Heat oven to 350°F (180°C). Bake covered, stirring occasionally, 1½ hours.

4. Serve warm or cold.

MARINATED HERRING
Makes 8 to 12 servings

6 herring fillets	½ lemon
Water	2 cups (500 mL) whipping cream
2 large onions, cut into quarters	
2 green apples (Granny Smith) pared, cored, cut into halves	¼ cup (60 mL) wine vinegar
	1 tablespoon (15 mL) olive oil
1 can (8¼ ounces or 235 g) beets, drained	4 bay leaves

1. Cover herring with water; refrigerate covered overnight. Drain herring; arrange in glass serving bowl.

2. Using slicing blade, slice onions, apples, beets and lemon. Add to herring.

3. Combine cream, vinegar, olive oil and bay leaves. Pour over herring. Refrigerate covered overnight. Serve cold.

Pancakes with Lingonberry Sauce and Chilled Cherry Soup

SWEET-AND-SOUR MACKEREL
Makes 8 to 10 servings

2 large onions, cut into
    quarters
1 lemon
2 to 3 pounds (900 to
    1350 g) mackerel
    fillets, cut into 2-
    inch (5 cm) pieces

1 cup (250 mL)
    gingersnaps
2 tablespoons (30 mL)
    vinegar
½ cup (125 mL) dark
    raisins
½ cup (125 mL) sugar
Water

1. Using slicing disc, slice onions and lemon. Place onions in bottom of large, heavy saucepan; add mackerel and lemon.

2. Using steel blade, process gingersnaps until finely ground. Add crumbs, vinegar, raisins and sugar to pan. Add water to cover.

3. Heat to boiling; reduce heat. Simmer covered until fish is tender, about 45 minutes. Refrigerate until cold.

PANCAKES WITH LINGONBERRY SAUCE

Makes 10 to 12 servings

Lingonberry Sauce
(recipe follows)
4 egg yolks, beaten
1 cup (250 mL) all-
purpose flour
1 cup (250 mL) half-
and-half
1 cup (250 mL) milk

3 tablespoons (45 mL)
sour cream
½ teaspoon (2 mL) salt
½ teaspoon (2 mL) sugar
4 egg whites
¼ cup (60 mL) butter or
margarine

1. Make Lingonberry Sauce.

2. Using steel blade, process egg yolks, flour, half-and-half, milk, sour cream, salt and sugar until mixed. Transfer to large mixing bowl.

3. Beat egg whites with electric mixer until stiff but not dry peaks form. Fold egg whites into batter.

4. Heat butter in large skillet. Pour 1 tablespoon (15 mL) of batter for each pancake into skillet. Fry until golden, turning once. Serve with Lingonberry Sauce.

Lingonberry Sauce

2 cups (500 mL) canned
lingonberries,
drained

¼ cup (60 mL) water
¾ cup (180 mL) sugar

1. Heat lingonberries and water in saucepan to boiling; reduce heat. Simmer uncovered 10 minutes.

2. Stir in sugar; simmer uncovered 5 minutes. Cool.

LUCIA BUNS

Makes 12

1 package active dry
yeast
1 teaspoon (5 mL)
sugar
¼ cup (60 mL) warm
water (about 110 °F
or 43 °C)
⅛ teaspoon (0.5 mL)
saffron powder
1 teaspoon (5 mL)
water
¼ cup (60 mL) sugar
½ teaspoon (2 mL)
ground cardamom

1 egg
3 cups (750 mL) all-
purpose flour
¾ cup (180 mL) milk
¼ cup (60 mL) butter
or margarine,
melted
1 egg, slightly beaten
Sugar
12 dark raisins
¼ cup (60 mL) blanched
slivered almonds

1. Dissolve yeast and 1 teaspoon (5 mL) sugar in warm water. Let stand 5 minutes.

2. Mix saffron and 1 teaspoon (5 mL) water.

3. Insert steel blade. Place ¼ cup (60 mL) sugar, the cardamom, 1 egg, flour, saffron, milk and butter in bowl. Process until mixed. With machine running, add yeast through feed tube. Process until ball of dough forms.*

4. Place dough in greased bowl; turn the dough to grease the top of the ball. Let rise covered until double, about 1 hour. Punch down and knead for 3 minutes. Divide dough into 12 pieces. Roll each piece into 4-inch (10 cm) rope. Coil into circles, leaving small hole in center; place on greased baking sheet.

5. Brush with beaten egg; sprinkle with sugar. Place a raisin and almond in each center hole. Let rise 1 hour. Heat oven to 375 °F (190 °C). Bake until golden, 20 minutes.

*Notes: *Because of the texture of this dough, 3 cups (750 mL) of flour can be processed at one time.*

Recipe can be doubled. Process in 2 batches. Stack coils of dough in 2 layers on greased baking sheet. (Distribute raisins and almonds among centers of buns.) Let rise, and bake as directed.

Lucia Buns can be made 1 day in advance. Store in tightly covered container. Heat wrapped in aluminum foil at 350°F (180°C) about 10 minutes.

CHILLED CHERRY SOUP

Makes 8 servings (about 1 cup or 250 mL each)

3 cans (16 ounces or
450 g each) pitted
tart cherries,
drained, juice
reserved from 1
can
1½ cups (375 mL) water
6 tablespoons (90 mL)
sugar
½ teaspoon (2 mL)
ground cinnamon
½ teaspoon (2 mL)
ground allspice

⅛ teaspoon (0.5 mL)
salt
2 lemon slices
2 cups (500 mL) half-
and-half
2 tablespoons (30 mL)
all-purpose flour
1½ cups (375 mL) dry
red wine
1 cup (250 mL)
whipping cream,
whipped
Nutmeg

1. Using steel blade, process half the cherries until chopped; repeat with remaining half (reserving 8 whole cherries for garnish, if desired). Combine cherries in large saucepan.

2. Stir reserved juice, the water, sugar, cinnamon, allspice, salt and lemon into cherries. Heat to boiling; reduce heat. Simmer covered 5 minutes.

3. Using steel or plastic blade, process half-and-half and flour until mixed.

4. Stir flour mixture and wine into cherries. Heat to boiling; cook, stirring constantly, 3 minutes. Refrigerate until cold.

5. Spoon soup into bowls; garnish with whipped cream and sprinkle with nutmeg.

Note: Chilled Cherry Soup can be made up to 2 days in advance. Refrigerate covered.

Around the Mediterranean

Shrimp with Feta and Stuffed Grape Leaves

Joyous Greek Dinner

Stuffed Grape Leaves with Egg-Lemon Sauce

Pastitsio

Shrimp with Feta

Stewed Green Beans

Greek Sesame Bread

Baklava

The unique sunniness of the Greek islands and the legendary warmth of the people are reflected in the ebullient and unpretentious cooking of Greece. This generous menu highlights traditional ingredients and dishes.

Greek food adapts well to the food processor because it features many ground-meat stuffings and fillings—the ingenious Greek solutions to the mountainous country's lack of pasture for beef and pork production. Lamb is by far the most accessible meat of the region and its delicate flavor is well complemented by the herbs that flourish on Greek hillsides as well as local olive oil, red wine, fruits and spices.

Stuffed Grape Leaves with Egg-Lemon Sauce wraps a subtly seasoned lamb stuffing in the popular grape leaves. The leaves are widely available; they often come rolled up in a jar and packed in brine. You must rinse off the salt brine before you proceed with the recipe. The food processor ensures that the classic Greek Egg-Lemon Sauce will be as smooth and satiny as it should be—the machine has mastered the art of holding the chicken stock, eggs and lemon juice together in what is otherwise a tricky emulsion.

Pastitsio is a marvelous rich casserole of meat sauce, macaroni and cream sauce. You'll find this recipe to be a great addition to your file of hearty, inexpensive family dishes; it displays the typically Greek practice of scenting meat dishes with cinnamon. Shrimp with Feta features two other standard ingredients: the brine-aged sheep's milk cheese called feta and the age-old anise liqueur, ouzo. Greece's world-renowned honey supply flavors the crusty white bread as well as Baklava, the beloved fillo dessert filled with an amalgam of sweetened and spiced walnuts. Be sure to score the top of the Baklava before you bake it or you'll never be able to cut the pastry without shattering the crisp fillo.

Greeks were producing wine when Homer wrote of the "wine-dark sea"; so, not surprisingly, they have created an excellent light wine, Roditis, to go with this diverse menu.

STUFFED GRAPE LEAVES WITH EGG-LEMON SAUCE
Makes 40 rolls

½ cup (125 mL) parsley
   sprigs
1 large onion, cut into
   quarters
1 pound (450 g) lamb,
   cut into 1-inch (2.5
   cm) cubes
2 tablespoons (30 mL)
   olive oil
½ cup (125 mL)
   uncooked white rice
⅓ cup (80 mL) pine nuts
   or slivered almonds
⅓ cup (80 mL) dark
   raisins

1 teaspoon (5 mL) dried
   mint leaves
½ teaspoon (2 mL) dill
   seeds
1 teaspoon (5 mL) salt
¼ teaspoon (1 mL)
   pepper
1 jar (16 ounces or
   450 g) grape leaves
3 tablespoons (45 mL)
   lemon juice
1 quart (1 L) water or
   enough to cover
Egg-Lemon Sauce
   (recipe follows)

1. Using steel blade, process parsley, onion and lamb (½ pound or 225 g at a time) separately, using on/off technique, until chopped.

2. Sauté onion in oil in skillet until tender, about 10 minutes.

3. Combine all ingredients except grape leaves, lemon juice, water and Egg-Lemon Sauce in large mixing bowl.

4. Gently unroll grape leaves; rinse well. Drain on paper toweling. Carefully separate about 40 whole leaves. Set aside leaves that are broken or torn.

5. Place 1 leaf, vein-side up, on a surface; place 1 tablespoon (15 mL) meat mixture at base of leaf. Fold in sides, and roll to completely seal filling. Repeat process with remaining leaves and filling.

6. Place layer of remaining whole and torn leaves in bottom of large saucepan. Arrange stuffed rolls in 2 layers; top with another layer of leaves.

7. Add lemon juice and enough water to cover all but 1 inch (2.5 cm) of leaves. Heat to boiling; reduce heat. Simmer covered for 30 minutes.

8. Make Egg-Lemon Sauce.

9. Remove stuffed grape leaves to serving platter. Pour Egg-Lemon Sauce over all.

Note: Stuffed grape leaves can also be served cold as an appetizer. Omit Egg-Lemon Sauce, garnish with lemon slices and cherry tomatoes. Spear with toothpicks.

Egg-Lemon Sauce
Makes 1½ cups (375 mL)

2 tablespoons (30 mL)
   butter or margarine
2 tablespoons (30 mL)
   all-purpose flour
1 cup (250 mL) hot
   chicken stock

2 eggs
3 to 4 tablespoons
   (45 to 60 mL)
   lemon juice
2 tablespoons (30 mL)
   cold water

1. Melt butter in saucepan. Stir in flour to make smooth paste; cook over medium heat, stirring constantly, 2 to 3 minutes. Stir in hot stock. Heat to boiling; cook, stirring constantly, until thickened, about 3 minutes.

2. Using steel or plastic blade, process eggs until foamy. Add lemon juice and water. With machine running, add chicken stock mixture through feed tube in a slow steady stream, process until blended.

PASTITSIO
Makes 10 to 12 servings

¼ **pound (115 g) Parmesan cheese, cut into 1-inch (2.5 cm) cubes**	½ **teaspoon (2 mL) ground cinnamon**
½ **cup (125 mL) parsley sprigs**	¼ **teaspoon (1 mL) ground nutmeg**
1 **clove garlic**	½ **teaspoon (2 mL) salt**
2 **onions, cut into quarters**	¼ **teaspoon (1 mL) pepper**
2 **tablespoons (30 mL) olive oil**	4 **eggs**
2 **pounds (900 g) beef or lamb, cut into 1-inch (2.5 cm) cubes**	1 **pound (450 g) elbow or tube macaroni, cooked**
1 **can (16 ounces or 450 g) tomato sauce**	5 **tablespoons (75 mL) butter or margarine, melted**
1 **cup (250 mL) dry red wine**	¼ **teaspoon (1 mL) salt**
	⅛ **teaspoon (0.5 mL) pepper**
	Cream Sauce (recipe follows)

1. Insert steel blade. With machine running, drop Parmesan cheese through feed tube; process until finely grated; reserve. Using steel blade, process parsley until chopped; reserve.

2. Insert steel blade. With machine running, drop garlic through feed tube; process until minced. Add onions to bowl; process, using on/off technique, until chopped.

3. Sauté garlic and onions in oil in large skillet until tender, about 5 minutes.

4. Using steel blade, process meat, ½ pound (225 g) at a time, until finely chopped. Add to onions; cook until no longer pink, 10 minutes.

5. Stir in reserved parsley, the tomato sauce, wine, cinnamon, nutmeg, ½ teaspoon (2 mL) salt and ¼ teaspoon (1 mL) pepper. Heat to boiling; reduce heat. Simmer uncovered until most of liquid has evaporated, 20 to 30 minutes.

6. Using plastic or steel blade, process eggs until foamy.

7. Combine eggs, macaroni, butter, ¼ teaspoon (1 mL) salt and ⅛ teaspoon (0.5 mL) pepper and ½ cup (125 mL) of the reserved Parmesan cheese in large mixing bowl.

8. Make Cream Sauce.

9. Heat oven to 350°F (180°C). To assemble, spread half the macaroni mixture in bottom of buttered 16 × 11-inch (40 × 28 cm) pan. Top with half the meat mixture. Sprinkle with ¼ cup (60 mL) Parmesan cheese. Top with remaining macaroni and meat mixtures. Sprinkle with ¼ cup (60 mL) Parmesan cheese. Pour Cream Sauce over casserole.

10. Bake until top is puffy and golden, about 1 hour.

Cream Sauce

½ **cup (125 mL) butter or margarine**	2 **cups (500 mL) cottage or ricotta cheese**
6 **tablespoons (90 mL) all-purpose flour**	⅛ **teaspoon (0.5 mL) ground nutmeg**
4 **cups (1 L) milk**	
3 **eggs**	

1. Melt butter in saucepan. Stir in flour to make smooth paste; cook over medium heat, stirring constantly, 2 to 3 minutes. Remove pan from heat; stir in milk gradually. Heat to boiling; cook, stirring constantly, until thickened, about 5 minutes. Cool.

2. Using plastic or steel blade, process eggs until foamy.

3. Stir eggs, cottage cheese and nutmeg into sauce.

SHRIMP WITH FETA
Makes 6 to 8 servings

½ **cup (125 mL) parsley sprigs**	1 **bay leaf**
1 **clove garlic**	¼ **cup (60 mL) whipping cream**
1 **onion, cut into quarters**	¼ **teaspoon (60 mL) pepper**
1 **tablespoon (15 mL) olive oil**	2 **pounds (900 g) uncooked shrimp, shelled, deveined**
*½ **pound (225 g) feta cheese**	2 **tablespoons (30 mL) olive oil**
1 **can (16 ounces or 450 g) tomatoes, drained**	**½ **cup (60 mL) ouzo or anise-flavored liqueur**
⅓ **cup (80 mL) dry white wine**	

1. Using steel blade, process parsley until chopped; reserve. With machine running, drop garlic through feed tube; process until minced. Add onion to bowl; process, using on/off technique, until chopped.

2. Sauté garlic and onion in 1 tablespoon (15 mL) oil in skillet for 5 minutes.

3. Using steel blade, process feta and tomatoes separately, using on/off technique, until coarsely chopped; reserve feta. Add tomatoes, wine and bay leaf to onion mixture.

4. Cook onion mixture uncovered over medium heat until thickened, about 20 minutes. Stir in cream and pepper.

5. Sauté shrimp in 2 tablespoons (30 mL) oil in skillet until pink and tender, 5 to 8 minutes.

6. Heat ouzo in small saucepan; ignite. Shake pan until flames die out.

7. Heat oven to 425°F (220°C). Transfer shrimp to ungreased baking dish. Cover shrimp with sauce; pour ouzo over sauce. Sprinkle feta over top.

8. Bake until cheese melts, about 10 minutes. Sprinkle with reserved parsley.

*Notes: *Mozzarella cheese can be substituted for the feta.*

**Ouzo is a Greek aperitif that can be purchased in specialty or liquor stores.

STEWED GREEN BEANS
Makes 6 to 8 servings

½ cup (125 mL) parsley sprigs	2 pounds (900 g) fresh green beans, trimmed, cut into 2-inch (5 cm) pieces
2 onions, cut into quarters	
⅓ cup (80 mL) olive oil	
1 can (16 ounces or 450 g) tomatoes, undrained	⅛ teaspoon (0.5 cm) ground cinnamon
1 cup (250 mL) tomato juice	1 teaspoon (5 mL) salt
	¼ teaspoon (1 mL) pepper

1. Using steel blade, process parsley and onions separately, using on/off technique, until chopped.

2. Sauté onions in oil in large saucepan until tender, 5 minutes.

3. Using steel blade, process tomatoes, using on/off technique, until chopped.

4. Add chopped tomatoes and remaining ingredients to saucepan.

5. Heat to boiling; reduce heat. Simmer covered over medium heat until beans are tender, 45 to 60 minutes.

GREEK SESAME BREAD
Makes two 9-inch (23 cm) loaves

2 packages active dry yeast	1 tablespoon (15 mL) salt
1 cup (250 mL) warm water (about 110°F or 43°C)	1 egg
	5½ to 6 cups (1375 mL to 1.5 L) all-purpose flour
1 cup (250 mL) milk, scalded	Cornmeal
¼ cup (60 mL) honey	1 egg white
¼ cup (60 mL) butter or margarine, melted	1 tablespoon (15 mL) cold water
	¼ cup (60 mL) sesame seeds

1. Add yeast to warm water. Stir until dissolved.

2. Mix milk, honey, butter and salt in 1-quart (1 L)

measuring cup; cool to lukewarm.

3. Using steel blade, process egg until foamy. Add egg and yeast mixture to milk mixture.

4. Insert steel blade. Add 2 cups (500 mL) of the flour to bowl. With machine running, add half the milk mixture through feed tube; process until blended, 5 seconds. With machine running, add ¾ cup (180 mL) of the flour, ¼ cup (60 mL) at a time. Process until dough forms into slightly sticky, smooth ball, adding ¼ cup (60 mL) more flour, if necessary. Process 20 to 30 seconds longer. Knead dough briefly on lightly floured surface into smooth ball.

5. Place dough in greased bowl; turn the dough to grease the top of the ball.

6. Repeat steps 4 and 5 with remaining flour and milk mixture.

7. Let dough stand covered in warm place until doubled, 1½ to 2 hours.

8. Punch down dough. Turn onto lightly floured surface; shape each mass of dough into ball.

9. Grease two 9-inch (23 cm) round pans; sprinkle with cornmeal. Place dough balls into pans.

10. Brush each loaf with egg white beaten with cold water. Sprinkle each loaf with 2 tablespoons (30 mL) sesame seeds.

11. Let stand covered in warm place until doubled, 1½ to 2 hours.

12. Heat oven to 350°F (180°C). Bake until loaves are golden and sound hollow when tapped, about 40 minutes. Remove from pans; cool on wire racks.

BAKLAVA
Makes about 40 pieces

1½ pounds (675 g) walnuts	*1 pound (450 g) fillo leaves
½ cup (125 mL) sugar	
2 teaspoons (10 mL) ground cinnamon	1 pound (450 g) butter or margarine, melted
1 teaspoon (5 mL) ground cloves	Cinnamon-Honey Syrup (recipe follows)
½ teaspoon (2 mL) ground nutmeg	

1. Using steel blade, process walnuts, ½ pound (225 g) at a time, until coarsely chopped.

2. Combine chopped walnuts, the sugar, cinnamon, cloves and nutmeg in large mixing bowl; mix.

3. Unroll fillo leaves. Cut to fit 16 × 11-inch (40 × 28 cm) pan. Keep fillo leaves covered with damp towel to prevent them from drying.

4. Brush pan with melted butter. Layer 6 fillo leaves in pan, brushing each with melted butter. Sprinkle ¼ of

the walnut mixture, about 1¼ cups (310 mL), over fillo. Top with 4 fillo leaves, brushing each with melted butter. Sprinkle with ¼ walnut mixture. Repeat layers 2 more times, using 4 fillo leaves for each layer. After last layer of walnut mixture, top with 6 fillo leaves, brushing each with melted butter.

5. Heat oven to 350°F (180°C). Cut baklava into 2-inch (5 cm) diamonds with very sharp knife. Bake until golden, about 1 hour.

6. Make Cinnamon-Honey Syrup.

7. Pour slightly cooled Cinnamon-Honey Syrup over Baklava. Let stand at least 8 hours before serving.

*Notes: *Frozen fillo or strudel leaves can be purchased at specialty food stores. Thaw before using; refreeze unused portion. Baklava is best made at least 1 day in advance. It will keep 10 days tightly wrapped at room temperature. Do not store Baklava in refrigerator.*

Cinnamon-Honey Syrup
Makes about 3 cups (750 mL)

2 cups (500 mL) sugar	1 cup (250 mL) honey
1½ cups (375 mL) water	¼ cup (60 mL) lemon
3 cinnamon sticks	juice
(about 2-inches or	3 tablespoons (45 mL)
5 cm long)	rum or brandy
Grated rind of 1	
lemon	

1. Combine sugar, water, cinnamon sticks and lemon rind in heavy saucepan. Heat to boiling; cook until syrup thickens slightly, about 10 minutes.

2. Remove pan from heat; remove cinnamon sticks. Stir in honey, lemon juice and rum.

Refreshing Israeli Luncheon

Avocado Leek Soup

Falafel Stuffed in Pita Bread

Citrus-Yogurt Dessert

The little country of Israel, poor in farmland and cattle, has become known for its imaginative vegetarian fare. With irrigation and advanced farming technology, Israelis have converted part of the desert area into gardens renowned for the quality of their produce.

Falafel is the best known Israeli dish and these crisply fried, spicy garbanzo bean-bulgur wheat balls can become positively addictive. But don't worry—they are also highly nutritious. Stuff them into half loaves of Pita Bread with crisp vegetables and douse them with yogurt-dill sauce and you may discover that hamburgers can't compare to this sandwich treat.

Yogurt, a staple throughout the Middle East, gives the Citrus-Yogurt Dessert both a creaminess akin to cheesecake and a lightness like that of a mousse. But this dessert also has a unique tanginess; if you can get Jaffa oranges, they would fit the flavor and spirit of this lightly sweetened recipe quite well. The food processor handles the Graham Cracker Nut Crust with ease and the fabulous crunch of the ground pecans and crackers, spiced with cinnamon and nutmeg, accents the creaminess of the filling. You could use the same crust recipe to line an eight-inch pie pan for your favorite banana cream pie.

Serve Avocado Leek Soup either hot or cold. Either way, the marriage of sharp leeks and buttery avocados provides a memorable opening for this menu.

You might not want to serve wine with this informal lunch, but if you do, you'll find an Israeli Vin Rouge Supérieur to be an excellent choice.

AVOCADO LEEK SOUP
Makes 6 servings

1 small lemon	1 tablespoon (15 mL)
3 medium leeks	lemon juice
1 tablespoon (15 mL)	1 cup (250 mL)
butter or	half-and-half
margarine	½ to ¾ teaspoon (2 to
2½ cups (625 mL)	3 mL) salt
chicken broth	⅛ teaspoon (0.5 mL)
2 medium avocados,	white pepper
pared, cut into	Paprika
chunks	

1. Using slicing disc, slice lemon; reserve.

2. Using slicing disc, slice leeks, using white part and about 1 inch (2.5 cm) of green top. Sauté leeks in butter in small saucepan 2 to 3 minutes. Add 1 cup (250 mL) of the chicken broth. Heat to boiling; reduce heat. Simmer covered 5 minutes.

3. Using steel blade, process chicken broth mixture and avocados until pureed. Return to saucepan. Stir in remaining 1½ cups (375 mL) chicken broth, the lemon juice, half-and-half, salt and pepper. Heat until hot.

Falafel Stuffed in Pita Bread

4. Ladle soup into bowls. Garnish each serving with lemon slices; sprinkle with paprika.

Note: Soup is also excellent served cold.

FALAFEL STUFFED IN PITA BREAD
Makes 6 servings

*¼ cup (60 mL) bulgur
    wheat
1 cup (250 mL) hot
    water
½ cup (125 mL) cherry
    tomatoes
2 small green or red
    peppers
1 medium cucumber,
    pared, cut into
    quarters
¼ head iceberg lettuce,
    cut into wedges
1 clove garlic
2 cups (500 mL)
    canned garbanzo
    beans, drained
3 tablespoons (45 mL)
    dry bread crumbs
1 egg
1 tablespoon (15 mL)
    sesame seeds

1 teaspoon (5 mL)
    lemon juice
½ teaspoon (2 mL) salt
½ teaspoon (2 mL)
    ground cumin
⅛ teaspoon (0.5 mL)
    black pepper
⅛ teaspoon (0.5 mL)
    ground red pepper
Vegetable oil
1½ cups (375 mL) plain
    yogurt
1 tablespoon (15 mL)
    chopped fresh or
    1½ teaspoons (7
    mL) dried dillweed
6 Pita Breads, cut in
    half (see Index for
    page number)
Hot pepper sauce

1. Place bulgur wheat in a small bowl and cover with hot water. Let stand 30 minutes; drain.

2. Using slicing disc, slice tomatoes, peppers, cucumber and lettuce separately. Place vegetables in separate bowls or arrange on platter.

3. Insert steel blade. With machine running, drop garlic through feed tube; process until minced. Add beans to bowl. Process until mixture is pureed. Add bulgur wheat, bread crumbs, egg, sesame seeds, lemon juice, salt, cumin and black and red peppers. Process, using on/off technique, until well blended.

4. Shape mixture into 36 balls, about 1-inch (2.5 cm) each; refrigerate 20 minutes.

5. Heat 2 inches (5 cm) oil in skillet or deep-fat fryer to 375 °F (190 °C). Fry garbanzo balls, 6 at a time, until golden, about 3 minutes. Drain on paper toweling; keep warm in oven.

6. Mix yogurt and dillweed. Place about 3 garbanzo balls in each bread half. Top with 1 tablespoon (15 mL) yogurt mixture. Add assortment of sliced vegetables and another tablespoon yogurt mixture. Sprinkle with few drops hot pepper sauce.

*Note: *Bulgur wheat can be purchased at health food stores and Middle Eastern groceries.*

CITRUS-YOGURT DESSERT
Makes 8 to 10 servings

Graham Cracker Nut
    Crust (recipe
    follows)
1 small orange, cut in
    half
1½ tablespoons (22 mL)
    unflavored gelatin
½ cup (125 mL) water
½ cup (125 mL) fresh
    orange juice
3 eggs, separated
½ cup (125 mL) sugar
1 teaspoon (5 mL)
    grated orange rind

1 teaspoon (5 mL)
    grated lemon rind
1 teaspoon (5 mL)
    vanilla
2 packages (8 ounces
    or 225 g each)
    cream cheese,
    room temperature,
    cut into 4 pieces
2 cartons (8 ounces or
    225 g each) lemon
    or orange-flavored
    yogurt

1. Make Graham Cracker Nut Crust.

2. Using slicing disc, slice orange; reserve.

3. Stir gelatin into water; let stand 5 minutes. Place gelatin mixture, orange juice, egg yolks and sugar in top of double boiler. Cook over simmering water, stirring constantly, until mixture thickens slightly, 15 to 20 minutes. Remove from heat. Stir in orange and lemon rinds and vanilla. Cool 10 minutes.

4. Using steel blade, process cheese 5 seconds. Add ¼ cup (60 mL) of the gelatin mixture; process 5 seconds. Add remaining gelatin mixture; process until smooth. Transfer to large mixing bowl; stir in yogurt.

5. Beat egg whites with electric mixer until stiff but not dry peaks form. Stir ¼ of the cheese mixture into egg whites; fold in remaining cheese mixture. Pour into prepared crust. Refrigerate at least 4 hours.

6. Remove rim of springform pan. Garnish top with orange slices.

Graham Cracker Nut Crust

¼ cup (60 mL) pecans
5 whole graham
    crackers, broken
    into pieces
⅓ cup (80 mL) melted
    butter or margarine

½ teaspoon (2 mL)
    ground cinnamon
⅛ teaspoon (0.5 mL)
    ground nutmeg

1. Heat oven to 400°F (200°C). Using steel blade, process nuts and graham crackers until finely ground. Add butter, cinnamon and nutmeg to bowl. Process until combined.

2. Press mixture into bottom and ½ inch (1.5 cm) up side of 9-inch (23 cm) springform pan. Bake 8 minutes. Cool on wire rack.

Something Different— Moroccan Couscous

Eggplant Salad

Moroccan Whole Wheat Bread

Couscous

Date-Apricot Pastries

Moroccan food may be the world's most "discovered" cuisine. Every visitor to the northwest African country is both surprised and entranced by the superbly seasoned native fare. They all return home singing the praises of an odd-sounding dish called Couscous and glowing with tales of marvelous stews, salads, breads and pastries. The term "Couscous" is used to describe both the country's wheat staple—tiny beads of steamed semolina paste—and the hearty stew that cooks with the wheat. Moroccans use a special pot, called a couscousière, to prepare Couscous and the design of the vessel helps to explain the savory nature of the dish. The bottom half is a stew pot; it holds assorted meats and vegetables as they simmer in a fragrant broth. The top half is a very fine-holed colander; it supports the couscous grains so that they steam in the aromatic vapor of the broth below. Stew and grains are served together on a large platter with side dishes of the broth and a hot pepper sauce called Harissa. The Harissa contributes an appealing piquant note to the otherwise bountiful but bland array of food.

Morocco's "staff of life" is a marvelously rich whole-wheat loaf. The salads are legion; they usually feature a single vegetable dressed with a flattering blend of herbs and spices.

Fruits and nuts abound in Morocco's temperate plateaus and hot desert regions. Date-Apricot Pastries encase the wealth in translucent leaves of fillo pastry. You can buy frozen packages of this simple flour and water pastry at many supermarkets and at all Greek and Middle Eastern groceries. It is very easy to produce crisp, golden desserts with the packaged dough. The fillo must be completely thawed before you can use it (the unused portion can be refrozen) and it is very important that you not let the leaves dry out while you are working with them. Keep them covered with a damp towel, for they will shatter if they get too dry.

Moroccans usually take no beverage with meals, but drink copious amounts of mint-flavored tea afterward. You might prefer a versatile and full-bodied Château-neuf-du-Pape with your dinner.

EGGPLANT SALAD
Makes 2 cups (500 mL)

1 eggplant (about 1 pound or 450 g)
1 large clove garlic
½ cup (125 mL) parsley sprigs
½ small onion, cut in half
1 large tomato, peeled, seeded, cut into quarters
¼ cup (60 mL) olive oil
2 tablespoons (30 mL) lemon juice
½ teaspoon (2 mL) salt
¼ teaspoon (1 mL) pepper
Lettuce leaves
Tomato wedges
Greek olives

1. Heat oven to 350°F (180°C). Bake eggplant for 1 hour. Let cool; peel off skin.

2. Insert steel blade. With machine running, drop garlic through feed tube; process until minced. Add parsley to bowl; process until chopped. Add onion to bowl; process, using on/off technique, until chopped. Add tomato to bowl; process, using on/off technique, until coarsely chopped.

3. Cut eggplant into 2-inch (5 cm) pieces. Add eggplant, oil, lemon juice, salt and pepper to bowl; process, using on/off technique, until ingredients are combined. Do not overprocess; mixture should be chunky.

4. Refrigerate several hours or overnight before serving.

5. To serve, place eggplant salad on bed of lettuce and surround with tomato wedges and Greek olives.
   Note: This salad can also be served as a dip with raw vegetables or as a filling for Pita Bread (see Index for page number).

MOROCCAN WHOLE WHEAT BREAD
Makes 1 loaf

2 packages active dry yeast
¼ cup (60 mL) lukewarm water
1 cup (250 mL) milk
2 tablespoons (30 mL) butter or margarine, cut into pieces
1 tablespoon (15 mL) sugar
2 teaspoons (10 mL) salt
2 cups (500 mL) all-purpose flour
1½ to 2 cups (375 to 500 mL) whole wheat flour
2 tablespoons (30 mL) sesame seeds

1. Combine yeast and lukewarm water in 2-cup (500 mL) measuring cup. Stir until yeast is dissolved.

2. Mix milk, butter, sugar and salt in small saucepan. Heat until butter is melted and salt and sugar are dissolved. Cool to lukewarm. Stir into yeast mixture.

3. Insert steel blade. Place 1 cup (250 mL) all-purpose flour, ½ cup (125 mL) whole wheat flour and 1 tablespoon (15 mL) sesame seeds in bowl. With machine running, add half the liquid ingredients through feed tube; process a few seconds until blended. Add all or part of ½ cup (125 mL) whole wheat flour, a few tablespoons at a time, until dough forms slightly sticky ball. Let dough spin around bowl 20 to 30 seconds. Turn dough onto lightly floured surface. Knead briefly into smooth ball.

4. Repeat step 3 with remaining flour, sesame seeds and liquid mixture. Combine two balls of dough into one. Place dough in greased bowl; turn the dough to grease the top of the ball.

5. Let stand covered in warm place until doubled, about 1 hour.

6. Punch down dough. Shape into round loaf. Place on greased baking sheet. Let stand covered in warm place until doubled, about 1 hour.

7. Heat oven to 350°F (180°C). Bake until bread sounds hollow when tapped, 40 to 45 minutes. Remove from baking sheet. Cool on wire rack. Cut bread into wedges to serve.

COUSCOUS
Makes 6 to 8 servings

*12 dried red cayenne peppers
Water
2 pounds (900 g) lamb and/or beef, cut into 1-inch (2.5 cm) cubes
8 cups (2 L) water
1 chicken (3 pounds or 1350 g), cut into serving pieces
1 cup (250 mL) dried chick-peas
2 onions, cut into quarters
3 tomatoes, cut into quarters
3 carrots
3 zucchini
1 turnip or rutabaga, cut into 1-inch (2.5 cm) cubes
1 small head cabbage, cut into 3 to 4 wedges
1 teaspoon (5 mL) paprika
1 teaspoon (5 mL) ground cinnamon
½ teaspoon (2 mL) ground ginger
¼ teaspoon (1 mL) saffron threads or powder
½ cup (125 mL) dark raisins
2 to 3 teaspoons (10 to 15 mL) salt
½ teaspoon (2 mL) pepper
**1 pound (450 g) uncooked couscous (durum wheat Semolina)
¼ cup (60 mL) melted butter or margarine
1 clove garlic
¼ teaspoon (1 mL) salt
1 tablespoon (15 mL) olive oil
1 tablespoon (15 mL) lemon juice
Pinch ground cumin

1. Place peppers in small saucepan. Cover with water; heat to boiling. Remove from heat. Cover pan; let stand 3 hours.

2. Place meat and 8 cups (2 L) water in large couscousière or stock pot; heat to boiling; reduce heat. Simmer covered 1 hour.

3. Add chicken and chick-peas to pot.

4. Using steel blade, process onions and tomatoes separately, using on/off technique, until chopped; add to pot.

5. Using slicing disc, slice carrots and zucchini separately. Add carrots and turnip to pot; cook 45 minutes. Add more water if mixture is becoming dry.

6. Add zucchini, cabbage, paprika, cinnamon, ginger, saffron, raisins, 2 to 3 teaspoons (10 to 15 mL) salt and pepper to pot. Simmer until vegetables are tender, about 30 minutes. Remove 1 cup (250 mL) broth; reserve.

7. Cook couscous in top of couscousière or saucepan according to package instructions. When cooked, toss with melted butter.

8. Drain peppers; cut in half lengthwise and scoop out seeds.

9. Insert steel blade. With machine running, drop garlic, peppers and ¼ teaspoon (1 mL) salt through feed tube. Process until finely chopped. Add olive oil and lemon juice; process until peppers are minced. Add cumin and 1 cup (250 mL) reserved broth; process until blended.

10. To serve, mound couscous in center of large platter.

Couscous

Arrange meat and vegetables around it. Serve with pepper sauce and additional broth on the side.

> Notes: *Wear rubber gloves when handling peppers; don't touch skin or eyes.*
>
> **Couscous can be purchased in Middle Eastern groceries and specialty food stores.*

DATE-APRICOT PASTRIES
Makes 24

¼ pound (115 g) pitted dates (about ½ cup or 125 mL)
6 ounces (170 g) dried apricots (about 1 cup or 250 mL)
½ cup (125 mL) walnuts
¼ cup (60 mL) orange marmalade or apricot preserves
Grated rind of 1 orange

2 tablespoons (30 mL) sugar
¼ teaspoon (1 mL) ground cinnamon
*12 fillo leaves (about ½ pound or 225 g)
½ cup (125 mL) butter or margarine, melted
Honey Syrup (recipe follows)

1. Using steel blade, process dates, apricots, walnuts, orange marmalade, orange rind, sugar and cinnamon, using on/off technique, until chopped and blended.

2. Unroll fillo leaves; cut lengthwise in half. Keep fillo leaves covered with lightly dampened towel while working to prevent drying. Brush 1 half-leaf with melted butter (see photo 1). Fold lengthwise in half. Place heaping teaspoonful of fruit mixture near bottom edge (see photo 2). Fold bottom over filling, fold in sides and roll up (see photo 3). (Pastries should be about 2 inches or 5 cm long.) Brush with melted butter. Repeat with remaining leaves and filling. Place on ungreased baking sheet.

3. Heat oven to 350°F (180°C). Bake until pastries are puffed and golden, about 30 minutes.

4. While pastries are baking, make Honey Syrup.

5. When baked, soak hot pastries in warm Honey Syrup 2 to 3 minutes. Transfer to serving plate.

> Note: *Frozen fillo or strudel leaves can be purchased at specialty food stores. Thaw before using; refreeze unused portion.*

Honey Syrup
Makes 1½ cups (375 mL)

⅔ cup (160 mL) sugar
⅔ cup (160 mL) water
⅔ cup (160 mL) honey

2 tablespoons (30 mL) lemon juice

1. Combine sugar and water in small saucepan. Heat to boiling; reduce heat. Simmer uncovered 5 minutes. Stir in honey and lemon juice. Simmer 5 minutes.

Photo 1. Cut fillo leaf lengthwise in half; brush the half-leaf with melted butter.

Photo 2. Fold buttered fillo leaf in half lengthwise and place a heaping teaspoonful of fruit mixture near bottom edge.

Photo 3. Fold bottom of leaf over filling, fold in the sides and roll up. (Filling will be completely encased in fillo leaf.)

Dinner of Turkish Delights

Chick-Pea Spread

Pita Bread

Mint Meatballs with Yogurt Sauce

Cracked Wheat Salad

Almond-Raisin Pudding

Turkish food is one of the best kept secrets of the international culinary circuit. It features not only the myriad ingredients of an agriculturally wealthy country, but also the legacy of sophisticated dishes developed by the chefs at Topkapi Palace, where Ottoman sultans dined amidst extraordinary splendor. The wonderful thing about Turkish food is the intriguing mosaic of flavors in each dish—and the food processor makes such compositions easy to accomplish.

You'll find Pita Bread to be an excellent alternative to everyday sandwich bread as well as the natural accompaniment to a Turkish meal. Also called "pocket bread," the flat, round loaves puff up in the oven; each one, cut in half, yields two half-moon sandwich holders. The airy Pita bakes quickly and olive oil gives it unusual flavor.

Unlike any other side dish, Cracked Wheat Salad holds a haunting counterpoint of hearty cracked wheat and cool mint flavors. Bulgur is wheat that has been par-boiled and sun-dried; it contains the whole wheat germ and some of the bran, making it quite nutritious. Try to use fresh mint leaves in this recipe and remember this salad the next time you plan a picnic—it's a good traveler.

The Ottoman Empire ruled the Balkans for over 500 years and strongly influenced the cuisines of those countries. Therefore, a full-bodied Yugoslavian wine from Macedonia or Slovenia would stand up well to this Turkish feast.

CHICK-PEA SPREAD
Makes about 3 cups (750 mL)

2 cans (15 ounces or 425 g each) chick-peas, undrained	***⅓ cup (80 mL) tahini paste**
3 cloves garlic	**2 teaspoons (10 mL) dried mint leaves**
⅓ cup (80 mL) lemon juice	**½ teaspoon (2 mL) salt**
	Fresh mint sprigs
	Pita Bread (see Index for recipe)

1. Drain chick-peas; reserve 3 to 4 tablespoons (45 to 60 mL) liquid.

2. Insert steel blade. With machine running, drop garlic through feed tube. Process until minced. Add chick-peas, lemon juice, tahini paste, dried mint and salt. Process until mixture is smooth. Add reserved chick-pea liquid for desired consistency.

3. Mound Chick-Pea Spread on serving platter or place in bowl. Garnish with fresh mint.

4. Serve with Pita Bread.

Note: *Tahini paste is ground hulled sesame seeds; it can be purchased in Middle Eastern groceries and many supermarkets.

PITA BREAD
Makes 12

1 package active dry yeast	**1 tablespoon (15 mL) olive oil**
1¼ cups (310 mL) warm water (105 to 115°F or 40 to 45°C)	**2½ to 3 cups (625 to 750 mL) all-purpose flour**
1½ teaspoons (7 mL) salt	**Cornmeal**

1. Combine yeast and ¼ cup (60 mL) warm water; stir until dissolved. Let stand 5 minutes.

2. Combine 1 cup (250 mL) warm water, salt and olive oil in 2-cup (500 mL) measuring cup; stir until salt is dissolved. Stir in yeast mixture.

3. Insert steel blade. Place 2 cups (500 mL) of the flour in bowl. With machine running, add liquid ingredients through feed tube; process until blended. Add ½ to 1 cup (125 to 250 mL) flour, ¼ cup (60 mL) at a time, until dough forms into slightly sticky ball. Let dough spin around bowl 20 to 30 seconds. Knead dough 2 to 3 minutes on lightly floured surface until smooth and elastic; form into smooth ball.

4. Place dough in greased bowl; turn the dough to grease the top of the ball. Let rise covered in warm place until dough is double in size, about 1½ hours.

5. Punch down dough. Let rise covered until dough has doubled in size again, about 1 hour.

6. Heat oven to 500°F (260°C). Form dough into long loaf; divide into 12 equal pieces. Flatten and knead dough into smooth 3-inch (8 cm) circles. Roll circles on generously floured surface until 6 inches (15 cm) in diameter and ¼-inch (0.5 cm) thick.

7. Place ungreased baking sheets in oven 5 minutes. Sprinkle baking sheets with cornmeal; place 6 dough circles on each.

8. Bake at 500°F (260°C) until bread is puffy and light brown, about 5 minutes. Cool on wire rack.

MINT MEATBALLS WITH YOGURT SAUCE
Makes 6 to 8 servings (about 50 meatballs)

2 slices fresh bread, broken into pieces	**1 onion, cut into quarters**
½ cup (125 mL) parsley sprigs	**¼ cup (60 mL) olive oil**

1 pound (450 g) round steak, cut into 1-inch (2.5 cm) pieces
½ pound (225 g) pork or veal, cut into 1-inch (2.5 cm) pieces
⅓ cup (80 mL) pine nuts
2 teaspoons (10 mL) dried mint leaves
1 teaspoon (5 mL) dried oregano leaves
¼ teaspoon (1 mL) ground cinnamon
2 eggs
1½ teaspoons (7 mL) salt
¼ teaspoon (1 mL) pepper
Flour
Yogurt Sauce (Recipe follows)
½ head lettuce, cut into wedges
2 tomatoes, cut into quarters

1. Using steel blade, process bread and parsley separately until finely chopped; reserve. Process onion, using on/off technique, until chopped.

2. Sauté onion in 1 tablespoon (15 mL) olive oil in large skillet until tender, about 5 minutes.

3. Using steel blade, process beef and pork, ½ pound (225 g) at a time, until chopped.

4. Mix bread crumbs, parsley, onion, meat, pine nuts, dried mint, oregano, cinnamon, eggs, salt and pepper thoroughly in large bowl. Shape meat mixture into walnut-size balls. Coat meatballs with flour; cook in remaining olive oil in large skillet over medium heat until brown and cooked through, 10 to 15 minutes.

5. Make Yogurt Sauce.

6. Using slicing disc, slice lettuce; place on serving platter.

7. Using steel blade, chop tomatoes. Place on top of sliced lettuce.

8. Arrange cooked meatballs on top of tomatoes. Pour Yogurt Sauce over all.

Yogurt Sauce
Makes 2 cups (500 mL)

½ cup (125 mL) parsley sprigs
½ teaspoon (2 mL) dried mint leaves
½ teaspoon (2 mL) salt
2 cups (500 mL) plain yogurt

1. Using steel blade, process parsley until chopped. Add remaining ingredients to bowl. Process until blended. Refrigerate until ready to use.

CRACKED WHEAT SALAD
Makes 6 servings

*1½ cups (375 mL) cracked or crushed bulgur wheat
Cold water
4 to 6 green onions and tops, cut into 1-inch (2.5 cm) pieces
2 cups (500 mL) parsley sprigs
3 tomatoes, cut into quarters
¼ cup (60 mL) olive oil
⅓ cup (80 mL) lemon juice
2 tablespoons (30 mL) fresh mint, chopped, or 2 teaspoons (10 mL) dried mint leaves
1 teaspoon (5 mL) salt
¼ teaspoon (1 mL) pepper
Lettuce leaves
Tomato wedges
Ripe olives

1. Place bulgur wheat in large bowl; add cold water to cover. Let soak until grains are soft, 10 to 15 minutes for fine grain, 2 to 2½ hours for coarse grain. Drain well.

2. Wrap bulgur in dishtowel; squeeze as dry as possible. Transfer to medium bowl.

3. Using steel blade, process green onions and parsley until finely chopped. Add to bulgur.

4. Using steel blade, process 3 tomatoes, using on/off technique, until finely chopped.

5. Add chopped tomatoes, olive oil, lemon juice, mint, salt and pepper to bulgar; toss to combine.

6. Serve salad on lettuce leaves. Garnish with tomato wedges and ripe olives.

*Note: *Bulgur wheat can be purchased at health food stores and Middle Eastern groceries.*

ALMOND-RAISIN PUDDING
Makes 6 servings

6 ounces (170 g) blanched almonds
2 cups (500 mL) whipping cream
2½ cups (625 mL) milk
¾ cup (180 mL) sugar
½ cup (125 mL) golden raisins
1 teaspoon (5 mL) vanilla extract
½ teaspoon (2 mL) almond extract
½ cup (125 mL) milk
¼ cup (60 mL) all-purpose flour
3 egg yolks, slightly beaten
⅛ teaspoon (0.5 mL) salt
Pinch ground nutmeg
Ground cinnamon

1. Using steel blade, process almonds until finely chopped.

2. Combine almonds, cream, 2½ cups (625 mL) milk and the sugar in saucepan; heat to boiling. Remove from heat; let stand covered 20 minutes.

3. Strain mixture; discard almonds. Return mixture to saucepan. Add raisins, vanilla and almond extracts.

4. Mix ½ cup (125 mL) milk and the flour; stir until smooth. Stir milk-flour mixture and egg yolks gradually into saucepan. Heat to boiling; cook, stirring constantly, until mixture is thick and smooth. Stir in salt and nutmeg.

5. Pour into individual bowls or 1½-quart (1.5 L) ungreased casserole. Sprinkle with cinnamon. Refrigerate until chilled, about 3 hours.

MEXICO & PERU

Hearts of Palm Salad and Enchiladas with Green Sauce

Elegant Peruvian Supper

Beef in Wine

Potatoes and Cheese Casserole

Orange Salad

Cold Coffee Soufflé

The sixteenth-century Spanish conquerers remarked of Peru that "no one went hungry in that land." More to the point, the Incan civilization probably enjoyed a cuisine more sophisticated than that of most of Europe in those days.

Among the spoils of the Spanish Conquest was the potato, which was first cultivated in the high valleys of the Andes Mountains, where corn or beans would not grow. The Spanish brought the potato back to Europe; and they introduced the ancient art of cheesemaking to the Incas. The impact of this exchange on Old World cooking is well known; the result in Peru was a beautiful, pale gold dish called Papas a la Huancana, or Potatoes and Cheese Casserole. A sauce of cheese, cream, chilies and other seasonings elevates the now commonplace potato to heights of Andean glory.

Incan cooks knew that the secret of tenderizing the tough meat of their mountain-grazing cattle was to cut it into small pieces and simmer it slowly with wine. You are sure to enjoy the sample on this Peruvian menu, Beef in Wine, which features a spectrum of flavorings ranging from piquant garlic and onion to sweet sausage and raisins.

Most Latin Americans consume awesome amounts of coffee. In Peru, the beverage is brewed thick and drunk black. We've added cream and turned the staple into an ethereal, fluffy dessert, Cold Coffee Soufflé.

This menu is very easy to serve. The Beef in Wine can be cooked early in the day and reheated. The potato casserole can be arranged in advance, left in the refrigerator for the flavors to fuse and baked shortly before dining. Make and refrigerate the soufflé and the salad dressing ahead of time. Arrange the salads at the last minute and look forward to a leisurely, uninterrupted evening with guests. Cocktails made with pisco, the Peruvian brandy, would be appropriate, as would a soothing Peruvian red wine or a Chilean Cabernet.

BEEF IN WINE
Makes 6 to 8 servings

1 clove garlic
1 large onion, cut into quarters
1 tomato, cut in half
1 tablespoon (15 mL) vegetable oil
¼ pound (115 g) mild sausage
2 strips bacon, cut into 1-inch (2.5 cm) pieces
2 pounds (900 g) pot roast, cut into 1-inch (2.5 cm) cubes
½ teaspoon (2 mL) dried oregano leaves
¾ cup (180 mL) red wine
¾ cup (180 mL) water
3 tablespoons (45 mL) red wine vinegar
⅓ cup (80 mL) raisins

1. Insert steel blade. With machine running, drop garlic through feed tube; process until minced.

2. Using slicing disc, slice onion and tomato separately.

3. Heat oil in Dutch oven. Add garlic, onion, sausage and bacon; cook 3 minutes, stirring occasionally.

4. Add beef, tomato, oregano, wine and water; simmer covered until meat is tender, about 1 hour.

5. Add vinegar and raisins; simmer uncovered about 30 minutes.

POTATOES AND CHEESE CASSEROLE
Makes 6 to 8 servings

8 medium potatoes, pared, cut into quarters
Water
2 medium onions, cut in half
½ pound (225 g) mild Cheddar cheese
*1 can (4 ounces or 115 g) mild chilies, drained, seeded, washed in cold water
⅓ teaspoon (1 mL) salt
¼ teaspoon (1 mL) ground white pepper
¼ teaspoon (1 mL) ground turmeric
½ cup (125 mL) whipping cream
3 tablespoons (45 mL) olive oil
¼ cup (60 mL) pitted ripe olives

1. Place potatoes in large saucepan; add water to cover. Boil covered until tender, 20 minutes. Drain and cool. Using slicing disc, slice potatoes and onions; arrange in ungreased 2-quart (2 L) casserole.

2. Using shredding disc, shred cheese; sprinkle over potatoes.

3. Heat oven to 350°F (180°C). Using steel blade, chop chilies. Add salt, pepper and turmeric to bowl. With machine running, add cream and oil. Pour sauce over casserole; top with olives.

4. Bake uncovered until hot, about 30 minutes.
   *Note: *Wear rubber gloves when handling chilies; do not touch skin or eyes.*

ORANGE SALAD
Makes 6 to 8 servings

6 oranges, peeled, cut in half
2 medium red onions, cut into quarters
½ cup (125 mL) pitted ripe olives
½ pound (225 g) romaine
1 tablespoon (15 mL) fresh or 1 teaspoon (5 mL) dried mint leaves
2 parsley sprigs

2 tablespoons (30 mL) fresh or 1 teaspoon (5 mL) dried basil leaves
½ teaspoon (2 mL) salt
⅛ teaspoon (0.5 mL) pepper
6 tablespoons (90 mL) olive oil
2 tablespoons (30 mL) wine vinegar

1. Using slicing disc, slice oranges, onions and olives. Arrange on romaine on salad plates. **T48** **T56**

2. Using steel blade, process mint, parsley and basil until minced.

3. Add salt, pepper, oil and vinegar to bowl; process until blended. Sprinkle over salad.

COLD COFFEE SOUFFLÉ
Makes 8 to 10 servings

1 cup (250 mL) water
1½ envelopes unflavored gelatin
¾ cup (180 mL) sugar
½ cup (125 mL) coffee liqueur
2 tablespoons (30 mL) lemon juice

8 extra-large eggs, separated
1 cup (250 mL) blanched almonds
3 cups (750 mL) whipping cream
⅛ teaspoon (0.5 mL) salt

1. Mix water and gelatin until dissolved.

2. Mix ½ cup (125 mL) of the sugar, the coffee liqueur, lemon juice, egg yolks and gelatin mixture in medium saucepan. Cook over low heat, stirring frequently, until mixture coats spoon. Refrigerate until just beginning to thicken.

3. Using steel blade, process almonds until ground. Fold almonds into cooled custard. **T44**

4. Whip cream with electric mixer; reserve 1 cup (250 mL) for garnish. Fold remaining cream into custard mixture. Beat egg whites and salt with electric mixer; add remaining sugar, 2 tablespoons (30 mL) at a time, beating until stiff but not dry peaks form. Fold egg whites into soufflé mixture.

5. Pour mixture into ungreased 2-quart (2 L) soufflé dish or individual coffee cups. Refrigerate 6 hours before serving. Garnish with reserved whipped cream.

Mexican Celebration

Tostados

Chicken Molé

Avocado Salad

Fresh Pineapple Pie

The molé is Mexico's holiday fare. Its name is derived from the Aztec word "Molli," meaning a sauce flavored with chilies; but the molé is far grander than most sauces. Some versions take up to three days to prepare in the traditional mortar and pestle, with all the requisite grinding of vegetables, chilies, nuts, seeds, fruits and spices. So the food processor certainly shows its mettle by reducing the elegant blend to a matter of minutes.

Indeed Molé Sauce is quite easy for us to serve because it can be made at least one day in advance and refrigerated. The chicken over which it is poured can also be cooked in advance. So only the last-minute baking remains to be done as the dinner hour approaches.

Tostados should be served hot from the oven. One of the antojitos, or "little whims" of Mexican food, they make a crisp, lively hors d'oeuvre and demonstrate vividly why Mexicans dote on tortilla snacks with all kinds of toppings. You'll find that canned mild chilies are just that—quite mild. But do be careful when handling them; the seeds and oils can irritate eyes and skin, even though the seeded peppers are not very ferocious.

Mexican cooking is known for its opulent use of fresh fruit. We can't think of two better examples than a buttery Avocado Salad and a Fresh Pineapple Pie, redolent of cinnamon and nutmeg. You can bake the pie in advance, but don't even consider slicing the ripe avocados until after guests have arrived.

This splendid dinner deserves an excellent wine. A Cabernet from central Chile remains true to the meal's Latin American theme, yet invokes the soft, deep mood of a good Bordeaux.

Tostados

TOSTADOS
Makes 12

2 cups (500 mL)
  vegetable oil
1 package corn tortillas
½ pound (225 g)
  Monterey Jack
  cheese
1 onion, cut into
  quarters
1 tomato, cut in half

1 medium avocado,
  pared, pitted, cut in
  half
*1 can (4 ounces or 115
  g) mild green
  chilies, drained,
  seeded, rinsed in
  cold water
1 cup (250 mL) canned
  refried beans

1. Heat oil in medium skillet to 375 °F (190 °C). Fry tortillas, 1 at a time, until golden, about 5 seconds on each side. Drain on paper toweling.

2. Using shredding disc, shred cheese.

3. Using slicing disc, slice onion, tomato and avocado separately.

4. Using steel blade, process chilies until chopped.

5. Heat oven to 375 °F (190 °C). Spread refried beans on tortillas; top as desired with cheese, onion, tomato, avocado and chilies.

6. Place on baking sheet; bake 5 minutes. Serve hot.
   *Note: *Wear rubber gloves when handling chilies; don't touch skin or eyes.*

CHICKEN MOLÉ
Makes 6 servings

1 large onion, cut into
  quarters
2 large chickens (3 to
  3½ pounds or 1350
  to 1600 g each), cut
  into serving pieces
4 cloves

Water
Molé Sauce (recipe
  follows)
¼ cup (60 mL) olive oil
4½ cups (1125 mL) hot
  cooked rice

1. Using slicing disc, slice onion.

2. Place chicken in stock pot; add onion, cloves and water to cover. Cook over medium-low heat until chicken is almost cooked, about 45 minutes.

3. Remove chicken; reserve stock.

4. Make Molé Sauce.

5. Heat oven to 350 °F (180 °C). Heat oil in large skillet; brown chicken on all sides. Place chicken in ungreased casseroles; ladle sauce over chicken. Bake 20 minutes. Serve with rice.

Molé Sauce
Makes about 3 cups (750 mL)

2 cloves garlic
1 medium onion, cut
  into quarters
2 large tomatoes, cut
  into quarters
1 green pepper, cut into
  quarters
2 toasted tortillas, cut
  into quarters
⅓ cup (80 mL) raisins
⅓ cup (80 mL) peanuts
¼ teaspoon (1 mL)
  ground allspice

¼ teaspoon (1 mL)
  ground cinnamon
¼ teaspoon (1 mL)
  ground cumin
2 teaspoons (10 mL)
  chili powder
1 tablespoon (15 mL)
  sugar
3 tablespoons (45 mL)
  vegetable oil
2 cups (500 mL)
  reserved chicken
  stock

1. Insert steel blade. With machine running, drop garlic through feed tube; process until minced.

2. Add onion, tomatoes, pepper and tortillas to bowl; process, using on/off technique, until minced.

3. Add raisins, peanuts, allspice, cinnamon, cumin, chili powder and sugar to bowl; process until smooth.

4. Heat oil in saucepan; stir in puree and chicken stock. Cook over medium heat 2 minutes.

AVOCADO SALAD
Makes 6 to 8 servings

1 large head romaine,
  stalk trimmed
4 large ripe avocados,
  pared, pitted, cut in
  half
2 cloves garlic
¼ cup (60 mL) olive oil
¼ cup (60 mL) vegetable
  oil

1 tablespoon (15 mL)
  lemon juice
¼ cup (60 mL)
  tarragon vinegar
¼ teaspoon (1 mL) salt
⅛ teaspoon (0.5 mL)
  pepper

1. Using slicing disc, slice romaine; place in salad bowl.

2. Using slicing disc, slice avocados; place in salad bowl.

3. Insert steel blade. With machine running, drop garlic through feed tube; process until minced. Add oils, lemon juice, vinegar, salt and pepper to bowl; process until blended. Pour over salad; toss.

FRESH PINEAPPLE PIE
Makes 6 servings

Pie Pastry (recipe
  follows
1 large pineapple,
  pared, cored, cut
  into quarters
½ teaspoon (2 mL)
  ground nutmeg
1 teaspoon (5 mL)
  ground cinnamon

¼ teaspoon (1 mL) salt
1½ cups (375 mL) sugar
3 tablespoons (45 mL)
  all-purpose flour
2 tablespoons (30 mL)
  butter or margarine

1. Make Pie Pastry.

2. Using slicing disc, slice pineapple. Combine pineapple, nutmeg, cinnamon, salt, sugar and flour in saucepan. Cook over medium heat, stirring frequently, until filling thickens. Stir in butter until blended; cool.

3. Heat oven to 400°F (200°C). Roll ⅔ pastry out on lightly floured board; ease into 9-inch (23 cm) pie plate. Pour filling into pie shell.

4. Roll out remaining pastry. Cut into strips; form lattice design with strips on top of pie. Trim and flute edges.

5. Bake 10 minutes; reduce temperature to 350°F (180°C). Bake until crust is golden, about 35 minutes.

Pie Pastry

2 cups (500 mL) all-purpose flour	3 tablespoons (45 mL) butter or margarine
¼ teaspoon (1 mL) salt	5 tablespoons (75 mL) ice water
1 teaspoon (5 mL) sugar	

1. Insert steel blade. Place flour, salt, sugar and butter in bowl; process until combined.

2. With machine running, add ice water through feed tube; process until dough forms ball. T50

3. Refrigerate dough in covered container 1 hour.

Festive Mexican Dinner

Cheese and Tomato Dip

Stuffed Peppers with Sauce

Hearts of Palm Salad

Enchiladas with Green Sauce

Mexican Chocolate Cake

There are more than 2000 dishes in the repertoire of Mexican cooking. This fact may surprise you if you associate the cuisine exclusively with tacos and beans. What comes as even more of a shock to most palates is the vast difference between Mexican restaurant food and home-style cooking. You will rarely encounter the best examples of Mexican dishes in restaurants. So good native recipes, especially ones adapted to the ease of the food processor, are truly something to treasure.

Chiles Rellenos, or Stuffed Peppers with Sauce, delights everyone with its varied textures: the light egg-batter coating yields to crunchy pepper and then to soft, melted cheese. Similarly, the Enchiladas Verdes, or Enchiladas with Green Sauce, holds the intrigue of a wine-enriched meat filling, fragrant tortillas and a chili-spiked sauce.

These dishes, like the Cheese and Tomato Dip, must be served fresh and hot. So time your preparations accordingly. Make the Flour Tortillas—a specialty of northern Mexico—ahead of time and keep them wrapped in a towel. Then prepare the Green Sauce and the meat filling for the enchiladas. Stuff the peppers with cheese and make the Hearts of Palm Salad; refrigerate both, but don't pour the dressing over the salad until you're ready to serve it. Make the Cheese and Tomato Dip just as guests are due to arrive; while they enjoy the dip you can complete the enchiladas, put them in the oven and complete the stuffed peppers. The effort required to coordinate these dishes is more than repaid by their incomparable flavor.

The Mexican Chocolate Cake can, of course, be made early in the day. This dark, wonderful cake reminds us that Mexican cooks—centuries ago—were the first to mate chocolate with the essence of the vanilla bean.

A California Zinfandel wine or a Petit Sirah will counter the piquancy of Mexican food. But perhaps not so well as icy Mexican beer.

CHEESE AND TOMATO DIP
Makes 8 to 10 servings

1 medium onion, cut into quarters	2 tablespoons (30 mL) butter or margarine
1 large tomato, peeled, cut in half	⅛ teaspoon (0.5 mL) salt
*1 can (4 ounces or 115 g) mild green chilies, drained, seeded	1 cup (250 mL) vegetable oil
½ pound (225 g) Cheddar cheese	1 package corn tortillas, cut into quarters
	Salt

1. Using slicing disc, slice onion and tomato.

2. Using steel blade, chop chilies.

3. Using shredding disc, shred cheese.

4. Heat butter in skillet. Add onion; sauté until soft, about 5 minutes. Add ⅛ teaspoon (0.5 mL) salt, the chilies, tomato and cheese. Simmer until cheese melts, 5 minutes.

5. Heat oil in heavy skillet to 380°F (190°C). Fry 6 pieces tortilla at a time until golden brown, about 5 seconds; drain on paper toweling. Sprinkle lightly with salt.

6. Serve tortilla chips with dip.
   *Note: *Wear rubber gloves when handling chilies; don't touch skin or eyes.*

STUFFED PEPPERS WITH SAUCE
Makes 8 servings

8 small bell peppers or 16 sweet finger peppers, slit and seeded
½ pound (225 g) Monterey Jack cheese, cut into ½-inch (1.5 cm) strips
3 eggs, separated
3 tablespoons (45 mL) all-purpose flour
2 cups (500 mL) vegetable oil
Flour

4 tomatoes, peeled, cut in half
1 small onion, cut in quarters
1 chicken bouillon cube
½ teaspoon (2 mL) dried oregano leaves
½ teaspoon (2 mL) salt
⅛ teaspoon (0.5 mL) pepper
1½ ounces (45 g) sharp Cheddar cheese

1. Stuff each pepper with Monterey Jack cheese, dividing cheese evenly.

2. Beat egg whites with electric mixer until soft peaks form. Beat egg yolks until blended; add to egg whites. Sprinkle 3 tablespoons (45 mL) flour on egg mixture; fold together.

3. Heat oil in heavy skillet to 380°F (190°C). Coat peppers with flour. Coat peppers with egg batter. Fry in oil until golden on all sides. Drain on paper toweling.

4. Heat oven to 350°F (180°C). Using steel blade, process tomatoes and onion, using on/off technique, until chopped. Place tomatoes, onion, bouillon cube, oregano, salt and pepper in saucepan; simmer covered, stirring occasionally, 8 minutes.

5. Place peppers in shallow baking dish. Spoon sauce over tops of peppers.

6. Using shredding disc, shred Cheddar cheese. Sprinkle over sauce. Bake uncovered until cheese melts, 15 to 20 minutes.

HEARTS OF PALM SALAD
Makes 8 servings

1 head lettuce, cut into wedges
4 large tomatoes, cut in half
1 can (14 ounces or 400 g) hearts of palm, drained
2 teaspoons (10 mL) sugar
1 teaspoon (5 mL) salt

¼ teaspoon (1 mL) ground turmeric
½ teaspoon (2 mL) ground cumin
⅛ teaspoon (0.5 mL) pepper
6 tablespoons (90 mL) olive oil
¼ cup (60 mL) lemon juice

1. Using slicing disc, slice lettuce. Arrange on 8 salad plates.

2. Using slicing disc, slice tomatoes. Arrange on lettuce.

3. Pack hearts of palm vertically in feed tube; using slicing disc, slice. Arrange on top of tomatoes.

4. Insert steel blade. Measure sugar, salt, turmeric, cumin, pepper, olive oil and lemon juice into bowl; process until blended. Pour over salads.

ENCHILADAS WITH GREEN SAUCE
Makes 8 servings

Flour Tortillas (recipe follows)
1 clove garlic
2 large onions, cut into quarters
1 green pepper, cut into quarters
1¾ pounds (800 g) chuck or round steak, cut into ¾-inch (2 cm) cubes
3 tablespoons (45 mL) vegetable oil
2 tablespoons (30 mL) chili powder

2 tablespoons (30 mL) chicken stock
1½ teaspoons (7 mL) cumin seeds
2 bay leaves
1 tablespoon (15 mL) crushed red pepper flakes
1 cup (250 mL) red wine
Green Sauce (recipe follows)
½ pound (225 g) sharp Cheddar cheese

1. Make Flour Tortillas.

2. Insert steel blade. With machine running, drop garlic through feed tube; process until minced. Add onions and green pepper to bowl; process until minced.

3. Using steel blade, process meat, ½ pound (225 g) at a time, using on/off technique, until chopped.

4. Sauté onion mixture in oil 6 minutes. Stir in meat and remaining ingredients except Green Sauce and cheese; simmer covered, stirring occasionally, 30 minutes. Remove bay leaves.

5. Make Green Sauce.

6. Heat oven to 350°F (180°C). Dip each tortilla in Green Sauce. Fill tortillas with meat mixture. Roll up and place seam-sides down in greased 13 × 9 × 2-inch (33 × 21 × 5 cm) casserole. Pour remaining Green Sauce over tortillas.

7. Using shredding disc, shred cheese; sprinkle over Green Sauce. Bake 30 minutes.

Flour Tortillas
Makes 16

5 cups (1250 mL) all-purpose flour
1 teaspoon (5 mL) salt

½ cup (125 mL) shortening, cut into chunks
1 cup (250 mL) hot water

1. Insert steel blade. Place half the flour, salt and shortening in bowl; process until small particles form. With machine running, slowly add ½ cup (125 mL) of the water through feed tube; process 10 seconds, until dough forms ball.

2. Repeat with remaining ingredients. Let dough stand covered 20 minutes.

3. Divide each ball of dough into 8 balls; roll out balls on lightly floured surface into 6-inch (15 cm) circles (see photo 1).

4. Fry 1 circle in ungreased frying pan, turning once, until light brown spots appear on each side (see photo 2). Repeat with remaining circles.

Photo 1. On a lightly floured surface, roll out each little ball of dough into a 6-inch circle.

Photo 2. Fry one tortilla at a time in ungreased frying pan, turning once, until light brown spots appear on each side.

Green Sauce

1 large onion, cut into quarters
2 large tomatoes, peeled, cut in half
*1 can (4 ounces or 115 g) mild green chilies, drained, seeded
3 tablespoons (45 mL) vegetable oil
2 cups (500 mL) sour cream

1. Using steel blade, process onion, tomatoes and chilies until pureed.

2. Heat oil in medium saucepan, add puree. Simmer, stirring frequently, 10 to 15 minutes.

3. Remove from heat; stir in sour cream.
   *Note: *Wear rubber gloves when handling chilies; don't touch skin or eyes.*

MEXICAN CHOCOLATE CAKE
Makes 8 to 10 servings

½ cup (125 mL) water
½ cup (125 mL) granulated sugar
3 tablespoons (45 mL) cocoa
½ cup (125 mL) butter or margarine
1 cup (250 mL) granulated sugar
2 large eggs
2 cups (500 mL) all-purpose flour
1 teaspoon (5 mL) baking soda
¼ teaspoon (1 mL) salt
1 cup (250 mL) milk
1 teaspoon (5 mL) white distilled vinegar
1 teaspoon (5 mL) vanilla
¼ pound (115 g) butter or margarine
2 squares (1 ounce or 30 g each) unsweetened chocolate
6 tablespoons (90 mL) milk
1 pound (450 g) powdered sugar
1 teaspoon (5 mL) vanilla

1. Heat oven to 375 °F (190 °C). Mix water, ½ cup (125 mL) granulated sugar and the cocoa in small saucepan. Cook over medium heat, stirring frequently, 5 minutes.

2. Using steel blade, process ½ cup (125 mL) butter, 1 cup (250 mL) granulated sugar and the eggs until mixed.

3. Add cocoa mixture to bowl; process until mixed. Transfer to large mixing bowl.

4. Mix flour, baking soda and salt. Add to mixing bowl; mix well.

5. Mix 1 cup (250 mL) milk, the vinegar and 1 teaspoon (5 mL) vanilla. Add to mixing bowl; mix well. (Batter will be thin.)

6. Pour batter into greased and floured 8-cup (2 L) ring mold. Bake until done, about 30 minutes. Invert on wire rack.

7. While cake is baking, mix ¼ pound (115 g) butter, the chocolate and 6 tablespoons (90 mL) milk in small saucepan; cook over low heat, stirring occasionally, until chocolate melts.

8. Insert steel blade. Place powdered sugar and 1 teaspoon (5 mL) vanilla in bowl. With machine running, add chocolate mixture through feed tube; process until mixed.

9. Frost cake while still warm.

Austria, Germany, Russia & Poland

Hot Potato Salad and Rye Bread

Austrian Dinner Party

Caraway Cheese Sticks

Liver Dumpling Soup

Veal Goulash

Asparagus Spears

Hazelnut Torte

Just as the Austro-Hungarian Empire once stretched from Vienna eastward across the Carpathian Mountains, north through Czechoslovakia and south through half of Yugoslavia, so the cuisine of Austria encompasses both the elegance of the capital and the simple delights of the rural areas.

One of the glories of Vienna, Liver Dumpling Soup, is actually rustic fare elevated by refinement rather than by origins. The measures of this dish are the lightness of the flavorful dumplings and the quality of the broth. In our recipe, the food processor guarantees the proper texture of the meat mixture—you don't have to worry about over-processing—and a splash of brandy adds grandeur even if you use canned beef stock.

Veal Goulash is another country preparation, boldly spiced with paprika; yet the use of veal and the smooth sauce produced by pureeing the onions gives the dish "citified" airs. Mushrooms are optional in this recipe, but they would bridge the flavors of veal, paprika and sour cream wonderfully. Asparagus Spears sprinkled with buttered bread crumbs, chopped egg and cheese exemplifies the Austrian practice of serving vegetables in partial disguise.

The Hazelnut Torte is a remarkable souvenir of the Hapsburg dynasty. Blanketed with profligate amounts of whipped cream, the layers are composed of ground hazelnuts and bread crumbs rather than flour. Egg whites are the only leavening; so be sure to use extra-large eggs.

Offer a glass of dry sherry, if you wish, with the Caraway Cheese Sticks before dinner (and be sure to save this piquant recipe for all cocktail hours). The well-seasoned goulash would take nicely to Hungary's famous red wine, Egri Bikavér—which translates to "bull's blood!"

CARAWAY CHEESE STICKS
Makes 3 dozen

1 ounce (30 g) Parmesan cheese, cut into 1-inch (2.5 cm) cubes
2 ounces (60 g) sharp Cheddar cheese
1 cup (250 mL) all-purpose flour
½ cup (125 mL) frozen butter or margarine, cut into pieces
¼ teaspoon (1 mL) salt
1 tablespoon (15 mL) caraway seeds
1 teaspoon (5 mL) dry mustard
Pinch paprika
Pinch cayenne pepper
Dash red pepper sauce
2 to 3 tablespoons (30 to 45 mL) milk, white wine or water

1. Insert steel blade. With machine running, drop Parmesan cheese through feed tube; process until finely grated; reserve. Using shredding disc, shred Cheddar cheese.

2. Insert steel blade. Place flour, butter and salt in bowl; process until butter is mixed into dry ingredients.

3. Add shredded Cheddar cheese, caraway seeds, mustard, paprika, cayenne pepper and red pepper sauce to bowl. With machine running, add milk through feed tube; process until mixture forms ball. Refrigerate dough in covered container 2 hours.

4. Heat oven to 425 °F (220 °C). Roll dough ¼-inch (0.5 cm) thick on floured surface; cut into 5 × ½-inch (13 × 1.5 cm) strips.

5. Place cheese strips on greased baking sheet; sprinkle with Parmesan cheese.

6. Bake until golden, 10 to 12 minutes.

LIVER DUMPLING SOUP
Makes 6 servings

5 slices dry bread, broken into pieces
¼ cup (60 mL) milk
¼ cup (60 mL) parsley sprigs
½ small onion, cut in half
1 tablespoon (15 mL) butter or margarine
½ pound (225 g) calves' liver, cleaned, trimmed, cut into 1-inch (2.5 cm) pieces
1 egg
⅛ teaspoon (0.5 mL) ground marjoram leaves
½ teaspoon (2 mL) salt
⅛ teaspoon (0.5 mL) pepper
Pinch ground nutmeg
6 cups (1.5 L) beef stock
1 tablespoon (15 mL) brandy

1. Using steel blade, process bread to fine crumbs (about 1 cup or 250 mL crumbs). Toss crumbs with milk.

2. Using steel blade, process parsley until chopped. Remove from bowl. Using steel blade, process onion, using on/off technique, until chopped. Sauté onion in butter in skillet until tender, about 5 minutes.

3. Using steel blade, process all ingredients except beef stock and brandy to paste-like consistency. Refrigerate 1 hour.

4. Heat beef stock and brandy to boiling in medium saucepan.

5. Shape liver mixture into 12 dumplings; add to hot stock. Simmer covered 15 to 20 minutes. Serve soup in individual bowls with 2 dumplings in each bowl.

Hazelnut Torte

VEAL GOULASH
Makes 6 servings

¼ cup (60 mL) parsley
    sprigs
3 onions, cut into
    quarters
¼ cup (60 mL) butter
    or margarine
3 pounds (1350 g) veal,
    cut into 1-inch (2.5
    cm) cubes
½ cup (125 mL) chicken
    stock
1 cup (250 mL) dry
    white wine
1 tablespoon (15 mL)
    paprika

2½ teaspoons (12 mL)
    salt
¼ teaspoon (1 mL)
    pepper
1 teaspoon (5 mL)
    lemon juice
2 tablespoons (30 mL)
    all-purpose flour
1 cup (250 mL) sour
    cream
6 cups (1.5 L) hot
    cooked noodles

1. Using steel blade, process parsley until chopped; reserve.

2. Using steel blade, process onions, using on/off technique, until chopped. Sauté onions in butter in Dutch oven until tender, about 10 minutes. Add veal to Dutch oven; cook 5 minutes, stirring frequently.

3. Add chicken stock, wine, paprika, salt and pepper to Dutch oven. Heat to boiling; reduce heat. Simmer covered until meat is tender, 1 to 1½ hours. Remove veal; strain sauce. Return liquid to Dutch oven.

4. Using steel blade, process strained onion mixture until smooth; add to Dutch oven. Stir in lemon juice.

5. Mix flour and sour cream; stir into sauce. Add veal to Dutch oven;* simmer uncovered 10 minutes.

6. Transfer goulash to serving dish and sprinkle with chopped parsley. Serve with noodles.
    *Note: *For variation, stir in ½ pound (225 g) sliced mushrooms sautéed in butter.*

ASPARAGUS SPEARS
Makes 6 servings

2 pounds (900 g) fresh
    asparagus, trimmed
Boiling water
½ teaspoon (2 mL) salt
2 slices dry bread,
    broken into pieces

1 ounce (30 g) Parmesan
    cheese, cut into
    1-inch (2.5 cm)
    cubes
1 hard-cooked egg, cut
    in half
¼ cup (60 mL) butter or
    margarine

1. Place asparagus in large skillet or saucepan. Cover with boiling water. Add salt. Cook covered over medium heat just until tender, 6 to 8 minutes. Drain and transfer to heated serving dish.

2. Using steel blade, process bread to fine crumbs; remove from bowl. Insert steel blade. With machine running, drop cheese through feed tube; process until finely grated. Remove from bowl. Using steel blade, process hard-cooked egg, using on/off technique, until finely chopped. **T28**

3. Sauté bread crumbs in butter until crumbs are light brown. Add Parmesan cheese. Spoon crumbs over asparagus; toss gently. Sprinkle chopped egg over the top.

HAZELNUT TORTE

Makes 10 to 12 servings

1 slice bread, crust removed, broken into pieces	1 teaspoon (5 mL) vanilla
2½ cups (625 mL) hazelnuts	¼ teaspoon (1 mL) salt
7 extra-large eggs, separated	2 cups (500 mL) whipping cream
1 cup (250 mL) sugar	¼ cup (60 mL) sugar
	¾ cup (180 mL) plum jelly

1. Heat oven to 350°F (180°C). Line bottoms of three 8-inch (20 cm) cake pans with waxed paper.

2. Using steel blade, process bread to fine crumbs; reserve.

3. Using steel blade, process all but 10 hazelnuts until finely chopped; remove ½ cup (125 mL) chopped nuts and reserve. Add egg yolks, ½ cup (125 mL) of the sugar and the vanilla to bowl; process until lemon colored. **T44**

4. Beat egg whites and salt with electric mixer until foamy. Add ½ cup (125 mL) sugar, 2 tablespoons (30 mL) at a time, beating until stiff but not dry peaks form. Fold bread crumbs into egg whites. Fold hazelnut mixture into egg whites.

5. Pour batter into pans. Bake until cake springs back when touched, 25 to 30 minutes. Invert onto wire racks.

6. Whip cream and ¼ cup (60 mL) sugar with electric mixer until soft peaks form.

7. Place 1 cake layer on serving plate; spread with ¼ cup (60 mL) jelly and ¾ cup (180 mL) whipped cream. Repeat with remaining layers. Cover completely with remaining whipped cream.* Sprinkle side of cake with reserved chopped nuts. Garnish top with whole hazelnuts. Refrigerate 3 to 4 hours before serving.

*Note: *If desired, some of the whipped cream may be piped in a decorative border around top of cake.**

Informal Austrian Supper

Liptauer Cheese

Sweet-and-Sour Spinach Salad

Stuffed Beef Rolls

Linzertorte

Austria is known, above all, for its magnificent pastries. And none is more famous than the spectacular Linzertorte that ends this menu. It is made with the most heavenly, cookie-like crust of chopped almonds flavored with cinnamon and cloves and enriched with butter and egg yolks. The butter must be frozen prior to processing or this rich dough will not hold together. Filled with raspberry jam, the shallow torte glistens with its overlay of a diamond-lattice crust framing the rosy jam. Sprinkle the torte generously with powdered sugar, serve it with cups of rich, freshly-brewed coffee and imagine yourself in Vienna.

That city was once the capital of an empire that spanned present-day Austria and Hungary, as well as large parts of other eastern European countries. So, not surprisingly, we find some of the same dishes in several of the regional cuisines. Liptauer Cheese takes its name from the town of Liptó in northern Hungary; it is not a cheese actually, but a classic cheese-based spread highly seasoned with paprika, caraway, mustard, anchovies and capers. It is quick, superb party food—sometimes served gilded with caviar.

Rouladen, or Stuffed Beef Rolls, are well known to every cook who has ever searched for an unusual, savory way to serve round steak; and the food processor adds to the popularity of this dish by making the stuffing so easy to prepare. You may be less familiar with Spaetzle, the small, meltaway dumplings that turn any gravy into a gourmet treat. They are so easy to make that you may never go back to ordinary noodles and rice.

Both the Liptauer Cheese and the rich beef rolls will be enhanced by a Pinot Noir wine from Austria's eastern provinces, the full, deep Blauburgunder.

Stuffed Beef Rolls with Spaetzle

LIPTAUER CHEESE
Makes 2 cups (500 mL)

8 ounces (225 g) cream cheese, cut into 3 pieces
½ cup (125 mL) butter or margarine, room temperature
1 to 2 anchovy fillets
1 teaspoon (5 mL) drained capers

1 teaspoon (5 mL) caraway seeds
2 teaspoons (10 mL) prepared mustard
2 teaspoons (10 mL) ground paprika
1 tablespoon (15 mL) dried chives
Pumpernickel bread

1. Using steel blade, process cream cheese and butter until smooth. Add anchovy fillets, capers, caraway, mustard and 1 teaspoon (5 mL) of the paprika. Process until thoroughly blended and smooth.

2. Transfer mixture to small bowl; refrigerate until slightly firm, about 1 hour.

3. Using a spatula, shape cheese into a mound on serving plate. Garnish with chives and remaining paprika. Serve with thin slices of pumpernickel.

SWEET-AND-SOUR SPINACH SALAD
Makes 6 servings

½ pound (225 g) bacon, cut into 1-inch (2.5 cm) pieces
Sweet-and-Sour Dressing (recipe follows)

1 pound (450 g) fresh spinach, stems trimmed
¼ pound (115 g) mushrooms

1. Cook bacon until crisp. Drain on paper toweling. Reserve 2 tablespoons (30 mL) bacon fat for the dressing.

2. Make Sweet-and-Sour Dressing.

3. Place spinach in salad bowl.

4. Using slicing disc, slice mushrooms; add to spinach.

5. Pour hot salad dressing over spinach and mushrooms; toss gently. Sprinkle bacon pieces over top.

Sweet-and-Sour Dressing
Makes 1½ cups (375 mL)

1 large onion, cut into eighths	3 tablespoons (45 mL) cider vinegar
2 tablespoons (30 mL) reserved bacon fat	⅓ cup (80 mL) sugar
2 tablespoons (30 mL) water	1 cup (250 mL) mayonnaise

1. Using steel blade, process onion, using on/off technique, until chopped. Cook in bacon fat until light brown, 5 to 8 minutes.

2. Combine water, vinegar and sugar in small saucepan; heat to boiling, stirring until sugar dissolves. Reduce heat.

3. Add mayonnaise and cooked onion; stir until smooth. Keep warm.

STUFFED BEEF ROLLS
Makes 6 servings

2½ pounds (1125 g) thinly cut round steak	¼ teaspoon (1 mL) pepper
2 slices fresh pumpernickel bread, broken into pieces	2 to 3 tablespoons (30 to 45 mL) Dijon-style mustard
½ cup (125 mL) parsley sprigs	2 dill pickles, each cut lengthwise into 8 slices
2 onions, cut into quarters	Flour
½ pound (225 g) pork, cut into 1-inch (2.5 cm) cubes	2 carrots, cut into 1-inch (2.5 cm) pieces
4 tablespoons (60 mL) butter or margarine	2 ribs celery, cut into 1-inch (2.5 cm) pieces
2 tablespoons (30 mL) drained capers	1 cup (250 mL) dry red wine
¼ teaspoon (1 mL) dried marjoram leaves	2 cups (500 mL) beef stock
¼ teaspoon (1 mL) salt	Spaetzle (recipe follows)
	Fresh parsley sprigs, if desired

1. Pound meat with a mallet until about ⅛-inch (0.5 cm) thick; cut meat into 5 × 3-inch (13 × 8 cm) pieces. There should be 12 to 15 pieces.

2. Using steel blade, process bread to fine crumbs. Remove from bowl. Process ½ cup (125 mL) parsley, 1 of the onions and the pork separately, using on/off technique, until chopped.

3. Sauté chopped onion in 1 tablespoon (15 mL) of the butter in Dutch oven until tender, about 5 minutes. Add pork; cook until brown, 10 minutes.

4. Using plastic or steel blade, process pork mixture, bread crumbs, parsley, capers, marjoram, salt and pepper, using on/off technique, until blended.

5. Spread each beef slice with a little mustard. Place a heaping tablespoon seasoned pork mixture and 1 slice pickle in center; roll tightly.* Secure with wooden toothpicks or tie with string. Coat beef rolls with flour.

6. Heat remaining butter in Dutch oven; brown beef rolls in butter. Remove from pan.

7. Using steel blade, process remaining onion, the carrots and celery until chopped. Add to pan; sauté about 5 minutes.

8. Place beef rolls over vegetables. Add wine and beef stock; heat to boiling; reduce heat. Simmer covered until meat is tender, about 1 to 1½ hours.

9. Make Spaetzle.

10. Transfer beef rolls to warm platter; discard toothpicks or string. Pour sauce over top. Garnish with parsley sprigs if desired. Serve with Spaetzle.

*Note: *Any leftover filling can be added to the sauce in Step 8.*

Spaetzle
Makes 6 servings

2½ cups (625 mL) all-purpose flour	2 tablespoons (30 mL) salt
1 teaspoon (5 mL) salt	3 tablespoons (45 mL) butter or margarine, melted
2 eggs	
½ cup (125 mL) water	
6 quarts (6 L) water	

1. Insert steel blade. Place flour and 1 teaspoon (5 mL) salt in bowl. With machine running, add eggs and ½ cup (125 mL) water through the feed tube; process until dough forms a ball. (This may require a few drops more water.) Let dough spin around bowl for 15 to 20 seconds.

2. Roll dough ⅛-inch (0.5 cm) thick on lightly floured surface. Using a sharp knife, cut off slivers of dough.

3. Heat 6 quarts (6 L) of water to boiling; add 2 tablespoons (30 mL) salt. Drop dough slivers into boiling water and cook about 5 to 10 minutes. They will float to the surface when cooked.

4. Remove with slotted spoon to colander. Drain. Transfer to heated serving dish and toss with butter.

Note: For a tasty variation, cooked Spaetzle can be tossed with any of the following ingredients: ¼ pound (115 g) sautéed mushrooms, 2 tablespoons (30 mL) chopped parsley, 2 chopped onions sautéed in butter until light brown, ¼ cup (60 mL) grated Parmesan cheese or 8 slices crumbled crisp bacon.

LINZERTORTE
Makes 8 servings

6 ounces (170 g) unblanched almonds	1 teaspoon (5 mL) ground cinnamon
1 cup (250 mL) all-purpose flour	¼ teaspoon (1 mL) ground cloves
½ pound (225 g) frozen butter or margarine, cut into 16 pieces	Pinch salt
	3 egg yolks
Rind of 1 lemon, cut into pieces	1 teaspoon (5 mL) vanilla
½ cup (125 mL) sugar	1 cup (250 mL) raspberry jam
	Powdered sugar

1. Using steel blade, process almonds until finely chopped.

2. Add flour and butter to almonds in bowl. Process until butter is mixed into dry ingredients. Add lemon rind, sugar, cinnamon, cloves, salt, egg yolks and vanilla to bowl; process until mixture forms ball. Refrigerate ¼ of the dough.

3. Pat remaining dough into bottom and 1 inch (2.5 cm) up side of ungreased 9-inch (23 cm) springform pan. (Crust is fairly thick.)

4. Spread raspberry jam evenly on crust.

5. Heat oven to 350°F (180°C). Roll remaining dough ½-inch (1.5 cm) thick on lightly floured surface. Cut into 6 strips, ½ to ¾-inch (1.5 to 2 cm) wide. Arrange 3 strips evenly spaced over top of jam. Rotate pan 45° (an eighth of a turn). Place 3 more strips evenly spaced over top. Spaces between strips should be diamond shaped rather than square (see photo 1).

Photo 1. Lay pastry strips on jam to form diamond pattern.

6. Bake until light brown, 45 to 50 minutes. Let stand 5 minutes; remove rim of springform pan. Cool to room temperature before serving. Sprinkle with powdered sugar.

Russian Midnight Supper

Mushroom and Potato Soup

Cucumber Salad

Kulebiac

Charlotte Russe

Moscow has given the world some of the best theater—and some of the best after-theater fare. Few dishes fit the bill for late-night dining as well as Kulebiac, a tantalizing pastry-wrapped loaf of salmon, mushrooms, chopped eggs and rice.

You can make the Kulebiac before you leave for the theater, under-bake it slightly and refrigerate it covered with aluminum foil until later. Finish baking it while guests enjoy appetite-appeasing bowls of steaming Mushroom and Potato Soup, which can be made a day in advance and reheated. Certainly it would not be amiss to drink a few toasts of icy cold vodka—with caviar and buttered black bread, perhaps— while the soup is simmering.

The Kulebiac looks much more complex than it is to prepare. The food processor takes care of all the chop-

ping, and there is no easier way to cook fish than by oven-poaching. If you refrigerate the flaky pastry, you'll have no trouble rolling it out; once the fillings are layered atop the pastry, all you have to do is fold in the sides envelope-fashion. Decoration is purely a matter of choice; the only imperative is that you cut slits or small circular holes in the pastry for steam to escape.

The supreme elegance of Charlotte Russe also belies its simple preparation. The filling is essentially an egg custard enriched with sour cream, almonds and whipped cream. Gelatin ensures that the mixture will set properly and un-mold easily. Be sure to butter the mold generously and if the ladyfingers are stale, so much the better.

Choose a very good Chablis (Grand Crus) or even Champagne for this romantic Russian supper.

MUSHROOM AND POTATO SOUP
Makes 8 servings

2 parsley sprigs	⅛ teaspoon (0.5 mL)
1 large carrot	pepper
1 pound (450 g)	3 tablespoons (45 mL)
mushrooms	butter or margarine
4 large potatoes, pared	2 tablespoons (30 mL)
2 onions, cut into	all-purpose flour
quarters	½ teaspoon (2 mL)
2 quarts (2 L) beef stock	caraway seeds
½ teaspoon (2 mL) salt	

1. Using steel blade, chop parsley.

2. Using shredding disc, shred carrot.

3. Using slicing disc, slice mushrooms, potatoes, and onions.

4. Place stock in 6-quart (6 L) kettle; add vegetables, parsley, salt and pepper. Heat to boiling; reduce heat. Simmer covered until vegetables are tender, about 40 minutes.

5. Heat butter in small skillet; add flour. Cook and stir over medium heat until smooth paste is formed. Mix ½ cup (125 mL) soup into flour and butter. Stir back into soup. Add caraway. Simmer, stirring occasionally until slightly thickened, about 5 minutes.
   Note: Leftover soup can be stored covered in refrigerator up to 1 week.
   Recipe can be halved to serve 4.

CUCUMBER SALAD
Makes 4 servings

2 large cucumbers,	1 tablespoon (15 mL)
pared, seeded	white wine vinegar
1 large onion, cut into	⅛ teaspoon (0.5 mL)
quarters	white pepper
1 teaspoon (5 mL) salt	½ teaspoon (2 mL) dill
1 cup (250 mL) sour	seeds or sprig fresh
cream or plain	dillweed
yogurt	

1. Using steel blade, slice cucumbers and onion. Sprinkle salt over cucumbers and onion. Let stand 30 minutes; rinse and drain.

2. Combine sour cream, vinegar and pepper; pour over cucumbers and onion. Refrigerate 30 minutes; garnish with dill seeds.

KULEBIAC
Makes 4 servings

1¾ cups (430 mL)	5 tablespoons (75 mL)
all-purpose flour	ice water
⅛ teaspoon (0.5 mL)	4 shallots, peeled
salt	½ pound (225 g)
¼ cup (60 mL) cold	mushrooms
butter or margarine,	2 tablespoons (30 mL)
cut into pieces	butter or margarine
3 tablespoons (45 mL)	3 hard-cooked eggs,
vegetable	cut into halves
shortening	

1½ cups (375 mL) cooked rice
½ cup (125 mL) parsley sprigs
2 slices bread, broken into pieces
1 pound (450 g) salmon fillet
3 cups (750 mL) red wine
2 bay leaves
1 egg, slightly beaten
Watercress sprigs
Lemon wedges
Sour cream

1. Insert steel blade. Place flour, salt, ¼ cup (60 mL) butter and the shortening in bowl; process until small particles form. With machine running, slowly add water through feed tube; process until dough forms ball. Refrigerate covered 1 hour.

2. Using steel blade, process shallots until chopped. Using slicing blade, slice mushrooms.

3. Sauté shallots in 2 tablespoons (30 mL) butter in skillet until soft, 3 minutes. Add mushrooms; sauté 1 minute.

4. Using steel blade, process hard-cooked eggs, using on/off technique, until chopped. Combine eggs and rice.

5. Using steel blade, mince parsley. Add bread to bowl; process to fine crumbs.

6. Heat oven to 350 °F (180 °C). Place salmon in pan; add wine and bay leaves. Bake covered until fish flakes with a fork, about 25 minutes. Cool; drain.

7. Roll dough on lightly floured surface into a rectangle, about 2½ times larger than salmon.

8. Place bread crumb mixture in center of pastry; place salmon on top of bread crumbs, egg mixture on salmon, and shallot mixture on eggs (see photo 2). Trim edges of pastry; reserve scraps. Fold edges of pastry over top; press seams to seal (see photo 3). Place seams-side down on greased baking sheet.

9. Heat oven to 350 °F (180 °C). Roll out pastry scraps and cut decorative shapes for top of pastry, if desired. Brush pastry with beaten egg. Cut 2 circles in pastry to allow steam to escape. Position decorative shapes on top of pastry (see photo 4); brush with beaten egg.

10. Bake until golden, about 45 minutes. Cut into slices; garnish with watercress and lemon. Serve with sour cream.

Kulebiac

Photo 2. In center of pastry, place bread crumb mixture; cover bread crumbs with salmon; place egg mixture on salmon; and top with shallot mixture.

Photo 3. Trim edges of pastry; fold edges over top of 4-layered filling. Press seams together to seal.

Photo 4. Cut 2 small circles in top of pastry. If desired, place decorative shapes (cut from pastry scraps) around circles.

CHARLOTTE RUSSE
Makes 6 to 8 servings

⅓ cup (80 mL) almonds	¼ cup (60 mL) cold water
⅔ cup (160 mL) sugar	14 ladyfingers, split
4 large egg yolks	½ cup (125 mL) sour cream
1⅓ cups (330 mL) milk	1 cup (250 mL) whipping cream
1 teaspoon (5 mL) vanilla	Warm water
2 packages unflavored gelatin	

1. Using steel blade, process almonds until chopped; reserve.

2. Using steel or plastic blade, process sugar and egg yolks until blended.

3. Place milk in heavy saucepan; heat until warm. Gradually stir in egg mixture. Cook over low heat until thickened; stir in vanilla.

4. Dissolve gelatin in cold water; stir into milk mixture. Refrigerate uncovered until set but not stiff, about 1 hour.

5. Butter 2-quart (2 L) charlotte mold or soufflé dish. Cut circle of waxed paper to fit bottom of mold. Butter both sides of paper and place in mold. Line bottom of mold with split ladyfingers, trimming ends to fit. Line sides of mold with ladyfingers (see photo 5).

Photo 5. Line bottom and all around sides of charlotte mold with split ladyfingers.

6. Mix sour cream and almonds into custard. Whip cream with electric mixer; fold into custard. Fill mold with mixture. Refrigerate 5 hours.

7. Dip mold briefly in warm water and unmold on serving platter.

Borscht

Country-Style Russian Dinner

Borscht

Piroshki

Chicken Stew with Dumplings

Cabbage and Onions

Honey Cake

The infamous cold winters of most of the Soviet Union have generated a cuisine of hearty "one-pot" dishes. These foods come as a gift to all cooks who look for satisfying, budget-minded fare during our own cold season. Based on the creative use of root vegetables, which can be cellar-stored through the winter, and the country's abundant dairy products, Russian food offers a stock of convenient family staples.

Borscht is Russia's best-known soul-warmer. There are probably as many versions, with or without meat, of this beet soup as there are cooks. It may be served hot, with boiled potatoes, or cold, with sour cream. Either way, the flaky, filled pastries called Piroshki are a classic accompaniment. Piroshki can be baked and kept frozen for several weeks.

Paprika and caraway give the Chicken Stew just enough tanginess to distinguish this blend from ordinary recipes. And the egg white-lightened dumplings, made with equal parts of all-purpose and instant flour, are the fluffiest imaginable. A caraway-seed accent makes Cabbage and Onions an excellent mate for the chicken, but you'll find that this side dish can perk up boiled beef, too. The recipe can be doubly recommended for the high vitamin content of the cabbage and its all-season availability.

The Honey Cake recipe is one of those quick culinary tricks that come in handy time and time again. Black coffee and orange rind are the secret ingredients that turn the cake's bouquet of spices into a rich kitchen perfume. This treat needs no frosting—just a samovar of hot tea for savoring pleasure.

Yugoslavia's Zilavka is a white wine that's both sufficiently dry and interesting to enhance this multi-flavored meal.

BORSCHT
Makes 6 servings

3 ribs celery	3 cups (750 mL) beef stock
2 pounds (900 g) beets, pared, cut into quarters, or 2 cans (16 ounces or 450 g each) whole beets, drained, cut into quarters	¼ cup (60 mL) dry red wine
	¼ teaspoon (1 mL) salt
	⅛ teaspoon (0.5 mL) pepper
	2 bay leaves
1 small onion, cut into quarters	1 cup (250 mL) sour cream, if desired
3 tablespoons (45 mL) butter or margarine	

1. Using slicing disc, slice celery and half the beets.

2. Using steel blade, separately process remaining beets and onion until finely chopped.

3. Sauté onion and celery in butter in skillet 3 minutes.

4. Combine vegetables, beef stock, wine, salt, pepper and bay leaves in Dutch oven. Heat to boiling; reduce heat. Simmer until vegetables are tender, about 1 hour.

5. Refrigerate until ready to serve. Remove bay leaves. Garnish each bowl of soup with dollop of sour cream, if desired.

PIROSHKI
Makes about 24

2 cups (500 mL) all-purpose flour	1 egg, slightly beaten
½ teaspoon (2 mL) baking powder	½ cup (125 mL) sour cream
½ teaspoon (2 mL) salt	Mushroom Filling (recipe follows)
¼ cup (60 mL) butter or margarine, cut into chunks	1 egg yolk, slightly beaten

1. Insert steel blade. Place flour, baking powder, salt and butter in bowl; process until small particles form. Add egg and sour cream; process until ball of dough forms. Refrigerate covered with plastic wrap 1 hour.

2. Make Mushroom Filling.

3. Roll out dough ⅛-inch (0.5 cm) thick on lightly floured surface. Cut into 2½-inch (6.5 cm) circles. Place 1 teaspoon (5 mL) filling in center of each circle. Fold in half and pinch edges to seal.

4. Heat oven to 375°F (190°C). Brush pastries with egg yolk. Place on greased and floured baking sheets. Bake 30 minutes.

Mushroom Filling

3 green onions and tops
½ pound (225 g)
    mushrooms
1 tablespoon (15 mL)
    butter or margarine
¼ teaspoon (1 mL) salt
⅛ teaspoon (0.5 mL)
    pepper

2 teaspoons (10 mL)
    all-purpose flour
1 teaspoon (5 mL) fresh
    or ½ teaspoon (2
    mL) dried dillweed
⅓ cup (80 mL) sour
    cream

1. Using steel blade, process onions and mushrooms until coarsely chopped.

2. Sauté onions and mushrooms in butter in skillet until soft, 2 minutes. Remove from heat.

3. Stir in salt, pepper, flour and dillweed. Cool to room temperature; stir in sour cream.

CHICKEN STEW WITH DUMPLINGS
Makes 6 servings

1 frying chicken (3½
    to 4 pounds or
    1600 to 1800 g),
    cut into pieces
¼ cup (60 mL) butter
    or margarine
½ teaspoon (2 mL) salt
½ teaspoon (2 mL)
    paprika
¼ teaspoon (1 mL)
    caraway seeds
1 large onion, cut into
    quarters
4 carrots
1 large turnip, pared
3 ribs celery

1½ cups (375 mL)
    chicken stock
2 tablespoons (30 mL)
    all-purpose flour
¼ cup cold water
¾ cup (180 mL) sour
    cream
¾ cup (180 mL) instant
    flour
¾ cup (180 mL) all-
    purpose flour
½ teaspoon (2 mL) salt
4 eggs, separated
3 tablespoons (45 mL)
    butter or
    margarine, melted

1. Place chicken, ¼ cup (60 mL) butter, ½ teaspoon (2 mL) salt, the paprika and caraway seeds in Dutch oven; brown chicken on all sides, about 15 minutes.

2. Using slicing disc, slice onion, carrots, turnip and celery.

3. Add sliced vegetables to Dutch oven; cook 3 minutes.

4. Add stock. Heat to boiling; reduce heat. Simmer 45 minutes. Remove chicken from Dutch oven. Mix 2 tablespoons (30 mL) all-purpose flour with the water; stir into stock mixture. Remove from heat; stir in sour cream. Return chicken to Dutch oven.

5. Using steel blade, process instant flour, ¾ cup (180 mL) all-purpose flour, ½ teaspoon (2 mL) salt, the egg yolks and 3 tablespoons (45 mL) melted butter until blended.

6. Beat egg whites with electric mixer until stiff but not dry peaks form. Fold egg whites into flour mixture. Heat stew to boiling; reduce heat. Drop dumplings by tablespoons onto top of stew. Simmer covered 5 minutes.

CABBAGE AND ONIONS
Makes 6 to 8 servings

2 large onions, cut into
    quarters
¼ cup (60 mL) butter or
    margarine
1 small head cabbage,
    cut into wedges

¼ teaspoon (1 mL) salt
⅛ teaspoon (0.5 mL)
    pepper
1 teaspoon (5 mL)
    caraway seeds

1. Using slicing disc, slice onions. Sauté onions in butter in skillet 3 minutes.

2. Using slicing disc, slice cabbage. Add to skillet; sauté until cabbage is tender, about 8 minutes.

3. Stir in salt, pepper and caraway seeds.

HONEY CAKE
Makes 6 servings

½ cup (125 mL) packed
    brown sugar
1 tablespoon (15 mL)
    orange rind
2 cups (500 mL) all-
    purpose flour
½ teaspoon (2 mL)
    baking powder
½ teaspoon (2 mL)
    baking soda
¼ teaspoon (1 mL)
    ground nutmeg

¼ teaspoon (1 mL)
    ground cinnamon
½ teaspoon (2 mL) salt
½ cup (125 mL) warm
    black coffee
¾ cup (180 mL) honey
¼ cup (60 mL) vegetable
    oil
2 large eggs
¼ teaspoon (1 mL)
    orange extract
½ cup (125 mL) dark
    raisins

1. Using steel blade, process sugar and orange rind until chopped.

2. Heat oven to 375 °F (190 °C). Add remaining ingredients except raisins to bowl; process until blended. Add raisins to bowl; process 1 second to combine.

3. Pour batter into greased and floured 9 x 9 x 2-inch (23 x 23 x 5 cm) pan. Bake 45 minutes. Cut into squares to serve.

German Sauerbraten Feast

Mushrooms in Cream Sauce on Toast

Green Salad with Buttermilk Dressing

Sauerbraten

Potato Pancakes

Sweet-and-Sour Red Cabbage

Mocha Mousse

Almond Crescents

Sauerbraten reigns supreme at a lavish German dinner. Its harmony of sweet and sour flavors, accented by spicy gingersnaps used to thicken the sauce, makes this embellished beef pot roast quite satisfying and popular with everyone. Marinating is critical to the flavor of the meat and you can leave the meat refrigerated in its bath of red wine longer than the time specified in the recipe—up to ten days, if you wish. Turn the meat over twice a day, and it will grow more tender and flavorful everyday. The food processor turns the vegetable-laden gravy, made with the tangy marinade, into a smooth, delicious puree.

Serve crisp Potato Pancakes as the perfect foil for the meat and sauce. Indeed, you may find yourself frying up these mouth-watering rounds of shredded potatoes to go with all kinds of entrees. If there is one food that shows off the food processor to better advantage than any other, it is the potato, because it is of the right size and texture for instant shredding, slicing, chopping and grating. If you like large potato pancakes, you need only shred the vegetable; if you prefer them small and fluffy, first shred the potato and then briefly chop the shreds.

Mocha Mousse is one of the richest desserts we've ever tasted. Butter, cream and three-quarters of a pound of chocolate make it an exemplar of the German sweet tooth. If you like chocolate mousse, you'll find that the coffee flavoring actually heightens the flavor of the chocolate. Some guests will want to indulge in both the mousse and the simple Almond Crescent cookies; others will opt for cookies and coffee only after this filling repast.

A spicy, full-bodied white wine, Bernkastel Mosel will engage well with the complex flavor of the Sauerbraten.

MUSHROOMS IN CREAM SAUCE ON TOAST
Makes 6 servings

1 large onion, cut into eighths
2 tablespoons (30 mL) butter or margarine
2 pounds (900 g) mushrooms
1 tablespoon (15 mL) all-purpose flour
3 tablespoons (45 mL) dry sherry
¾ to 1 cup (180 to 250 mL) whipping cream or half-and-half
1 teaspoon (5 mL) salt

⅛ teaspoon (0.5 mL) pepper
Pinch ground nutmeg
¼ pound (115 g) chicken livers
2 tablespoons (30 mL) butter or margarine
Pinch salt
Pinch pepper
⅛ teaspoon (0.5 mL) dried thyme leaves
6 slices toast, crusts removed, cut diagonally in half

1. Using steel blade, process onion, using on/off technique, until chopped. Sauté in 2 tablespoons (30 mL) butter until tender, 5 to 8 minutes.

2. Using slicing disc, slice mushrooms. Add to onions; cook covered until tender, 3 to 5 minutes.

3. Stir in flour; cook over medium heat, stirring constantly, 2 to 3 minutes. Stir in sherry, ¾ cup (180 mL) cream, 1 teaspoon (5 mL) salt, ⅛ teaspoon (0.5 mL) pepper and the nutmeg; cook until thickened and smooth, about 5 minutes. (If mixture is too thick, add more cream.) Keep warm.

4. Sauté chicken livers in 2 tablespoons (30 mL) butter in small skillet until no longer pink, 8 to 10 minutes.

5. Using steel blade, process chicken livers, salt, pepper and thyme until smooth.

6. Spread each slice of toast with about 1 tablespoon (15 mL) of liver mixture. Top with creamed mushrooms.

GREEN SALAD WITH BUTTERMILK DRESSING
Makes 6 servings

8 slices bacon, cut into 1-inch (2.5 cm) pieces
1 pound (450 g) romaine or mixed greens, cut into bite-size pieces

2 red apples, cored, cut into halves
½ cup (125 mL) buttermilk
1 tablespoon (15 mL) sugar
¼ teaspoon (1 mL) salt
1 teaspoon (5 mL) lemon juice

1. Cook bacon until crisp. Drain, reserving 3 tablespoons (45 mL) bacon fat. Crumble bacon. Toss lettuce with hot bacon fat in salad bowl.

2. Using slicing disc, slice apples; add to lettuce. Mix buttermilk, sugar, salt and lemon juice. Pour over lettuce and toss. Sprinkle bacon over top.

SAUERBRATEN
Makes 6 to 8 servings

Marinade (recipe
    follows)
4 pounds (1800 g)
    bottom round of
    beef
10 gingersnaps, broken
    in half
¼ cup (60 mL) butter or
    margarine
2 carrots, cut into
    1-inch (2.5 cm)
    pieces

2 onions, cut into
    quarters
2 ribs celery, cut into
    1-inch (2.5 cm)
    pieces
¼ cup (60 mL) parsley
    sprigs
1 teaspoon (5 mL) salt
¼ teaspoon (1 mL)
    pepper
1 tablespoon (15 mL)
    sugar

1. Make Marinade.

2. Pour Marinade over meat in glass baking dish; refrigerate covered, turning meat twice a day, 5 to 7 days.

3. Using steel blade, process gingersnaps to fine crumbs.

4. Remove meat from Marinade; reserve Marinade. Pat meat dry with paper toweling. Sauté meat in butter in large saucepan or Dutch oven until light brown on all sides, about 10 minutes. Remove meat.

5. Using steel blade, process carrots, onions, celery and parsley until finely chopped. Sauté chopped vegetables in pan drippings 5 minutes. Add meat to chopped vegetable mixture.

6. Strain Marinade; add strained Marinade to meat. Heat to boiling; reduce heat. Simmer covered until meat is tender, 3 to 4 hours. Turn meat occasionally.

7. Remove meat from sauce. Strain sauce. Using steel blade, process strained solids until smooth. Return to sauce. Stir in gingersnap crumbs, salt, pepper and sugar. Heat to boiling; cook until thickened.

8. Slice meat; arrange slices on a serving platter. Pour some sauce over top; serve remaining sauce on side.
    Note: This recipe makes more Sauerbraten than you will need for the six people served at this dinner. Enjoy it the next day. Simply reheat in sauce.

Marinade

1 onion, cut into
    quarters
4 cups (1 L) red wine
1 cup (250 mL) water
3 tablespoons (45 mL)
    lemon juice

1 bay leaf
3 whole cloves
4 peppercorns
¼ teaspoon (1 mL) dried
    thyme leaves
Pinch ground nutmeg

1. Using steel blade, process onion, using on/off technique, until chopped.

2. Combine all ingredients in saucepan. Heat to boiling; reduce heat. Simmer uncovered 5 minutes. Cool.

POTATO PANCAKES
Makes 6 to 8

3 large potatoes, pared
    Cold water
1 small onion, cut into
    quarters
2 eggs
3 tablespoons (45 mL)
    all-purpose flour

2 tablespoons (30 mL)
    melted butter or
    margarine
1 teaspoon (5 mL) salt
⅛ teaspoon (0.5 mL)
    pepper
Vegetable oil

1. Using shredding disc, shred potatoes. Transfer to medium bowl and add cold water to cover.

2. Using steel blade, process onion, using on/off technique, until finely chopped. Add eggs, flour, butter, salt and pepper to bowl. Drain potatoes, pat dry with paper toweling, and add to bowl. Process just until mixture is blended.

3. Heat ¼ inch (0.5 cm) oil in skillet. Spoon about ¼ cup (60 mL) potato mixture into skillet for each pancake; flatten with spatula. Fry until brown on both sides.

4. Drain pancakes on paper toweling and serve immediately.

SWEET-AND-SOUR RED CABBAGE
Makes 6 servings

1 onion, cut into
    quarters
2 tablespoons (30 mL)
    butter or margarine
2 tart apples (Granny
    Smith or Greening),
    pared, cored, cut
    into halves
2 pounds (900 g) red
    cabbage, cored, cut
    into wedges
¼ cup (60 mL) cider
    vinegar

¼ cup (60 mL) sugar
½ cup (125 mL) water or
    chicken stock
1 teaspoon (5 mL) salt
¼ teaspoon (1 mL)
    ground nutmeg
Pinch ground cloves
2 tablespoons (30 mL)
    red wine
2 tablespoons (30 mL)
    currant jelly

1. Using steel blade, process onion, using on/off technique, until chopped. Sauté in butter in large saucepan until soft, 5 minutes.

2. Using slicing disc, slice apples. Add apples to saucepan; cook 5 minutes.

3. Using slicing disc, slice cabbage. Stir sliced cabbage, vinegar, sugar, water, salt, nutmeg and cloves into saucepan. Heat to boiling; reduce heat. Simmer covered until cabbage is tender, about 1 hour.

4. Just before serving, stir in wine and jelly.

MOCHA MOUSSE
Makes 6 to 8 servings

¾ pound (340 g) semisweet chocolate, broken into pieces
2 tablespoons (30 mL) water
3 tablespoons (45 mL) instant coffee powder
1 ounce (30 g) semisweet chocolate
6 eggs, separated
¾ cup (180 mL) granulated sugar
2 tablespoons (30 mL) rum or orange-flavored liqueur
1 teaspoon (5 mL) vanilla
¾ cup (180 mL) butter or margarine, room temperature, cut into 12 pieces
Pinch salt
¼ teaspoon (1 mL) cream of tartar
1 cup (250 mL) whipping cream
2 tablespoons (30 mL) powdered sugar
½ teaspoon (2 mL) vanilla

1. Combine ¾ pound (340 g) chocolate, the water and coffee powder in top of double boiler. Heat over simmering water, stirring occasionally, until chocolate is melted and mixture is smooth. Cool.

2. Using shredding disc, shred 1 ounce (30 g) chocolate; reserve.

3. Using steel blade, process egg yolks and granulated sugar until thick and lemon colored, 3 to 4 minutes. Add melted chocolate mixture, rum and 1 teaspoon (5 mL) vanilla to bowl. Process until thoroughly blended.

4. With machine running, gradually add pieces of butter, 1 at a time, through feed tube. Let each piece become mixed before adding more. Transfer mixture to large mixing bowl.

5. Beat egg whites and salt with electric mixer until foamy. Add cream of tartar; beat until stiff but not dry peaks form.

6. Fold egg whites into chocolate mixture. Pour into greased 1½-quart (1.5 L) mold or dish. Refrigerate at least 6 hours.

7. Just before serving, dip mold in warm water for a few seconds. Run a knife around edges and invert onto serving platter.

8. Beat cream, powdered sugar and ½ teaspoon (2 mL) vanilla with electric mixer until stiff. Spread over top and side of mousse.

9. Sprinkle shredded chocolate over top and side of mousse.

ALMOND CRESCENTS
Makes about 50

3 ounces (85 g) blanched almonds
1½ cups (375 mL) all-purpose flour
½ cup (125 mL) granulated sugar
1 cup (250 mL) butter or margarine, cut into 12 pieces
3 egg yolks
1 teaspoon (5 mL) vanilla
¼ teaspoon (1 mL) almond extract
Powdered sugar

1. Using steel blade, process almonds to fine powder. Add flour, granulated sugar and butter to bowl. Process until butter is mixed into dry ingredients.

2. Add egg yolks, vanilla and almond extract to bowl. Process until mixture is thoroughly blended and starts to form into a ball. Refrigerate dough 1 hour.

3. Heat oven to 325°F (160°C). Break off pieces of dough about the size of a walnut. Roll and shape pieces into crescents. Place on buttered baking sheets.

4. Bake until cookies are dry and golden, 15 to 20 minutes.

5. Carefully place on rack to cool. Sprinkle with powdered sugar.

Simple, Hearty German Supper

Split Pea Soup

Rye Bread

German Meatballs

Hot Potato Salad

Apple-Cheese Tart

Many of the simple yet satisfying recipes on this menu will become everyday family favorites in your home. There is nothing like thick, hot Split Pea Soup with thick slices of hearty homemade Rye Bread on blustery, winter nights. And German Meatballs, with a complement of capers and anchovies to spike the ground meats, offer an almost instant answer to appetites bored at work or school. The Hot Potato Salad can turn a supper or snack of bratwurst or other sausage into a mini-feast. And the Apple-Cheese Tart, with its fragrance of nutmeg, cinnamon, raisins and rum, is an absolutely irresistible adjunct to coffee any hour of the day. So prepare this complete menu for the complete experience of German Gemütlichkeit, but keep the recipes handy for everyday treats.

Remember that the split peas for the soup have to be soaked overnight before you can cook them. And this soup always seems to taste better the day after it is made; so start it several days before you plan to serve it. Or make it and freeze it for absolute convenience.

One of the great things about owning a food processor is that you never have to suffer with whatever the traffic will bear in the way of packaged ground beef and pork. Not only is the product you process at home fresher and less fatty than the supermarket meat, but it also has a "meatier," less crumbly texture that shows up especially well in the German Meatballs.

There is no comparison between packaged bread and homebaked loaves. And if you, like most people, are turning to more whole grain bread for its bonus of flavor and nutrition, then you'll cherish these thick-crusted, caraway-seasoned rye loaves. The term "whole-grain" is always somewhat of a misnomer, because you would not enjoy the leaden quality of bread baked exclusively with rye or wheat flour; you need the balance of all-purpose flour for the dough to rise well.

The best German wines are white, but for this hearty menu, you need a pungent red wine, like Blatina from Yugoslavia.

SPLIT PEA SOUP
Makes 6 servings

1½ cups (375 mL) dried split peas Water	2 carrots 2 tablespoons (30 mL) butter or margarine
½ cup (125 mL) parsley sprigs	6 cups (1.5 L) chicken stock
1 onion, cut into quarters	6 slices cooked crisp bacon, crumbled
2 ribs celery, cut into 1-inch (2.5 cm) pieces	

1. Soak peas in water to cover overnight; drain.

2. Using steel blade, process parsley, onion and celery until finely chopped.

3. Using slicing disc, slice carrots.

4. Sauté parsley, onion, celery and carrots in butter in large saucepan until soft, about 5 minutes.

5. Add peas and chicken stock. Heat to boiling; reduce heat. Simmer covered until peas are tender, 1 to 1½ hours.

6. Using steel blade, process soup, 2 cups (500 mL) at a time, until smooth.* Return to saucepan and heat.

7. Ladle soup into individual bowls. Sprinkle each serving with crumbled bacon.

> *Note: *If a coarser consistency is desired, remove carrot slices and about 1 cup (250 mL) peas. Process remaining soup, return carrot slices and peas.*

RYE BREAD
Makes 2 loaves

2 packages active dry yeast	2 cups (500 mL) rye flour
¾ cup (180 mL) warm water (105 to 115°F or 40 to 45°C)	2½ to 3 cups (625 to 750 mL) all-purpose flour
1 cup (250 mL) milk	1 tablespoon (15 mL) caraway seeds
2 tablespoons (30 mL) molasses	Cornmeal
2 tablespoons (30 mL) vegetable oil	1 egg white 1 tablespoon (15 mL) cold water
2 teaspoons (10 mL) salt	Caraway seeds, if desired

1. Combine yeast and warm water in 1-quart (1 L) measuring cup; stir until dissolved. Let stand 5 minutes.

2. Add milk, molasses, oil and salt to yeast mixture; stir until salt is dissolved.

3. Insert steel blade. Place 1 cup (250 mL) of the rye flour, 1 cup (250 mL) of the all-purpose flour and ½ tablespoon (7 mL) of the caraway seeds in bowl. With machine running, add half the yeast mixture

through feed tube. Process a few seconds until blended. Add ¼ to ½ cup (60 to 125 mL) all-purpose flour, ¼ cup (60 mL) at a time, until dough forms a slightly sticky and smooth ball.

4. Place dough in greased bowl; turn the dough to grease the top of the ball.

5. Repeat steps 3 and 4 using remaining flour, yeast mixture and ½ tablespoon (7 mL) caraway seeds.

6. Let dough stand covered in warm place until doubled, 45 to 60 minutes.

7. Punch down dough. Shape each piece dough into long, wide loaf. Place on greased baking sheet lightly sprinkled with cornmeal.

8. Let stand covered in warm place until doubled, 45 to 60 minutes.

9. Heat oven to 375 °F (190 °C). Mix egg white with 1 tablespoon (15 mL) cold water. Brush each loaf with egg white. Sprinkle with caraway seeds, if desired.

10. Bake until golden and bread sounds hollow when tapped, 35 to 40 minutes. Remove from baking sheet; cool on wire racks.

GERMAN MEATBALLS
Makes 6 to 8 servings (about 24 meatballs)

4 slices dry bread, broken into pieces	1 tablespoon (15 mL) drained capers
¼ cup (60 mL) milk	2 eggs
1 onion, cut into quarters	Grated rind of ½ lemon
1 tablespoon (15 mL) butter or margarine	1 teaspoon (5 mL) lemon juice
1 pound (450 g) beef, cut into 1-inch (2.5 cm) cubes	Pinch ground nutmeg
	¾ teaspoon (4 mL) salt
½ pound (225 g) pork or veal, cut into 1-inch (2.5 cm) cubes	¼ teaspoon (1 mL) pepper
	6 cups (1.5 L) beef stock
2 to 3 anchovy fillets	Caper Sauce (recipe follows)

1. Using steel blade, process bread to fine crumbs. Toss with milk; reserve.

2. Using steel blade, process onion, using on/off technique, until chopped. Sauté in butter until tender, 5 to 8 minutes.

3. Using steel blade, process beef, ½ pound (225 g) at a time, until finely chopped; transfer to a large mixing bowl. Process pork, anchovy fillets and capers until finely chopped.

4. Mix all ingredients except beef stock and Caper Sauce in mixing bowl. Shape into 2-inch (5 cm) meatballs.

5. Heat stock to boiling in large saucepan. Add meatballs. Cook covered until meatballs rise to the surface, 15 to 20 minutes. Drain; reserve 3 cups (750 mL) stock for sauce.

6. Make Caper Sauce.

7. Add meatballs to Caper Sauce; simmer uncovered until hot, about 10 minutes.

Caper Sauce

2 shallots, peeled	1 tablespoon (15 mL) drained capers
¼ cup (60 mL) butter or margarine	1 teaspoon (5 mL) lemon juice
¼ cup (60 mL) all-purpose flour	½ teaspoon (2 mL) salt
½ cup (125 mL) white wine	⅛ teaspoon (0.5 mL) pepper
2 to 3 cups (500 to 750 mL) reserved stock	Pinch ground nutmeg

1. Using steel blade, process shallots until finely chopped. Sauté shallots in butter in large saucepan until soft, 3 to 5 minutes.

2. Stir in flour to make smooth paste; cook 2 to 3 minutes. Remove pan from heat; gradually stir in wine and 2 cups (500 mL) of the stock. Stir in remaining ingredients, except stock.

3. Heat to boiling; reduce heat. Simmer, stirring constantly, until thickened, 3 to 5 minutes. Add more stock if a thinner consistency is desired.

HOT POTATO SALAD
Makes 6 servings

6 slices bacon, cut into 1-inch (2.5 cm) pieces	2 teaspoons (10 mL) sugar
¼ cup (60 mL) parsley sprigs	¼ teaspoon (1 mL) dried thyme leaves
1 onion, cut into quarters	1 bay leaf
1 tablespoon (15 mL) all-purpose flour	1 teaspoon (5 mL) salt
¾ cup (180 mL) beef stock	⅛ teaspoon (0.5 mL) pepper
2 tablespoons (30 mL) cider vinegar	6 small potatoes (1½ pounds or 675 g), pared
	2 cups (500 mL) water
	½ teaspoon (2 mL) salt

1. Cook bacon until crisp; drain on paper toweling. Reserve 3 tablespoons (45 mL) bacon fat.

2. Using steel blade, process parsley until chopped; remove from bowl. Process onion, using on/off technique, until chopped.

3. Sauté onion in bacon fat until light brown, 8 to 10 minutes. Stir in flour to make smooth paste; cook and stir 2 to 3 minutes. Gradually stir in beef stock, vinegar, sugar, thyme, bay leaf, 1 teaspoon (5 mL) salt, the pepper and parsley; stir until smooth. Simmer covered 10 minutes.

4. While onion mixture is simmering, use slicing disc to slice potatoes. Cook in water and ½ teaspoon (2 mL) salt just until tender, about 15 minutes; drain. Place in serving dish.

5. Pour hot dressing over potatoes; toss gently. Sprinkle bacon over top.

APPLE-CHEESE TART
Makes 6 to 8 servings

Lemony Tart Pastry (recipe follows)	½ teaspoon (2 mL) ground nutmeg
3 apples, pared, cored, cut into halves	1 cup (250 mL) cottage cheese
⅓ cup (80 mL) sugar	½ cup (125 mL) sour cream
1 teaspoon (5 mL) cornstarch	⅓ cup (80 mL) sugar
½ cup (125 mL) dark raisins or currants	2 eggs
½ teaspoon (2 mL) ground cinnamon	3 tablespoons (45 mL) rum
	1 teaspoon (5 mL) vanilla

1. Make Lemony Tart Pastry.

2. Heat oven to 400°F (200°C). Using slicing disc, slice apples. Combine apples, ⅓ cup (80 mL) sugar, the cornstarch, raisins, cinnamon and nutmeg in mixing bowl; toss to coat apples.

3. Spread apple mixture in bottom of baked pastry. Bake 15 minutes.

4. While apples are baking, use plastic or steel blade to process cottage cheese, sour cream and ⅓ cup (80 mL) sugar until smooth. Add eggs, rum and vanilla; process until mixed. Pour cheese mixture over cooked apples.

5. Reduce oven temperature to 350°F (180°C); bake until cheese topping is firm, 30 to 35 minutes. Serve warm or cold.

Lemony Tart Pastry

1 cup (250 mL) all-purpose flour	Rind of 1 lemon, cut into pieces
⅛ teaspoon (0.5 mL) salt	¼ cup (60 mL) butter or margarine, cut into 4 pieces
¼ teaspoon (1 mL) baking powder	
¼ cup (60 mL) sugar	1 egg

1. Using steel blade, process flour, salt, baking powder, sugar, lemon rind and butter until butter is mixed into dry ingredients. Add egg; process until mixture forms ball.

2. Heat oven to 400°F (200°C). Press dough over bottom and 2 inches (5 cm) up sides of 9-inch (23 cm) springform pan. Refrigerate 15 minutes. Bake 10 minutes.

Tempting Polish Supper

Stuffed Cabbage Rolls

Pike in the Polish Style

Kasha with Mushrooms and Onions

Poppy Seed Cookies

A quartet of beautifully seasoned dishes illustrates the lovingly and ingeniously woven tapestry of Polish cooking. The influences of many cultures can be seen in the food of the much-invaded country; yet there is a distinctively joyous quality about Polish cuisine.

Stuffed Cabbage Rolls bubble with a clever counterpoint of sweet and sour tastes. The tartness of cabbage and tomato juice is offset by brown sugar and raisins, and gingersnap crumbs thicken the sauce with inimitable zest. This is one dish that benefits from advance preparation, and the recipe can easily serve four or five diners as a one-dish entree.

Pike abounds in Poland's lakes and dill is a popular seasoning. But a sauce of chopped eggs and lemon juice is truly admirable for its unusual use of the hard-cooked eggs to soften and temper the tangy ingredients to match the sweet-fleshed fish. A side dish of Kasha with Mushrooms and Onions delivers a nutritional bonus with the vitamin-packed buckwheat groats. You'll welcome this recipe as a substitute for rice or potatoes with chicken or beef dishes, too.

There has always been a cooks' controversy over whether Kolecky, the delicious, crumbly cookies of Poland, are better made with yeast or pastry dough. We've decided in favor of yeast dough with a poppy seed filling. And you will, too—once you taste these light cakes. You can use canned poppy seed filling, but it's easy enough to grind the seeds in an electric blender (don't worry if the blade jams—it's inevitable, and the seeds should be well enough ground by then) and enjoy the wonderful sweetness of this vanilla and honey flavored formula.

The surprising Italian note in Polish cooking, which was introduced in the sixteenth-century royal court, makes a pleasant, dry Italian wine—an Orvieto or a somewhat less dry Lugana—quite appropriate with Pike in the Polish Style.

STUFFED CABBAGE ROLLS

Makes 6 to 8 servings

1 large head cabbage (4
    pounds or 1800 g),
    cut in half, leaves
    separated
2 large onions, cut into
    quarters
1 large lemon
1½ pounds (675 g)
    chuck, cut into
    1-inch (2.5 cm)
    cubes
¾ cup (180 mL)
    uncooked rice

½ teaspoon (2 mL) salt
⅛ teaspoon (0.5 mL)
    pepper
1 large egg, slightly
    beaten
½ cup (125 mL) brown
    sugar
1 can (16 ounces or
    500 mL) tomato
    juice
10 gingersnaps
½ cup (125 mL) dark
    raisins

1. Steam cabbage leaves in 3 inches (8 cm) water until soft, 5 minutes; drain.

2. Using slicing disc, slice onions and lemon separately. Line bottom of large Dutch oven with onions.

3. Using steel blade, process beef, 1 cup (250 mL) at a time, using on/off technique, until chopped. Place in medium mixing bowl. Mix rice, salt, pepper and egg into meat.

4. Place 1½ tablespoons (22 mL) meat mixture on cabbage leaf; fold in ends and roll. Place cabbage roll, seam-side down, in Dutch oven. Repeat with remaining cabbage leaves and meat mixture. Place lemon, brown sugar and tomato juice over cabbage rolls.

5. Using steel blade, process gingersnaps until ground. Sprinkle gingersnaps and raisins over cabbage rolls.

6. Cook covered over medium heat 45 minutes. Heat oven to 350°F (180°C). Bake uncovered 1½ hours.
   Note: Stuffed Cabbage Rolls can be made 1 day in advance and reheated. Leftover cabbage rolls can be kept covered in refrigerator up to 2 days.

PIKE IN THE POLISH STYLE

Makes 4 to 6 servings

3 onions, cut into
    quarters
1 carrot
3 ribs celery
1 lemon
2 pounds (900 g) pike,
    cleaned, scaled, cut
    into 2-inch (5 cm)
    pieces
¾ teaspoon (4 mL) salt
½ teaspoon (2 mL) white
    pepper

3 cups (750 mL) water
3 hard-cooked eggs
6 tablespoons (90 mL)
    butter or margarine
3 tablespoons (45 mL)
    lemon juice
1 teaspoon (5 mL) dried
    dillweed
¼ teaspoon (1 mL) salt
⅛ teaspoon (0.5 mL)
    black pepper

1. Using slicing disc, slice onions, carrot, celery and lemon separately.

2. Layer onions, carrot and celery in Dutch oven. Add fish; top with ¾ teaspoon (4 mL) salt, the white pepper, lemon and water.

3. Cook covered over medium heat until tender, about 20 minutes.

4. While fish is cooking, using steel blade, process eggs, using on/off technique, until chopped.

5. Heat butter in small skillet. Add lemon juice, eggs and dillweed, stirring after each addition. Stir in ¼ teaspoon (1 mL) salt and the black pepper. Cook 2 minutes.

6. Transfer fish to serving plate; cover with sauce.

KASHA WITH MUSHROOMS AND ONIONS

Makes 4 to 6 servings

*1 cup (250 mL) roasted
    buckwheat groats
1 egg, slightly beaten
1 teaspoon (5 mL) salt
¼ teaspoon (1 mL)
    pepper
2 cups (500 mL) boiling
    water

2 large onions, cut into
    quarters
½ pound (225 g)
    mushrooms
1 green pepper, seeded,
    cut in half
¼ cup (60 mL) butter or
    margarine

1. Combine groats and egg in medium saucepan. Cook over medium heat, stirring frequently, until egg is absorbed, 2 to 4 minutes. Add salt, pepper and boiling water; cook covered over low heat until water is absorbed, about 30 minutes.

2. Using slicing blade, slice onions, mushrooms and green pepper separately.

3. Heat butter in skillet; sauté onions, mushrooms and green pepper until soft, about 3 minutes.

4. Stir vegetables into groats. Cook over medium heat until hot, about 5 minutes.
   *Note: *Buckwheat groats can be purchased in specialty departments of supermarkets or in health food stores.*

POPPY SEED COOKIES

Makes 18

½ package active dry
    yeast
2 teaspoons (10 mL)
    sugar
3 tablespoons (45 mL)
    warm milk
2 cups (500 mL) all-
    purpose flour
¼ cup (60 mL) sugar
¼ teaspoon (1 mL) salt

½ cup (125 mL)
    lukewarm milk
3 tablespoons (45 mL)
    butter or margarine,
    melted
1 teaspoon (5 mL)
    vanilla
* Poppy Seed Filling
    (recipe follows)

1. Combine yeast, 2 teaspoons (10 mL) sugar and the warm milk; let stand 5 minutes.

2. Using steel blade, process flour, ¼ cup (60 mL) sugar, the salt, lukewarm milk, butter, vanilla and yeast mixture until mixed. Transfer to large buttered mixing bowl; let rise covered 1 hour.

3. Make Poppy Seed Filling.

4. Punch down dough; roll out on floured board ¼-inch (0.5 cm) thick. Cut into 2-inch (5 cm) circles. Place on buttered baking sheet. Make indentation in middle of circles with back of teaspoon; fill indentations with filling. Let rise 45 minutes.

5. Heat oven to 400 °F (200 °C). Bake until light brown, about 20 minutes.

   *Note: *Canned poppy seed filling can be used.*

Poppy Seed Filling
Makes 1½ cups (375 mL)

1 cup (250 mL) poppy
   seeds, ground
⅓ cup (80 mL) milk
⅓ cup (80 mL) sugar
1 tablespoon (15 mL)
   butter or margarine

½ teaspoon (2 mL)
   vanilla
2 tablespoons (30 mL)
   honey

1. Combine poppy seeds and milk in medium saucepan; simmer, stirring occasionally, 5 minutes. Stir in remaining ingredients; simmer 2 minutes. Cool.

Index